Ouida

Collection of Britisch authors

Idalia by Ouida Vol I

Ouida

Collection of Britisch authors

Idalia by Ouida Vol I

ISBN/EAN: 9783742804600

Manufactured in Europe, USA, Canada, Australia, Japa

Cover: Foto ©Andreas Hilbeck / pixelio.de

Manufactured and distributed by brebook publishing software (www.brebook.com)

Ouida

Collection of Britisch authors

COLLECTION
OF
BRITISH AUTHORS.
VOL. 905.

IDALIA BY OUIDA.

IN TWO VOLUMES.

VOL. I.

CONTENTS

OF VOLUME I.

			Page
CHAPTER	I.	The Border Eagle	7
—	II.	Having broken his Bread	34
—	III.	"Souffrir au Roi"	49
—	IV.	"N'ôtes-vous pas du Paradis?"	66
—	V.	"An Ignis Fatuus Gleam of Love"	85
—	VI.	The Wisdom of Mother Veronica	99
—	VII.	The Badge of the Silver Ivy	114
—	VIII.	"Passion born of a Glance!"	132
—	IX.	Ritter Tannhäuser	156
—	X.	The Sovereign of the Round Table	174
—	XI.	Fairy-Gold	194
—	XII.	"La Belle Dame sans Merci"	225
—	XIII.	"She smiles them down Imperially"	252
—	XIV.	The Allegory of the Pomegranate	274
—	XV.	"Monsignore"	302
—	XVI.	"A Temple not made with Hands"	315
—	XVII.	"Cravest thou Arcady? Bold is thy Craving. I shall not contest it"	331
—	XVIII.	"The Light in the Dust lies Dead"	355
—	XIX.	"More great in Martyrdom than throned as Cæsar's Mate"	365

wing as the flocks rose among the sedges; and the sole
monarch of earth or sky was a solitary golden eagle
soaring upward to the sun.

With a single swoop the bird had come down from
his eyrie among the rocks, as though he were about to
drop earthward; then, lifting his head, he spread his
pinions in the wind that was blowing strong and fresh
from Scotland through the heat of the August day,
and sailed upward gloriously with slow majestic motion through the light. Far below him lay the white-
crested waves gleaming afar off, the purple stretch of
the dark moors and marshes, the black still tarns, the
rounded masses of the woods; higher and higher,
leaving earth beneath him, he rose in his royal
grandeur, fronting the sun, and soaring onward, and
upward, against the blue skies and the snowy piles
of clouds, rejoicing in his solitude, and kingly in his
strength.

With his broad wings spread in the sun-gleam, he
swept through the silent air, his eyes looking at the
luminance which blinds the eyes of men, his empire
taken in the vastness of the space that monarchs cannot gauge, and his plumes stretched in all the glory
of his god-like freedom, his unchained liberty of life.
Far beneath him, deep down among the tangled mass
of heather and brown moor grasses, glistened the lean
cruel steel of a barrel, like the shine of a snake's back,
pointing upward, while the eagle winged his way aloft;
there, in his proud kingship with the sun, how could
he note or know the steel tube, scarce larger, from his
altitude, than a needle's length, of his foe, hidden deep
among the gorse and reeds? The sovereign bird rose
higher and higher still, in stately flight. One sharp

sullen report rang through the silence; a single grey puff of smoke curled up from the heather; a death-cry echoed on the air, quivering with a human agony; the eagle wheeled once round, a dizzy circle in the summer light, then dropped down through the sunny air—stricken and dead.

Was it more murder when Cæsar fell?

The assassin rose from where he had knelt on one knee among the gorse, while his retriever started the wild-fowl up from the sedges of a pool, and strode through bracken and heath to the spot where his science had brought down the eagle, at a distance, and with an aim, which marked him as one of the first shots in Europe. A hundred yards brought him to the place where his quarry had fallen, and he thrust the heather aside with impatient movement; he was keen in sport as a Shikari, and he had looked for no rarer game to-day than the blackcocks or the snipes, or at very best a heron from the marshes.

On the moor the King-bird lay, the pinions broken and powerless, the breast-feathers wet and bathed in blood, the piercing eyes, which loved the sun, blind and glazed with film; the life a moment before strong, fearless, and rejoicing in the light, was gone. A feeling, new and strange, came on his slayer, as he stood there in the stillness of the solitary moor, alone with the dead eagle lying at his feet. He paused, and leaned on his rifle, looking downward:

"God forgive me. I have taken a life better than my own!"

The words were involuntary, and unlike enough to one whose superb shot had become noted from the jungles of Northern India to the ice-plains of Norway;

from the bear-haunts of the Danube to the tropic forests of the Amazons. But he stood looking down on the mighty bird, while the red blood welled through the blossoming furze, with something that was almost remorse. It looked strangely like *slaughter*, in the still golden gleam of the summer day.

If you wonder at it, wait until you see an eagle die on a solitary moorland that was his kingdom by right divine, with all the glorious liberty of life.

The skill which you would have challenged the first marksmen in Europe to have beaten, will look, for a second at least, oddly base, and treacherous, and cowardly, when the Lord of the Air lies, like carrion, at your feet.

Knee-deep in the purple heather, the destroyer leant on his gun, alone on the Scotch side of the Border, with the sea flashing like a line of silver light on his left, and the bold sweep of the Cheviot Hills fronting him. The golden eagle had fallen by no unworthy foe; he was a man of very lofty stature, and of powerful build and sinew, his muscles close knit, and his frame like steel, as became one who was in hard condition from year's end to year's end. His complexion was a clear bronze, almost as dark as an Arab's, though originally it had been fair enough; his black sweeping moustaches and beard were long, thick, and silken; his eyes, large, and very thoughtful, the hue of the eagle's he had shot. His features were bold, proud, and frank, while his bearing had the distinction of blood, with the dash of a soldier, the reposeful stateliness of the old régime, with the alert keenness of a man used to rapid action, clear decision, coolness under danger, and the wiles of the world in

all its ways. Standing solitary there on the brown
heath, his form rose tall and martial enough for one
of the night riders of Liddesdale, or the Knight of
Snowdon himself, against the purple haze and amber
light.

In the days of Chevy Chase and Flodden Field
his race had been the proudest of the nobles on the
Border-side, their massive keep reared in face of the
Cheviots, the lands their own, over miles of rock, and
gorse, and forest, lords of all the Marches stretching to
the sea. Now all that belonged to him was that wild
barren moorland, which gave nothing but the blackcock and the ptarmigan which bred in their wastes;
and a hunting-lodge, half in ruins, to the westward,
buried under hawthorn, birch, and ivy, a roost for
owls and a paradise for painters.

"A splendid shot, Erceldoune; I congratulate you!"
said a voice behind him.

The slayer of the golden eagle turned in surprise;
the moors, all barren and profitless though they were,
were his, and were rarely trodden by any step except
his own.

"Ah! your Grace? Good day. How does the
Border come to be honoured by a visit from you?"

"Lost my way!" responded his Grace of Glencairne, an inveterate sportsman and a hearty, florid,
stalwart man of sixty, clad in a Scotch plaid suit, and
looking like a well-to-do North-country farmer. "We're
staying with Fitzallayne, and came out after the black
game; lost all the rest somehow, and know no more
where we are than if we were at the North Pole.
You're a godsend. Let me introduce my friends to

you; Sir Fulke Erceldoune — Lord Polemore — Mr. Victor Vane."

The beggared gentleman raised his bonnet to the Duke's friends with much such frank soldier-like courtesy as that with which the Border lords, whose blood was in his veins, received Chatellherault and Hamilton in the wild free days of old.

"Shot an eagle, Erceldoune? By George! what a bird," cried the Duke, gazing down amazed and admiring on the murdered monarch.

"I envy you, indeed!" said his companion whom he had named as Victor Vane. "I have shot most things — men, and other birds of prey — but I never killed an eagle, not even in the Hartz or the Engadine."

Erceldoune glanced at him.

"They are rare, and when they do appear we shoot them to ensure their scarcity! Perhaps the eagle you would wish to kill is the eagle with two heads? What sport have you had, Duke?"

"Very bad! Birds wild as the — But, God bless my soul, *your* bag's full! I say, we're nearly famished; can't you let us have something to eat at your place yonder?"

"With pleasure, sir, if your Grace can honour an owl's roost, and put up with a plain meal of cold game," said Erceldoune, as he thrust the dead king, with all his pomp of plumage torn and blood-stained, into his bag with the blackcocks, ptarmigan, wild-duck, and snipes.

"My dear fellow! I'll thank you for a crust; I'm literally starving," cried the nobleman, who was pining so wearily for his luncheon that the words "cold game" sounded to him like paradise. "And, by-the-way, if you've any of your father's Madeira left, you might feast an emperor; there wasn't such a wine connoisseur in Europe as Regency Erceldoune."

A shadow swept over the face of the golden eagle's foe as he whistled his dogs, and led the way for his guests over the moor, talking with the Duke. Vane caught the look, and smiled to himself; he thought it was because the ruined gentleman shrank from taking them to his beggared home and his unluxurious table; he erred for once. Such a petty pride was wholly impossible to the bold Border blood of Erceldoune; he would have taken them to a garret quite as cordially as to a mansion; he would have given them, Arab-like, the half of all he had with frank hospitality if that all had been only an oaten cake, and would never have done himself such mean dishonour as to measure his worth by the weight of his plate, the number of his wines, or the costliness of his soups.

True, the world, he knew well enough, only appraised men by the wealth that was in their pockets; but the world's dictum was not his deity, and with its social heart-burnings his own wandering, athletic, adventurous, and hardy life had never had much to do. He loved the saddle better than the drawing rooms, and mountain and moorland better than the lust of fame or gold.

It was not more than half a mile to the King's Rest, as the sole relic of the feudal glories of the Border lords was named, from an old tradition dating back to one of Malcolm of Scotland's hunting raids; the place would have maddened an architect or a lover of new stucco, but it would have enraptured an archæologist or an artist. One half of it was in ruins—a mass of ivy and grey crumbling stone; the other half was of all styles of architecture, from the round quaint tower of earliest date, to the fantastic, peaked, and oriel window'd Elizabethan. Birds made their nests in most of the chimneys, holly and hawthorn grew out of the clefts in the walls, the terraces were moss-grown, and the escutcheon above the gateway was lost in a profusion of scarlet-leaved creepers. But there were a picturesqueness, a charm, a lingering grandeur it had still; it spoke of a dead race, and it had poems in every ruin, with the sun on its blazoned casements, and the herons keeping guard by its deserted weed-grown moat.

"God bless my soul! How the place has gone to rack and ruin since I was here twenty years ago!" cried the Duke, heedlessly and honestly, in blank amazement, as he stared about him.

Erceldoune smiled slightly:

"Our fortunes have gone to 'rack and ruin,' Duke."

"Ah, to be sure—yes, to be sure! Sad thing!—sad thing! No fault of yours, though, Erceldoune. Your father shouldn't have been able to touch the entail. He was a—Well, well! he's gone to his account now," said his Grace, pulling himself up short, with a perception that he was on dangerous ground, but continuing to gaze about him with a blank naïveté of astonishment. Men used to call him a "sexagenarian schoolboy;" it was too harsh, for the Duke was a thoroughly good man of business, and a manly and honest friend, but it was true that the simplicity and candour of boyhood clung very oddly to him, and a courtier or a fine gentleman his Grace of Glencairne had never become, though he was not without a frank dignity of his own when roused to it.

By an arched side-door, through a long corridor, they passed into a room in the southern and still habitable portion of the house; a long lofty room, lighted at the end with two magnificent painted windows, panelled with cedar picked out with gold, hung with some half-dozen rare pictures, a Titian, two Watteaux, a Teniers, a Van Tol, and a Memling, covered with a once rich crimson carpeting, now much worn, and with some gold and silver racing and hunting cups on the buffet. The chamber was the relic of the lavish and princely splendour which scarce thirty years ago had been at its height in the King's Rest.'

"Ah! dear me—dear me!" murmured the Duke, throwing himself into a fauteuil. "This is the old supper-room! To be sure—how well I remember George IV. sitting just there where you stand. Lord! how fond he was of your father—birds of a feather! Well, well! we might be wild, wicked dogs—we were, sir; but we had witty times of it. Regency Erceldoune was a very brilliant man, though he might be a—"

Erceldoune, with brief courtesy to the Duke, rang the bell impatiently to order luncheon, and turned to the other men:

"I hope your sport and our moorland air may have given you an appetite, for Border larders were never very well stocked, you know, except when the laird made a raid; and, unhappily, there is no 'lifting,' now-a-days, to add to our stock!"

"My dear sir!" laughed Vane, dropping his glass, through which he had been glancing at the Van Tol, "half a cold grouse when one is starving is worth all

the delicacies of a Carême when one is not *in extremis*.
I am delighted to make acquaintance with your highly
picturesque and mediæval abode; a landscape-painter
would be in raptures over it, if you might wish it a
trifle more water-proof!"

There was a certain dash of condescension and the
suspicion of a sneer in the light careless words; if they
were intended to wound, however, they missed their
mark.

"'Starving on the moors' would not be so very
terrific to you if you had been six days in the saddle
on a handful of maize, as has chanced to me in the
Pampas and the Cordilleras," said Erceldoune, curtly:
—there is nothing your "mighty hunter before the
Lord," who is known from the Libyan desert to La
Plata, holds in more profound contempt than "small
miseries."

"Eh! What? Were you talking about your father's
dinners?" broke in his Grace, who, lost in his reveries
as his eyes travelled over the familiar chamber, was
not very clear what was said. "They were the best
in Europe! I have seen Yarmouth, and Alvanley, and
Talleyrand, and Charles Dix, and the best epicures
we ever had, round that table; I was a very young
fellow then, and the dinners were splendid, Erceldoune!
He liked to outdo the king, you know, and the king
liked to be outdone by him. I don't believe he'd
have gone quite the pace he did if it hadn't been for
George."

Erceldoune moved impatiently; these latter royal
memories connected with the King's Rest were no
honour to him; they were so many brands of an extravagant vice, and a madman's ostentation, that had

made him penniless, and bought a sovereign's smile with disgrace.

"I dare say, sir. I never knew any use that monarchs were yet, save in some form or another to tax their subjects."

Glencairne laughed: he had not seen much of the man who was now his host, but what he had seen he liked; the Duke abhorred the atmosphere of adulation in which, being a Duke, he was compelled to dwell, and Erceldoune's utter incapability of subservience or flattery refreshed him.

At that moment luncheon was served: the promised cold game in abundance, with some prime venison, some potted char, and a pile of superb strawberries; plain enough, and all the produce of the moorlands round, but accompanied by pure claret, and served on antique and massive plate which had been in the King's Rest for centuries, and was saved out of the total wreck of its fortunes, and at which Lord Polemore looked envyingly; he was of the new creation, and would have given half his broad lands and vast income to have bought that "high and honourable ancientness" which was the only thing gold could not purchase for him.

"You have a feast for the gods, Erceldoune. If this be Border penury, commend me to it!" cried Glencairne, as he attacked the haunch with a hearty and absorbed attention; like Louis Seize, he would have eaten in the reporter's box at the Assembly while Suleau was falling under twenty sword-thrusts for his sake, and the Swiss Guard were perishing in the Cour Royale.

"I am sure we are infinitely indebted!" murmured

Polemore, languidly, gazing at a Venetian goblet given to an Erceldoune by the Queen Regent, Mary of Guise.

"Nay, it is I who am the debtor to a most happy hazard. Try this wine," said Erceldoune, with that stately courtesy which was blent with his frank, *bref*, soldier-like manners;—sociality was not his nature, but cordial hospitality was.

The Duke looked up.

"Eh! Tokay? What, the very wine Leopold gave your father? Tiny bottles? all cobwebbed? *That's* it! The real imperial growth; can't get it for money. Ah! how much have you got of it left?"

"But little—only a dozen or so, I believe; but of what there is I would ask the pleasure of your Grace's acceptance, if the wine find favour with you."

"Favour with me? Hear the man. Why, it's Leopold's own growth, I tell you," cried his Grace. "As for giving it away, thank you a thousand times, but I couldn't—I wouldn't rob you of it for anything."

"Indeed I beg you will, my dear Duke," said Erceldoune, with a slight smile. "To a rich man you may refuse what you like, but to a poor man you must leave the pleasure of giving when he can."

"Really, on my soul, you're very good," said the Duke, whose heart was longing after the imperial vintage. "I thank you heartily, my dear fellow; but you're too generous, Erceldoune; give your head away, like all your race!—like all your race! If your ancestors had had their hands a little less free at giving, and their heads a little longer at their expenditure, you wouldn't have this place all tumble-down as it is about you now!"

"Generosity, if I can ever make claim to it, will not imperil me. Who has nothing can lose nothing," said Erceldoune, briefly. He did not feel particularly grateful for this discussion of his own fortunes and his father's follies before two strangers, and Vane, noticing this by tact or by chance, glided in with a question admiringly relative to a small gold salver singularly carved and filagreed.

"No, you are quite right, it is not European," answered his host, glad to turn the Duke's remarks off himself, the person he liked least to hear talked of, of any in the world. "It is Mexican. An Erceldoune who was in Cuba at the time Cortes sailed, and who went with him through all the Aztec conquest, brought it home from the famous treasures of Ayaxacotl. He bored a hole in it and slung it round his neck in the passage of the Noche Triste; there is the mark now."

"Very curious!" murmured Polemore, with a sharp twinge of jealousy; he felt it hard that this man, living in an owl's roost on a barren moor, should have had ancestors who were nobles and soldiers in the great Castilian conquest, while he, a viscount and a millionnaire, could not even tell who his fathers were at that era, but knew they had been wool-carders, drawers, butterers, cordwainers, or something horrible and unmentionable!

"Out with Cortes!" echoed Vane. "Then we have a link in common, Sir Fulke. I have some Mexican trifles that one of our family, who was a friend of Velasquez de Leon, brought from the conquest. So a Vane and an Erceldoune fought side by side at Otumba

2*

and in the temple of Huitzitopotchli? We must be friends after such an augury?"

Erceldoune bowed in silence, neither accepting nor declining the proffered alliance.

The sunlight poured through the scarlet creepers round the oriel windows into the chamber, on to the red pile of the fruit in its glossy leaves, the rich-hued plumage of the dead birds where they were hastily flung down, the gold and antique plate that was in strange contrast with the simplicity of the fare served on it; and on the dark martial head of the border-laird, where he sat with his great hounds couched about him in attitudes for Landseer. He looked, on the whole, more to belong to those daring, dauntless, fiery, steel-clad Cavaliers of the Cross, who passed with Cortes through the dark belt of porphyry into the sunlit valley of the Venice of the West, than to the present unheroic, unadventurous, unmoved, unadmiring age. Near him sat Victor Vane, a man of not more than thirty years, rather under the middle size and slightly built; in his bearing easy and aristocratic, in feature although not by any means handsome, very attractive, with blue eyes that were always smiling with pleasant sunshine, hair of the lightest hue that glanced like silk, and a mouth as delicate as a woman's, that would have made him almost effeminate but for the long amber moustaches that shaded it, while his face, though very fair, was perfectly colourless, which lent to it the delicacy, but also the coldness, of marble.

As the two men sat together—host and guest—antagonism seemed more likely between them than alliance; and in such antagonism, if it arose, it would have been hard to say which would be the victor. In

a fair and open fight, hand to hand, the blood of the Northern Countrie would be sure of conquest, and Erceldoune would gain it with the same ease and the same strength as that with which those in whose veins it had run before him had charged "through and through a stand of pikes," and stood the shock of the English lances; but in a combat of finesse, in a duel of intrigue, where the hands were tied from a bold stroke, and all the intricate moves were made in the dark, it would be a thousand to one that the bright and delicate Southron stiletto would be too subtle for the straight stroke and dauntless chivalry of the stalwart Border steel.

At that moment a despatch was handed to Erceldoune by the single servant who lived in the King's Rest, and served him when he was there. The letter was sealed with the royal arms, and marked "On her Majesty's Service." Its contents were but two lines:

"Sir Fulke Erceldoune on service immediately. Report to-morrow by 11 A.M. at F. O."

"From the office?" asked the Duke, as his host tossed the despatch aside.

"Yes. On service immediately. East Europe, I dare say."

"Ah! the Cabinet brewing more mischief with their confounded pedagogue's pettifogging, I will bet!" cried his Grace. (The existing Government was his pet foe.) "When are you ordered?"

"To-morrow. I shall take the night express, so I shall not need to leave here till midnight," answered Erceldoune, to set at rest any fears his guests might feel that they detained him. "I wish they had sent Buller or Phil Vaughan; I wanted a month more of the deer and the blackcock; but I must console myself with the big game in Wallachia, if I can find time."

"You serve her Majesty?" inquired Vane, who knew it well enough, as he knew all the state messengers in Europe.

"'The F. O., rather," laughed Erceldoune. "Salaried to keep in saddle! Paid to post up and down the world with a state bag honoured with Havannahs, and a despatch-box marked 'Immediate,' and filled with char, chocolate, or caviare!"

"Come, come, Erceldoune, that's too bad!" laughed the Duke.

"Not a whit, sir! I went out to New York last year with royal bags imposing enough to contain the freedom of Canada, or instructions to open an American war, but which had nothing in the world in them save a dinner-service for his Excellency, and some French novels and Paris perfumes for the First Secretary."

The Duke laughed:

"Well, that will hardly be the case now. Matters are getting very serious eastward; everywhere over there the people are ripe for revolt; I expect Venetia, and Galicia, and Croatia, and all the rest of them, are meditating a rising together. I happen to know those bags you take out will contain very important declarations from us; the Cabinet intend to send instructions to invite Turkey, command her rather, to———"

"My dear Duke, it is not for me to know *what* I take out; it is sufficient that I deliver it safely," laughed Erceldoune, to check the outpourings of his Grace's garrulous tongue. "I am no politician and diplomatist, as you know well. I prefer hard riding to soft lying in either sense of the word."

"Wish everybody else did!" said the Duke. "If men would keep to their own concerns and live as they ought, with plenty of sport and fresh air, everything would go smoothly enough. There'd be no marring or meddling then; as for this Cabinet, it's just what Clarendon said of Bristol: 'For puzzling and spoiling a thing, there was never his equal.' If the despatches you will carry to Moldavia don't embroil Europe, it won't be his fault, but there'll be sure to be a postscript to 'em all, meaning, 'N. B. In no case will *we* fight!'"

"Who is severe now, Duke? On my honour, you will make me feel as if I were Discord incarnate flying over Europe with her firebrand. I never took so poetic a side of the service before."

He strove to arrest the reckless course of incautious revelations of the intentions in high places, but it was useless. The Scotch Duke was off on the Foreign Office ill-deeds, and no power could have stopped him; no power did until he had fairly talked himself hoarse, when he drank a deep glass of claret, and rose, with reiterated thanks for his impromptu entertainment as sincere as they were voluble, and with cordial invitation to his castle of Benithmar, a stately pile upon the Clyde.

"And I hope you will allow me also to return your hospitalities in kind," said Vane, with his brightest smile. "Since you have the mania of *pérégrinomanie*, as Guy Patin calls it, and are always going up and down Europe, you must pass continually through Paris. I can only hope, both there and in Naples, you will very soon allow me the pleasure of showing you how much I hold myself the debtor both for the hospitality of to-day, and the acquaintance to which it has been so fortunate for me as to lead."

Erceldoune bent his head, and thanked him courteously but briefly—he had no love for honeyed speeches—and offered them, as a modern substitute for the stirrup-cup, some cigars of purest flavour, brought over by himself from the West Indies.

"How does Mr. Vane come in your Grace's society?" he asked the Duke, as he accompanied them across his own moor to put them *en route* for Lord Fitzallayne's, the two others having fallen slightly behind them.

"How? Eh? Why—I don't know—because he's staying at Fitz's, to be sure."

"Staying there!"

"Yes. Fitz swears by him, and all the women are in love with him, though he's a pale insignificant face, to my thinking. What do you know of him? Anything against him—eh?"

"Sufficiently *about* him to advise you, if you will allow me, not to let him glean from you the private intentions and correspondence of the ministry, or any instructions they may have given their representatives abroad. Only talk to him on such matters generally; say no more to him than what the public knows."

"What? Ah! indeed. I apprehend you. I thank you, sir—I thank you," said his Grace, hurriedly, conscious that he had been somewhat indiscreet, but curious as any old gossip in a Breton knitting and spinning gossipry. "But he stands very well; he comes of good blood, I think. He is a gentleman; you meet him at the best Courts abroad."

"Possibly."

"Then what the deuce is there against him?"

"I am not aware that I said there was anything. Simply I know his character; I know he is an adventurer—a political adventurer—associated with the ultra parties in Italy and Hungary. I do not think his social status is anything very remarkable, and I repeat my advice: do not take him into political confidence."

"If the man can't be trusted, the man's a blackguard!"

"My dear Duke! *la haute politique* will not admit of such simplifications. A man may be a great man, a great minister, a great patriot, but all the same he may be—politically speaking—a great cheat! Indeed, is there a statesman who is not one?"

"True, true—uncomfortably true," growled his Grace; "but of Victor Vane—what's there against him? What do you know—what would you imply?"

"I 'imply' nothing; it is the most cowardly word in the language. I know very little, and that little I have said to place your Grace on your guard; and it is no secret; Mr. Vane is well known abroad to be the determinate foe of Austria, and to be widely involved in political intrigues. Of his career I know no further; and of what I have said he is welcome to hear every word," said Erceldoune, with a dash of decision and impatience, while he paused and pointed to a road running round a bend of grey gorse-covered rock beside a brown and rapid moor stream, which would lead them by a short cut across the fells homewards.

There they parted in the bright warm August afternoon, as the sun began to sink towards the westward; his guests soon lost to sight behind the wild woodland

growth of the half savage glen, while the last of the
Border lords turned backward to his solitary and ruined
homestead, sweeping over the heather with the easy
swinging step of the bred mountaineer, followed by his
brace of staghounds and two black and tan setters.

"Salaried to keep in saddle! Paid to post up and
down Europe!" he had said, with a certain disdain, for
Erceldoune was nothing more or less than a Queen's
messenger; a State courier, bound to serve at a State
summons; holding himself in readiness for Russia or
Teheran, for ice-fields or sun-scorched tropics, for the
swamps of Mexico or the rose plains of Persia, at a
second's notice. But he suited the life, and the life
suited him; for he was a keen sportsman, and the first
rider in Europe; was equally at his ease in an Arab
camp and a Paris café, in a Polish snow-storm, with
the wolves baying in wrath and famine about the sleigh,
and in the chancellèrie of a British plenipotentiary over
the dainty dishes of a First Secretary's dinner; and
had an iron constitution, a frame steeled to all changes
of climate or inroads of fatigue, and that coolness under
close peril, and utter indifference to personal indulgence,
which made him renowned in the messenger service,
and as much at home in the Desert as a Sheikh. Indeed, the Desert life could not have been bolder, and
freer, and simpler than that which Erceldoune had led
from his boyhood, partly from nature, partly from
habit; he had as much of the barbaric chief in him as
he had of the man of the world.

His father—Regency Erceldoune, as he was called,
from his alliance with "the mad Prince and Poynings"

—had been a gambler, a debauchee, and a drunkard, though a gentleman with it all, Such orgies as George Rox had at the Cross Deep, his friend and favourite had at King's Rest, mad, witty, riotous, and shameless as the worst days of lascivious Rome. Lands and money went in them till there were neither left; and his son, brought to them and taught them, while he was nothing but a child, had sickened of the vice in which he was steeped as thoroughly as, had he been brought up by precisians, he would have craved and loved it. He saw men levelled with brutes, and made far more bestial than the beasts; and his nature reared itself out of the slough, and refused the slavery of sensuality. If he were too early contaminated, he was all the earlier revolted.

When he was twenty-two his father died; and he was left the last Master of King's Rest (by the old title long dropped in desuetude), with some miles of moorland and a beggared fortune, not a single relative, and not a chance of a career. A certain wild and witty peer, who had been prominent in the orgies of the Roissy of the Border—saying nothing to him, for the Erceldoune stock was famous for a pride, which perished rather than bend—got him offered a messengership; and his first meeting with officials at the Foreign Office was characteristic, and had not a little influence on his career. In the Board-room, at the hour when he was being received by those sleepy and solemn personages the Heads of a Department, there lounged in a minister, as celebrated for his cheery and facetious humour as for his successful and indomitable statesmanship; for his off-hand good nature as for his foreign policies. The Heads bowed submissive before my lord; my lord gave his rapid, lucid orders, and, as he was lounging out again, put up his eye-glass at Erceldoune.

"Messengership? We've too many messengers already," he said, cutting in two the reply of the Board to his interrogation. "Only ride over one another's way, and lose half the bags among them. Who are you, sir?"

"Fulke Erceldoune," said the Border lord, with no birthright but some barren acres of heather, returning the great Minister's stare as calmly and as haughtily; insolence he would not have brooked from an emperor.

"Erceldoune! God bless my soul, your father and I were like brothers once," said his lordship, breaking off his sharp autocratic cross-examination for the *sans façon* good-hearted familiarity of tone, most usual and congenial to him. "Not a very holy fraternity either! Monks of Medmenham! Who sent you up for a messengership? Lord Longbourn? Ah! very happy to appoint you. Go in for your examination as soon as you like."

"I thank you, my lord, no. You have said, 'You have too many messengers already.'"

The minister stared a minute, and then laughed.

"Pooh, pooh! Never mind what I said! If you're like what your father was, you won't complain of a sinecure."

The boy-master of King's Rest bowed to the cabinet councillor.

"I am *not* what he was; and I do not take money from the State, if the State do not need my services. I did not come here to seek a pension!"

The great statesman stared at him a second with a blank amazement; his condescension had never met with such a rebuff and such a scruple in all his length of years and of office. The grave and reverend Heads that bent to the earth in docility and servility before the Foreign Secretary, gazed at the offender with such horror of reprobation as the members of the Inquisition might have bestowed on a blasphemer who had reviled the Host and rebelled against the Holy See. Erceldoune stood his ground calmly and indifferently; he had said simply what he meant, and, in the pride of his youth and his ruin, he was grandly careless whether he had closed the door of every career upon himself, and condemned himself to starve for life on his profitless acres of tarne and gorse.

The Minister looked at him, with his keen blue eyes reading the boy through and through; then a rich humour lighted up their glittering azure light, and he laughed aloud—a mellow, ringing, Irish mirth, that startled all the drowsy echoes and pompous stillness of Downing-street.

"You hit hard and straight, my young Sir Fulke? Very dangerous habit, sir, and very expensive: get rid of it! Go before the commissioners to-morrow, and pass your examination. I'll give you an attachéship, if you like it better, but I don't think you'll do for diplomacy! I shall see you again. Good day to you."

The minister nodded, and left the Board-room with as much dash and lightness in his step when he ran down-stairs, as if he were still a Harrow boy; and, in that two minutes' interview in the Foreign Office, Erceldoune had made a friend for life in one who—if he had a short political memory, and took up policies, or treaties, and dropped them again with a charm-

ing facility and inconstancy, as occasion needed—
was adored by every man he employed, and was as
loyal to his personal friendships as he was staunch to
his personal promises.

True to his word, he gave Erceldoune his choice of
an attachéship, a messengership, a commission, or one
of those fashionable and cozy appointments in Downing-street where younger sons and patrician protégés
yawn, make their race books, discuss the points of
demi-reps and rosières, circulate the last epigram round
the town, manufacture new and sublimated liqueur
recipes, and play at baccarat or chicken hazard in the
public service. Erceldoune took the messengership;
from a motive which strongly coloured his character
and career even then—honour.

His father, deep in a morass of embarrassments,
had lived like a prince of the blood; his son had taken,
in sheer revulsion, an utter abhorrence of all debt.
He had been steeped in dissolute vices and lawless
principles from his earliest years; and the mere wildness of men of his own years looked childish, and was
without charm, beside the orgies through which he had
passed his noviciate while yet in his youngest boyhood.
He had seen men of richest wit, highest powers, brightest talents, noblest blood, suddenly disappear into darkness and oblivion, to drag on an outlawed life in some
wretched continental town, through that deadly curse of
usury, which had given their heritage to the Hebrews,
and let them glitter leaders of fashion for a decade,
only to seize their lives more surely at the last; and
he had sworn never to give his own life over to the
keeping of that vampire which lulls us into an opium-
like dream for one short hour, to drain our best blood

drop by drop with its brute fangs and its insatiate thirst. Had he gone into the army, where his own wishes would have led him, or had he taken one of the diplomatic or civil fashionable appointments offered him, the circles into which he would have been thrown must have flung him into debt, and into every temptation to it, however he might have resisted: he must have lived as those about him lived; the mere bare necessities of his position would have entailed embarrassments from which the liberty of his nature revolted as from a galley-slave's fetters. In Erceldoune's creed a landless gentleman was worthy of his blood so long as he was free—no longer.

Therefore he entered the messenger service; and, on the whole, the life, which he had now led for about a score of years, suited him as well as any, save a soldier's, could have done; the constant travel, the hard riding, the frequent peril, the life of cities alternating with the life of adventure—these were to his taste. And while in the capitals of Europe there was not a woman who could beguile, or a man who could fool him, the Mexican guachos found in him a rider fleet and fearless as themselves; the French Zéphyrs knew in him a volunteer, fiery and elastic as any their battalions held; the fishers of Scandinavia had lived with him through many a blinding icy midnight sea-storm; the Circassians had feasted and loved him in their mighty mountain strongholds; and the Bedaweens welcomed as one of themselves the Frank, who rode as they rode, without heeding the scorch of the brazen skies and sands; who could bring down a vulture on the wing whirling right betwixt his sight and the burning sun, a black speck on the yellow glare;

who could live like themselves, if needs be, on a draught of water and a handful of maize or of dates, and who cared for no better bed than their desert solitudes, with his saddle beneath his head, and the desert stars shining above.

Love he had known little of; no human life had ever become necessary to his, or ever obtained the slightest sway over, or hold upon, his own; in this he was exceptionally fortunate. What were dear to him were those profitless, useless moorland wastes of heath and heron-creeks, of yellow gorse, and brown still pools, the sole relics of his barren Border heritage, and which self-denial and renunciation had kept free from claim or burden.

The sun was shining full on the King's Rest as he returned, and he leaned over the low gate of the stable entrance, looking at the ivy-hidden ruins, which were all which remained to him of the possessions of a race that had once been as great as the Hamilton, the Douglas, or the Græme, and of which an empty title alone was left him, as though to make his poverty and its decay more marked. These did not often weigh on him; he cared little for riches, or for what they brought; and in the adventure and the vigour of a stirring wandering life there were a richness of colouring and a fullness of sensation which, together with a certain simplicity of taste and habit that was natural to himself, prevented the pale hues and narrow lines of impoverished fortunes from having place or note. But now the Duke's words had recalled them; and he looked at the King's Rest with more of melancholy than his dauntless and virile nature often knew. There, over the lofty gateway, where the banner of a great feudal

line had floated, the scarlet leaves of the Virginian
parasite alone were given to the wind. In the moat,
where on many a summer night the night-riders had
thundered over the bridge to scour hill and dale with
the Warden of the Marches, there were now but the
hoot of the heron, the nests of the water-rat, and the
thick growth of sedges and water-lilies. In the chambers where James IV. had feasted, and Mary Stuart
rested, and Charles Edward found his loyalest friends
and safest refuge, the blue sky shone through the open
rafters, and the tattered tapestry trembled on the walls,
and the fox and the bat made their coverts; the grand
entrance, the massive bastions, the stately towers which
had been there when the bold Border chieftains rode
out to join the marching of the clans, had vanished
like the glories of Alnaschar's dream, all that remained
to tell their place a mound of lichen-covered ruin, with
the feathery grasses waving in the breeze;—it was the
funeral pile of a dead race.

And the last of their blood, the last of their title,
stood looking at it in the light of the setting sun with
a pang at his heart.

"Well! better so than built up with dishonoured
gold! The power and the pomp are gone, but the
name at least is stainless," thought Erceldoune, as he
looked away from the dark and shattered ruins of his
heritage, across the moorland, golden with its gorse,
and towards the free and sunlit distance of the seas,
stretching far and wide.

CHAPTER II.

Having broken his Bread.

"What did you think of that man?" said Lord Polemore to Victor Vane that evening over his coffee in the drawing-rooms, out of the Duke's hearing.

"Think of him? think of him? Well!—I think he will die a violent death."

"Good gracious!" said the peer, with a little shiver. Why?"

"I never analyse!" laughed Victor, softly. "I think so,—because I think so. He will get shot in a duel, perhaps, for saying some barbaric truth or other in the teeth of policy."

"Who is that you are prophesying for with such charmingly horrible romance?" asked a very pretty woman.

"Fellow we met on the moor," answered Polemore. "Queer fellow? Beggar, you know,—holes in the carpets, rats in the rooms,—and yet, on my honour, Venice goblets and Mexican gold! Absurd!"

"What! a beggar with holes in his coat and rats in his pockets with Venice glass and Mexican ingots!" cried the beautiful blonde, who had been listening languidly.

"No, no! Not *that* sort of beggar, you know," interposed the peer. "Man that lives in a lot of ruins. Messenger fellow—lunched with him to-day. Wretched place; only fit for bats; no household, no cook, no anything; odious dungeon! And yet, on my word, if the fellow isn't ridiculous enough to serve up his dry bread on gold salvers, and pour his small beer into Cinque Cento glasses!"

"Come! we had very fair wine considering it was a Barmecide's feast," laughed Vane.

"Height of absurdity, you know!" went on Polemore, waxing almost eloquent under the spurs of the twinges of envy he had felt while at luncheon. "Fancy, Lady Augusta! here's a man nothing but a courier, he says himself, always racing up and down Europe with bags; so hard up that he has to shoot for himself everything that he eats, and living in a wretched rathole I wouldn't turn a dog into; yet keeps gold and silver things fit for a prince, and tells you bombastical stories about his ancestors having been caciques of Mexico! For my part, I don't doubt he stole them all!"

"Bravo! Bravissimo!" laughed Victor Vane. "And what is much more, Lady Augusta, this Border savage wears deer-skins in the rough, 'lifts' cattle when the moon's dark, and has a fricassee of young children boiling in a cauldron. Quite à l'antique, you see!"

"But who *is* the creature?" asked the lady, a little bewildered, a little interested, and a good deal amused.

"Oh—let me see—ah! he calls himself Fulke Erceldoune," said Polemore, with an air of never having heard the title, and of having strong reasons for believing it a false one.

A man standing near, turned at the name.

"Fulke? You are talking of Fulke Erceldoune? Best fellow in the world, and has the handsomest strain of black-tan Gordon setters, bred on the Regent and Rake cross, going anywhere."

"Oh—ah—do you know him, then?" murmured Polemore, a little discomfited.

"Rather! First steeple-chaser in the two countries; tremendous pots always on him. Know him!—ask the Shire men. Saved my life, by the way, last year—fished me out of the Gulf of Spezzia, when I was all but spent; awful tempest at the time; very nearly drowned himself. Is he here, do you say?"

"He's at that wretched rat-hole of his," grumbled Polemore, sorely in wrath.

"King's Rest? Didn't know that. Go and see him to-morrow."

"What remarkably conflicting statements!" murmured Lady Augusta, with languid amusement. "A beggar and a savage!—a preux chevalier and a paladin of chivalry! Singular combination this—what is it?—Fulke Erceldoune."

"Nay," laughed Vane, "it was a combination common enough in the old days of chivalry, and our friend seems to me better suited to the Cinque Cento than the present century. Just the sort of man to have been a Knight Templar with Cœur de Lion, or an adventurer with Pizarro, with no capital and no credit but his Toledo blade."

"Trash!" said the absent man's defender, with impatient disdain that almost roused him into energy, "Erceldoune is a splendid fellow, Lady Augusta. I only wish you could see him ride to hounds. In saddle; in sport; on a yacht deck in a storm; with any big game you like—pigs, bisons, tigers; swimming in the Turkish waters in mid-winter; potting lions with the Kabyles and the Zouaves—put him where you will, he's never at a loss, never beaten, and can do more than twenty men put together. Dash and science, you know; when you get the two together, they always win. As for money—all the good old names are impoverished now, and it's the traders only who have any gilding."

With which fling at Polemore—whose fathers were of the Cottonocracy—the champion, something disgusted at having been entrapped into such a near approach to anything like interest and excitement, turned away, and began to murmur pretty nothings, in the silkiest and sleepiest of tones, into the ear of a Parisian marquise.

"Extreme readiness to break your neck, and extreme aptitude for animal slaughter, always appear to be the English criterion of your capabilities and your cardinal virtues," murmured Vane, with his low light laugh, while Polemore, sulkily aggrieved, muttered to himself:

"Man that's a beggar to keep Mexican things and have his bare bones served up on gold dishes—ridiculous, preposterous! If he's so poor, he must be in debt; and if he's in debt he ought to sell them, out of common honesty. Cheats his creditors—clearly cheats his creditors!"

And so—having broken his bread and eaten his salt—they talked of him: there are a few rude nomad Arab virtues that have died out with civilisation; and the Sheikh will keep faith and return your hospitalities better than Society.

That evening, a Dalmatian, who was the body-servant of Victor Vane, a very polished and confidentially useful person, rode over to the little station nearest Lord Fitzallayne's, and sent a telegram, which he read from a slip of paper, to Paris. It ran thus, save that it was in a polyglot jumble of languages which would have defied any translation without a key:

"The Border Eagle flies eastward. Clip the last feather of the wing. Only La Picciola. Idalia or pearls of lead, as you like. Take no steps till beyond the King's. Then make sure, even if—White coats in full muster; Crescent horns up; Perfide, as usual, brags but won't draw. N. B. The Eagle will give you beak and talons."

Which, simply translated, meant—

"Erceldoune, Queen's Courier, will take the F. O. bags into the Principalities. Relieve him of the last despatches he has with him. We only want the smallest bag. I leave you to choose how to manage this; either with a successful intrigue or a sure rifle-shot. Do not stop him till he is beyond Turin. Secure the papers, even if you have to take his life to get them. The Austrians are in strong force everywhere; matters in Turkey, as regards the Principalities, are against us; England, as usual, bullies, but will not be drawn into a war. N. B. This Erceldoune will give you trouble, and fight hard."

And being translated by the recipient in all its intricacies of implication and command, would mean far more.

The tired telegraph clerk, who yawned and did nothing all day long in the little out-of-the-world Border station, save when he sent a message for the lodge to town, rubbed his heavy eyes, stared, told off the jumbled Babel of phrases with bewildered brain, and would barely have telegraphed them all in due order and alphabet but for the dexterous care of the Dalmatian.

While the message was being swelled out, the night-express dashed into the station, with red lamps gleaming through the late moonless night, and its white steam cloud flung far out on the gloom, flashing on its way from Edinburgh across the Border land,— a tall man, dressed in a dark loose coat of soft Canadian furs, with a great cheroot in his mouth, ran up the station stairs, and threw down his gold:

"First class to town;—all right."

He took his ticket, flung open a door of an unoccupied carriage, and threw himself into a seat with the rapidity of one used never to idle time and never to be kept waiting by others, and the train, with a clash and a clang, darted out into the darkness, plunging down into the gloom as into the yawning mouth of Avernus, its track faintly told by the wraith-like smoke of the wreathing steam and the scarlet gleam of the signal-lamps.

The Dalmatian had looked after him with some curiosity:

"Who is that?" he asked the clerk.

"Erceldoune, of the King's Rest. He is a Queen's messenger, you know, always rushing about at unearthly times, like a wandering Jew. I say, what the dickens is that word; Arabic, ain't it?"

The Dalmatian, with a smile, looked after the train, then turned and spelt out the words.

"Such gibberish! If that ain't a rum start somehow or other, I'm a Dutchman," thought the telegraphist, with a yawn, returning to his dog-eared green-covered shilling novel, relating the pungent adventures of a soiled dove of St. John's Wood, and showing beyond all doubt—if anybody ever doubted it yet—that virtue, after starving on three-halfpence a shirt, will be rewarded with pneumonia and the parish shell, while vice eats her truffles, drinks her wines, and retires with fashionable toilettes, and a competence, to turn repentant and respectable at leisure. Meanwhile, the night-express rushed on through silent hills, and sleeping hamlets, over dark water-pools and through bright gaslit cities, and above head the electric message flashed, outstripping steam, and flying, like a courier of the air, towards France before the man it menaced.

With noon on the morrow the best-known messenger in the service reported himself at the Foreign Office, received despatches for Paris, Turin, and Jassy, and started with the F. O. bags as usual express.

Had any prophet told him that as he lay back in the mail-train, with a curled silver Eastern pipe coming out of his waving beard, and papers of critical European import in the white bags lying at his feet, Chance was drifting him at its wanton caprice as idly and as waywardly as the feathery smoke it floated down on the wind, Erceldoune would have contemptuously denied that Chance could ever affect a life justly balanced and rightly held in rein. He would have said Chance was a deity for women, fatalists, and fools; a Fetish worshipped by the blind. The Border chiefs of the King's Rest had believed in the might of a strong arm and in the justice cleft by a long two-edged sword, and left weaklings to bow to Hazard:—and the spirit of their creed was still his.

Yet he might have read a lesson from the death of the moorland eagle;—one chance shot from the barrel hid in the heather, and power, strength, liberty, keen sight, and lordly sovereignty of solitude were over, and the king-bird reeled and fell!

But to draw the parable would not have been at all like his vigorous nature;—a state courier has not much habitude or taste for Oriental metaphors and highly-spiced romances, and he had too much of the soldier, the Shikari, the man of the world and the Arab combined, to leave him anything whatever of the poet or the dreamer. Men of action may have grave, but they never have visionary thoughts, and life with Erceldoune was too gallant, strong, and rapid a stream —ever in incessant motion, though calm enough, as deep waters mostly are—to leave him leisure or inclination to loiter lingeringly or dreamily upon its banks. Reflection was habitual to him, imagination was alien to him.

By midnight he reached Paris, and left his despatches at the English Embassy. There was no intense pressure of haste to get Turin-wards so long as he was in the far Eastern Principalities by the Friday, and he waited for the early mail train to the South, instead of taking a special one, as he would otherwise have done, to get across the Alps. If a few hours were left under his own control in a city, Erceldoune never slept them away; he slept in a railway carriage a travelling carriage, on deck, in a desert, on a raft rushing down some broad river that made the only highway through Bulgarian or Roumelian forests— anywhere where novelty, discomfort, exposure, or danger would have been likely to banish sleep from most men; but in a city he neglected it with an independence of that necessity of life which is characteristic of the present day. There is a café, whether in the

Rue Lafitte, Rivoli, Castiglione, or La Paix, matters not; here, in the great gilded salon, with its innumerable mirrors and consoles and little oval tables, or in the little cabinets, with their rosewood and gilding, and green velvet and rose satin, if there be a bouquet to be tossed down on the marble slab, and the long eyes of a Laure or Aglaë to flash over the wines, while a pretty painted fan taps an impatient rataplan or gives a soft blow on the ear—may be found after midnight a choice but heterogeneous gathering. Secretaries of all the legations, Queen's messengers, Charivari writers, Eastern travellers, great feuilletonists, great artists, princes if they have any wit beneath their purples, authors of any or all nations—all, in a word, that is raciest, wittiest, and, in their own sense, most select in Paris, are to be met with at the Café Minuit, if you be of the initiated. If you be not, you may enter the café of course, since it is open to all the world, and sup there off what you will, but you will still remain virtually outside it.

Erceldoune was well known here: it is in such republics only that a man is welcomed for what he is, and what he has done—not for what he is worth. He was as renowned in Paris because he was so utterly unlike the Parisians, as he was renowned in the East because he so closely resembled the Arabs; and he entered the Café Minuit for the few hours which lay between his arrival at the Embassy and his departure for Turin.

None of his own special set had dropped in just then; indeed, there were but few of them in Paris. As he sat at his accustomed table, glancing through a journal, and with the light from the gaselier above

shed ful on his face—a face better in unison with
drooping desert-palms, and a gleaming stand of rifles,
and the dusky glow of a deep sunset on Niger or on
Nile, for its setting and background, than with the
gilt arabesques and florid hues and white gaslight of a
French café—a new comer, who had entered shortly
afterwards and seated himself at the same table, addressed him on some topic of the hour, and pushed him
an open case of some dainty scented cigarettes.

Erceldoune courteously declined them: he always
smoked his own Turkish tobacco, and would as soon
have used cosmetiques as perfumed cigars; and, answering the remark, looked at the speaker. He was
accustomed to read men thoroughly and rapidly, even
if they carried their passports in cipher. What he saw
opposite him was a gracefully made man, of most
picturesque and brilliant beauty of a purely foreign type,
with the eyes long, dark, and melting, and features
perfectly cut as any cameo's—a man who might have
sat to a painter for Lamoral d'Egmont, or for one of
Fra Moreale's reckless nobly-born Free Lances, and
might have passed for five-and-thirty at the most, till
he who should have looked closely at the lines in the
rich reckless beauty, and caught a certain look in the
lustrous half-veiled eyes, would have allotted him,
justly, fifteen full years more.

Erceldoune gave him one glance, and though there
was little doubt about his type and his order, he had
known men of both by the hundreds.

"Paris is rather empty, monsieur? Sapristi! The as-
phalte in August would be too much for a salamander,"
pursued the stranger, over his bouilla-baisse. He spoke

excellent French, with a mellifluous southern accent, not of France.

Erceldoune assented. Like all travellers or men used to the world, he liked a stranger full as well as a friend for a companion—perhaps rather the better; but he was naturally silent, and seldom spoke much, save when strongly moved or much prepossessed by those whom he conversed with: then he would be eloquent enough, but that was rare.

"Thousands come to Paris this time of the year, but only to pass through it, as I daresay you are doing yourself, monsieur?" went on the Greek, if such he were, as Erceldoune judged him by the eyes and the features, worthy of Phidias' chisel, rarely seen without some Hellenic blood.

"For the season the city is tolerably full; travellers keep it so, as you say," answered Erceldoune, who was never to be entrapped into talking of himself.

"It is a great mistake for people to travel in flocks, like swallows and sheep," said his vivacious neighbour, whose manners were very careless, graceful, and thoroughly polished, if they had a dash of the Bohemian, the Adventurer, and the Free Lance. "A terrible mistake! Overcrowds the inns, the steamers, and the railway carriages; thins the soups, doubles the price of wines, and teaches guides to look on themselves as luxuries, to be paid for accordingly; makes a Nile sunset ridiculous by being witnessed by a mob; and turns Luxor and Jupiter Ammon into dust and prose by having a tribe of donkeys and dragomen rattled over their stones. A fearful mistake! If you are social and gregarious, stay in a city; but if you are speculative and Ishmaelesque, travel in solitude. Eh, monsieur?"

"If you can find it. But you have to travel far to get into solitudes in these days. Have you seen this evening's *Times?*"

"A thousand thanks! Wonderful thing, your *Times!* Does the work in England that secret police do in Vienna, spies and bayonets do here, and confetti to the populace and galleys to the patriots do in Rome."

"Scarcely! The *Times* would rather say it prevents England's having need of any of those continental arguments," said Erceldoune, as he tossed the brandy into his coffee.

The other laughed, as from under his lashes he flashed a swift glance at the Queen's Messenger. He would have preferred it if there had been less decision about the broad, bold, frank brow, and less power in the length of limb stretched out, and the supple wrist, as it lay resting on the marble slab of the café-table.

"Basta! Governments should give the people plenty to eat and plenty to laugh at; they would never be troubled with insurrections then, or hear anything more about 'liberty!' A sleek, well-fed, happy fellow never turned patriot yet; he who takes a dagger for his country only takes it because he has no loaf of bread to cut with it, or feels inclined to slit his own throat. Make corn and meat cheap, and you may play tyrant as you like."

"A sound policy, and a very simple one."

"All sound things are simple, monsieur! It is the sham and rotten ones that want an intricate scaffolding to keep them from falling; the perfect arch stands without girders. 'Panem et Circenses' will always be the first article of good governments; when the people are in good humour they never seethe into malcontents."

"Then I suppose you would hold that cheap provisions and low taxes would make us hear no more of this present cry of 'nationalities?'" His companion was piquant in his discourse and polished in his style, but he did not particularly admire him; and when he did not admire people, he had a way of holding them at arm's length.

"'Nationalities?' Ridiculous prejudices! Myths that would die to-morrow, only ministers like to keep a handy reason on the shelf to make a raid on their neighbour, or steal an inch or two of frontier when the spirit moves them," laughed the other, and his laugh was a soft silvery chime, very pleasant to the ear. "Pooh! a man's nationalities are where he gets the best wage and the cheapest meat, specially in these prosaic profoundly practical times, when there is no chivalry, no dash, no colour; when the common-place thrives; when we turn Egyptian mummies into railway fuel, and find Pharaoh's dust make a roaring fire; when we change crocuses into veratrin for our sore-throats, and violets into sweetmeats for our eating! A detestable age, truly. Fancy the barbarism of crystallising and crunching a violet! The flower of Clémence Isaure, and all the poets after her, condemned to the degradation of becoming a bonbon! Can anything be more typical of the prosaic atrocity of this age? Impossible!"

"With such acute feelings, you must find the dinner-card excessively restricted. With so much sympathy for a violet, what must be your philanthropy for a pheasant!" said Erceldoune, quietly, who was not disposed to pursue the Monody of a Violet in the Café Minuit, though the man to a certain extent amused him.

At that moment the foreigner rose a little hastily, left his ice-cream unfinished, and, with a gay graceful adieu, went out of the salon, which was now filling. "A handsome fellow, and talks well," thought Erceldoune, wringing the amber Moselle from his long moustaches, when he was left alone at the marble table in the heat, and light, and movement of the glittering café. "I know the fraternity well enough, and he is one of the best of the members, I dare say. He did not waste much of his science on me; he saw it would be profitless work. On my word, the wit and ability and good manners those men fritter away in their order would make them invaluable in a Chancellerie, and fit them for any State office in the world."

The First Secretary of the English Legation and a French diplomatist entered and claimed his attention at that instant, and he gave no more thought to the champion of the crystallised flowers, whom, justly or wrongly as it might chance, he had classed with the renowned Legion of Chevaliers d'Industrie, and whose somewhat abrupt departure he had attributed either to his own lack of promise as a plausible subject for experimentalising upon, or to the appearance on the scene of some *mouchard* of the Secret Bureau, whom the vivacious bewailer of the fate of sugared violets in this age of prose did not care to encounter.

Erceldoune thought no more of him then and thenceforward: he would have thought more had the mirrors of the Café Minuit been Paracelsus' or Agrippa's mirours of grammarye.

The long console-glass, with its curled gas-branches and its rose-hued draperies, and its reflex of the gilding, the glitter, the silver, the damask, the fruit, the wines, and the crowds of the Paris café, would have been darkened with night-shadows and deep forest foliage, and the tumult of close struggles for life or death, and the twilight hush of cloistered aisles, and the rich glow of Eastern waters, and the silent gloom of ancient God-forgotten cities; and, from out the waving, shadowy, changing darkness of all, there would have looked a woman's face, with fathomless, luminous eyes, and hair with a golden light upon it, and a proud, weary sorceress smile on the lips—the face of a temptress or of an angel?

But the mirror had no magic of the future; the glass reflected nothing save the gas-jets of the ormolu sconces; and Fulke Erceldoune sat there in Paris that night, drinking his iced Rhine wines, and smoking his curled Arabian meerschaum, knowing nothing of what lay before him, a blind wanderer in the twilight, a traveller in strange countries, as we are at best in life.

CHAPTER III.

"Souffrir en Roi."

Heaven forbid that the Principalities should be better governed: they would be like all the rest of the world in no time. They may be ruinous to themselves very probably, and a nest of internecine discord for Eastern Europe; but they are delightful for the stranger, and the bird of passage should surely have one solitude left wherein to find rest; regions where the refined tortures of the post cannot reach; where debts can be defied and forgotten across the stretch of those dense pine-woods which sever you from the rest of mankind; where the only highway to your quarters is a rapid surging river, with a timber-raft drifting down it; where, whirled along by gipsy horses and gipsy drivers through vast wooded tracks, you halt and wake with a pleasant wonder to find yourself in the broad streets and squares of a populous city, of which, though you are not more geographically ignorant than your brethren, you had not the haziest notion, and whose very name you do not know when you hear it, waking at the cessation of the horses' gallop and the gipsy Jehu's shouts, to open your eyes upon the clear Moldavian or Wallachian night, with the sound of music from some open casement above. Regions such as these are the Principalities, and who would not keep them so, from the Danube to the Dniester, from the Straits of Otranto to the Euxine, for the refuge of necessitous wanderers who have an inconvenient connection, a tiresome run upon them from the public, or a simple desire for a paradise where a woman will not follow them, where

letters will not come, where the game districts are un
beaten, and the deep woods and wild valleys as yet
unsketched and unsung?

Through the Principalities, Erceldoune travelled in
as brief a time, from the early dawn when he had left
Paris, as mail trains, express specials, rapid relays of
horses, and swift river passages could take him, across
Tyrol and Venetia, Alps and Carpathians, Danube and
Drave, calling at Belgrade with despatches, and pushing
straight on for Moldavia. Every mile of that wild and
unworn way was as familiar to the Queen's Messenger
as the journey between London and Paris is familiar
to other men. Where steam had not yet penetrated,
and there was no choice but between posting and the
saddle, he usually rode; if the roads were level, and
the route unsightly, he would take the luxurious rest of
a "Messenger's carriage," and post through the nights
and days; but, by preference, hard riding carried him
over most of his ground, with pace and stay that none
in the service could equal, and which had made the
Arabs, when their horses swept beside his through the
eastern sunlight, toss their lances aloft, and shout,
"*Fazzia! Fazzia!*" with applause to the Giaour. He
rode so now, when, having passed direct from Belgrade
across the lower angle of Transylvania, and crossed the
Carpathian range, he found himself fairly set towards
Moldavia, with only a hundred miles or so more left
between him and Jassy, which was his destination.

The Principality was in ferment; Church and civil
power were in conflict and rivalry; England, France,
Austria, and Russia were all disturbing themselves after
the affairs of this out-of-the-way nook, conceiving that
with Greece in insurrection, and Italy in a transition

state, and Poland quivering afresh beneath her bonds, even Moldavia might be the match to a European conflagration, and open up the scarce-healed Eastern question; and an English envoy was then at Jassy, charged with a special mission, to whom the despatches which Erceldoune bore carried special instructions, touching on delicate matters of moment to the affairs of central and eastern Europe, and to the part which would be played by Great Britain in the event of the freedom of the southern states, and the success of the liberal party in Athens, Hungary, or Venetia. This one bag, with the arms of England on the seal, and the all-important instructions within, was all that he carried now, slung round his neck and across his chest by an undressed belt of chamois leather. He was wholly alone; his mountain guides he had dismissed at the foot of the Carpathians, for he had gone through the most dangerous defiles and thief-invested passes all over the world caring for no other defence than lay in his holster pistols. He had been stopped two or three times, once by the "Bail-up!" of Tasmanian bushrangers, once by a Ghoorka gang in Northern India, once by a chieftain who levied black mail in the rocky fastnesses of Macedonia,—but his shots had always cleared him a passage through, and he had ridden on with no more loss than the waste of powder and ball. He was too well known, moreover, in both hemispheres, to be molested, and the boldest hill-robbers would have cared as little to come to close quarters with one whose strength had become proverbial, as to get themselves into trouble by tampering with the State courier of a great power.

It had been a splendid day in the young autumn, and it was just upon its close as he went through the forests, his mare, a pure-bred sorrel, scarcely touching the ground as she swept along, swift as a greyhound or a lapwing. The air was heavily scented with the fragrance of the firs; the last lingering rays of light slanted here and there across the moss through dark fanlike boughs, cone-laden; aisles of pines stretched in endless and innumerable lines of paths scarce ever trodden save by the wolf, or the wild boar, or the charcoal-burner, barely more human than the brute; and, in the rear, to the westward, towered the Carpathians, with their black rugged sides reared in the purple sunset, the guard of the Magyar fatherland.

Now and then, at rare intervals, a little hamlet buried in the recesses of the forest, whose few wretched women wore the Turkish yashmák, spoke of Moldavia, or he came on a camp of naked wild-eyed gipsies of the country; but as evening closed in, and Erceldoune advanced into a narrow rocky defile, the nearest passage through dense pine solitudes, even these signs of human life in its most brutalised phase, ceased wholly. There was only the rapid ring of his mare's hoofs, given back by a thousand hollow echoes, as he swept down the ravine, with high precipitous walls of rock rising on either side, while the river thundered and foamed beside him, and the trees closing above-head made it well-nigh dark as night, though beyond, the summits of the Hungarian range were still lit by the last rays of the sun gleaming golden on eternal snows. Sitting down in his saddle, with his eyes glancing, rapid and unerring as a soldier's, on either side where the shelving rocks sloped upward in the gloom, Erceldoune dashed along the defile at a pace such as the blood horses of the desert reach—the surging of the torrent at his side, the winds rising loud and stormy among the black pine-boughs above, the intense stillness and solitude around, that are only felt in the depths of a forest or the hush of a mountain-side.

These were what he loved in his life: these nights and days of loneliness, of action, of freedom, alone with all that was wildest and grandest in nature, under no law but the setting and rising of the sun, riding onward, without check or pause, a fresh horse ready saddled when the jaded one drooped and slackened; these were what suited the passionate need of liberty, the zest to do and dare, the eagle-love of solitude ingrained in his Border-blood, and as latent in him as in the chieftains of his name when they had borne fire and sword far away into stout Northumberland, or harried the Marches in their King's defiance.

The pressure of his knees sufficing for her guidance without curb or spur, the sorrel scoured the winding ravine, fleet and sure of foot, as though the rocky and irregular ground had been a level stretch of sward, her ears pointed, her pace like the wind, all the blood and mettle there were in her roused; she knew her master in her rider. Dashing onward through the gloom thus, suddenly his hand checked her; his eyes had seen what hers had not. Thrown back on her haunches in the midst of her breathless gallop, she reared in snorting terror; any other she might have hurled senseless to the earth; he sat as motionless as though horse and man were cast together in bronze.

Across the narrow and precipitous path lay the felled trunk of a pine, blocking the way. She rose erect; and stood so for a second, her rider in his saddle firm as on a rock—a sculptor would have given ten years of his life to have caught and fixed that magnificent attitude;—then down she came with a crash on her fore feet, while from the black barricade of the levelled pine, through the thick screen of stiffened branches, shone the gleam of half a dozen rifles, the long lean barrels glistening in the twilight.

The brigands lay in ambush waiting him; and the hoarse shout of arrest was pealed back by the echoes.

"Your papers—or we fire!"

And the steel muzzles covered him front and rear, while the challenge rang out down the vault of the hollowed rocks.

Swiftly as lightning his eyes swept over the rifles and numbered them—eight against one; rapidly as the wind he drew his pistol from his holster and fired among them; a shrill shriek pierced the air, a man reeled headlong down into the gorge of the river foaming below, and without breath, without pause, Erceldoune put the bay at the leap, trusting the rest to her hunter's blood, and facing the levelled death-dealers full in the front. The gallant beast deserved his faith; she rose point-blank at the barricade, and leapt with one mighty bound the great pine-barrier and the glittering line of steel. She landed safe;—a second, and she would have raced onward, distancing all shot and defying all pursuit; but with a yell that rang from rock to rock, the murderous barrels she had overleapt and cleared, covered her afresh; the sharp crack of the shots echoed through the pass, three balls pierced her breast and flanks, bedding themselves where the life lay, and with a scream of piteous agony she threw her head upward, swayed to and fro an instant, and fell beneath him—dead. He sprang from the saddle ere her weight could crush him, and, with his back against the ledge of granite, turned at bay; hope he had not, succour there could be none in those dense mountain solitudes, those wastes of vast unpeopled pine-woods; in that hour he had but one thought—to sell his life dearly, and to deserve his country's trust.

The echoes of the conflict rang in quick succession on the stillness, thundered back by the reverberations of the hills, it was hot, close, mortal work in that narrow choked defile, Erceldoune, with his back against the granite, and his dead bay at his feet between him and his foes, had the strength and the fury of a legion, now that his wrath was up in all its might, and the blood-thirst wakened in him. A ball broke his right arm above the wrist; it fell useless at his side. He laughed aloud:

"Blunderers! why don't you hit through the lungs?"

And as he changed his pistol into his left hand, he raised it, and the man who had shot him fell with a crash—a bullet through his brain. He could not load again; his arm was broken, and the hoarse yell of men, infuriated to be defied, and exasperated at their comrades' loss, told him his minutes were numbered, as one cry alone grated on the night air from many voices; in Romaic, in French, in Venetian, in Hungarian;—varied tongues, but one summons alone.

"Your papers or your life! Death, or surrender!"

There was a moment's hush and pause; they waited for their menace to do their work without the bloodshed that they shirked from caution and from wisdom, rather than from humanity; and at that instant the moon, through one break in the black pine roofing above-head, poured its light through the pass. Round him in a half-circle, broken from their barricade and ambush now that his fire was spent, pressed his assassins, their faces masked by the crape drawn over them, their rifles covering him with pitiless purpose. With his right arm hanging powerless, and with the mare lying at his feet, the sole barrier between him and the cross-fire levelled at him, stood Erceldoune, reared to his full height, motionless as though he were a statue.

"Death, or surrender!"

The summons hissed through the silence with a deadly meaning, a hoarse snarl such as the hounds give when the stag holds them too long at bay. Erceldoune stood erect, his eyes glancing calmly down on the semi-circle of the long shining lines of steel, each of whose hollow tubes carried his death-warrant; a look upon his face before which the boldest, though they held his life in their hands and at their mercy, quailed; he knew how he should save his trust and his papers, though he knew that his life must pay the forfeit. He calmly watched the levelled rifles, and a half smile passed over his face;—they had brought eight against one! —it was a distinction, at least, to take so much killing.

"The devil will never give in!" swore with savage Hungarian oaths the farthest of the band. "Seize him, and bind him!—we don't want his blood."

"Take the papers, and gag him. Carl is right; we want them, not him," muttered another, in whose southern German the keen ear of him whose life they balanced caught the foreign accent of a Gallician.

One who seemed the leader of the gang laughed— a rolling, mellow, harmonious laugh, which thrilled through the blood of Erceldoune as menace and challenge had never done: he had heard it a few nights before in the gaslit salon of the Parisian café.

"Basta, basta! 'Too many words, my masters.' Kill the Border Eagle and strip him afterwards! His beak won't peck when he's shot down!"

"Stop—stop!" muttered a milder Sicilian. "Give him his choice; we only want the despatches."

"The papers then, or we fire!"

The moon shone clearer and whiter down into the ravine, while they pressed nearer and nearer till the half-circle of steel glittered close against him, within a yard of his breast;—and the Greek who in the Café Minuit had lamented so softly the prosaic fate of the violet bonbons, pressed closest of all. He stood quietly, with no change in his attitude, and his broken wrist dripping blood on the stone at his feet; the dark scorn of fiery passions had lowered on his face, stormy, dangerous, menacing as the wrath that lightens up a lion's eyes, while on his lips was a laugh—a laugh for the coward caution of his assassins, the womanish cruelty which compassed him with such timorous might of numbers, fearing one man unarmed and wounded!

"Death, or surrender!"

The cry echoed again, loud and hoarse now as the hounds' bay, baffled and getting furious for blood.

His back was reared against the rock; his left arm pressed against his breast, holding to him the seals that were his trust; his eyes looked down upon them steadily as he answered:

"*Fire!*"

And while his voice, calm and unfaltering, gave the word of command for his own death-volley, with a swift sudden gesture, unlooked-for and unarrested by

them, he lifted his left hand, and hurled far away
through the gloom, till they sank with a loud splash
into the bed of the swollen rushing river, the white
bag of the English despatches;—lost for ever in the
deep gorge, and whirled on into darkness with the passage of foaming waters, where no spy could reach and
no foe could rob them.

Then, as the ravenous yell of baffled force and infuriated passion shook the echoes of the hills, the report
of the rifles rang through the night with sullen murderous peal, and Erceldoune fell as one dead.

All was still in the heart of the forest.

The snowy summits of the Carpathians gleamed
white in the moonlight; the cry of the wild dog or the
growl of the wild boar, the screech of the owl or the
rush of the bat's wing, alone broke the silence; above
the dark silent earth the skies were cloudless, and
studded with countless stars, whose radiance glistened
here and there through dense black shadow, on moss,
and boulders, and cavernous gorges, and torrents plunging downward through the night. In the narrow channel of the defile, with gnarled pines above and waters
roaring in their pent-up bed below, there lay the stiffened corpse of the mare, and across her body, bathed
in her blood and in his own, with his head fallen
back, and his face turned upward as the starlight fell
upon it, was stretched the Queen's Messenger, where
they had left him for dead.

The night had passed on and the hours stolen apace,
till the stars had grown large in the heavens, and the
morning planet risen in the east before the dawn; and
he had lain there, as lifeless and motionless as the

sorrel beneath him, through all the watches of the night which parted the sunset of one day from the daybreak of the next. His right arm, broken and nerveless, was flung across the neck of the mare, as though, Arab-like, his last thought as he fell had been of the brute-friend whom he had lost, and who had died for him; the blood had poured from a deep chest wound till the black velvet of his riding-coat was soaked through and through, and the mosses and the grasses were dyed with the stream that bore his life away; his face was stern yet serene, like many faces of the dead upon a battle-field, and only a deep-drawn laboured breath, that quivered at long intervals through all his frame, showed that existence had not wholly ceased with the murderous volley which had brought him to the earth, as his own shot had brought the kingly fearless strength of the golden eagle reeling downward to its fate. Either the aim of his assassins had been uncertain from the fury with which they had levelled and fired when they had seen their errand baffled, and the despatches flung beyond all reach into the mountain gorge, or they had been blinded by the flickering shadows of the moon, and the lust of their vengeance on him, for two shots alone had touched him out of the five which had been fired at him. One ball had pierced his breast and brought him down senseless, and, to all semblance, lifeless; it had been aimed by the leader of the band who had trifled with his ice, and mourned over the conserve of violets in Paris a few nights before. The other bullet, which had struck him in the chest, and would have cut its way straight through the lungs, had been turned aside by the solid silver of his meerschaum, in whose bowl the ball was bedded, though the force of its concussion

would have stretched him insensible without a wound.
He had fallen as one dead, and they had left him for
such in the narrow defile, hastening themselves to leave
the pine-forest far behind them, and put the range of
the Carpathians between them and Moldavia, taking
their own wounded with them, and plunging into the
recesses of the woods, where all pursuit could be baffled,
all detection defied. Whether they were mountain
banditti, or masked nobles, or insurgent conspirators,
those vast solitudes would never reveal, since the deed
would tell no tales and bear no witness; his assassination, if ever known, would be traced, they deemed, to
gipsies or charcoal-burners, while the odds were a million to one that the fate of the English State courier
would never be heard of, but would remain in the
shroud of an impenetrable mystery, whilst he lay in the
lonely and untrodden ravine, till the bears and the vultures left his bones to whiten unburied when they had
sated their hunger on the sinewy limbs of the man who
had fallen to avoid the surrender of his honour and
his trust.

Darkness closes thus over the fate of many; he is
"missing," and we know no more.

Nearly lifeless thus, Erceldoune had remained
through the long hours where his assassins had left
him; about him only the shrieking of the owls, the
sough of the winds among the pines, and the distant
roar of the beasts of prey, to whom his enemies had
trusted for the completion and the burial of their work.
Weaker men would have succumbed to less danger
than he had often brooked and passed through scathless; and even now the athletic strength within him refused to perish. The flowing of the blood had stopped,

a laboured sigh now and then gave sign of vitality, though not of consciousness; then, as the night was waning, a shudder ran through all his frame, and his eyes unclosed, looking upward, without light or sense, to the starlit vault above.

He remembered nothing.

The deep skies and "the stars in their courses" whirled giddily above him; the pine-boughs flickered in phantom shapes before his sight; the sounds of the winds and of the falling torrents smote dully on his ear; he had no sense but of suffocation from the congealed blood upon his chest, and the sharp agony of every breath; he wondered dimly, dreamily, who he was, and where he lay. An intense thirst parched his throat and oppressed his lungs—a thirst he suffered from without knowing what the torture could be—and the plunge and splash of the cascades in the gorge below filled his brain with vague thronging images of cool still lakes, of rushing brooks, of deep brown tarns among his native moorlands, and through them all he stood ever up to the lips in the cold delicious waters, yet ever powerless to stoop and taste one drop! The sweep of a night-bird's wing touched his forehead as it flew low under the drooped pine-branches; at the touch consciousness slowly and confusedly awoke; the night ceased to whirl round him in a chaos of shadow, the planets grew clear and familiar, and looked down on him from the dizzy mists circling above. By sheer instinct he sought to raise his right hand; it was powerless, and as he stretched out his left arm he felt the chill, stiffened body of his lost mare, and the grasses wet with her blood and his own; then thought and recollection awoke from the mists of death, and he remembered all.

He knew that he was lying there wounded unto death, beyond all appeal for aid, all hope of succour, powerless to drive from him the frailest insect that with the morning light should begin the fell work of corruption and destruction, alone in his last hour in the desolation of the Carpathians, with no companion save the beast of prey, no watcher but the carrion kite.

Dread of death he had never known; there was no such coward weakness in him now, in his worst extremity, when he knew that he was dying, in the best years of his manhood, slaughtered by the baseness of treacherous assassination, alone in the pent defile where his murder had been planned, and where no human step would ever come, except it were that of some mountain plunderer, who would strip off the linen and the velvet that the birds of prey would have left untouched, while his bones should lie there through summer drought and winter storm unburied, unlamented, unavenged. Fear was not on him even now in his dying hour, but a mortal sense of loneliness that his life had never known stole over him as he wakened in the hush of the forest night, paralysed, powerless, strengthless, felled in his full force, slain, like the golden eagle, by a single shot. The heavens, studded with their stars, looked chill and pitiless; the rocks towered upward in the moonlight, shutting him out from all the peopled slumbering world; no sound smote the stillness save the distant sullen moan of the brutes seeking their prey, and the winds sweeping and wailing through the endless aisles of pines;—he died in solitude.

The night wore on; a profound and awful silence

reigned around, only broken by the growl of wolves or the scream of foxes from their distant haunts; the ravening cry borne on the blast of those who, with each second which passed away, might scent blood from afar off, and track it in their hunger, and come down to rend, and tear, and devour, finishing the work of slaughter. He heard that sullen bay all through the night where he lay, across the dead mare motionless; he could not have stirred a limb, though the fangs of the wild boar had been at his throat, or the wolves in a troop been upon him. Hope or thought of succour he had none; he was in the deep heart of the mountains, where none could come; and he knew too well the lore of desert and camp not to know that all chance of life was over, that his last hour was here, and that if the vulture and the boar did not track him out, he would die of the loss of blood alone; or that if his frame bore up against the exhaustion of his wounds through the day which would soon dawn, he would perish but the more slowly, and the more agonisingly of famine and of thirst.

Time wore on; the stars grew large as the morning drew near, and his eyes gazed upward at them where he lay in the pass of the defile; a thousand nights on southern seas, in tropic lands, in eastern aisles of palm, through phosphor-glittering waters while his ship cleft her way, through the white gleam of snow steppes while the sleigh bells chimed, through the torchlit glades of forests while the German boar or the French stag was hunted to his lair, drifted to memory as the moon shone down on him through the break in the massed pine-boughs;—for he had ever loved the mere sense and strength of life; all

> "the wild joys of living, the leaping from rock to rock,
> The strong rending of boughs from the fir-tree, the cool river shock
> Of a plunge in a pool's living water,—the hunt of the boar,
> And the sultriness showing the lion is couchant in his lair."

And he knew that this glory was dead in him for ever, and that when those stars rose on another night, and shed their brightness upon earth and ocean, forest and sea, his eyes would be blind to their light and behold them no more, since he would be stricken out from the world of the living.

At last,—it seemed that an eternity had come and gone,—the day reached him, dawning from the splendour of Asia far away.

The light streamed in the east, the darkness of the shadows was broken by the first rays of warmth, the night birds fled to their roost, and above the clouds rose the sun, bathing the sleeping world in its golden gladness, and shining full on the snow peaks of the mountains. The forest-life awoke; the song of countless birds rose on the silence, the hum of myriad insects murmured beneath the grasses, the waters of innumerable torrents glistened in the sunbeams;—and, alone in the waking and rejoicing world, he lay, dying.

About him, where never sunlight came, were dank grasses, and the gloomy foliage of pines, but above-head, far aloft through the walls of granite, was the blue and cloudless sky of a summer dawn. His eyes looked upward to it heavily, and with the film gathering fast over them; in his physical anguish, in his sore extremity, there were still beauty and solace in the day.

Yet, as he gazed, the heavens were darkened, the sunlit morning became more loathsome than all the

solitude and darkness of the night; wakened in the
dawn and poised in air, drawn thither by the scent of
blood, he saw the flocks of carrion-birds, the allies
whom the assassins trusted to destroy all trace of their
work, the keepers of the vigil of the dead! Cleaving
the air and wheeling in the light, they gathered there,
vulture and kite, raven and rock-eagle, coming with the
sunrise to their carrion feast, sweeping downward into
the defile with shrill and hideous clamour till they alit
beside him, in their ravenous greed, upon the body of
the mare, striking their beaks into her eyes and whet-
ting their taste in her flesh, rending and lacerating,
and disputing their prey.

Thus he had seen them, many a time, making
their feast on the lion or camel of the East: and a
sickness of loathing came upon him, and a horror un-
utterable;—bound in the bonds of death, and powerless to lift his arm against them, he must lie, half
living and half dead, whilst the hungry hordes tore at
his heart.

A cry broke from him, loud and terrible—a shout
for help, where help there could be none. Its echo
pealing from the rocks, scared and scattered the ravening birds one instant from their lust; they wheeled and
circled in the sunlit air, then settled once more on
their spoil.

A single vulture, driven from the rest, poised above
him—waiting. Looking upward, he saw the bird,
with its dark wings outstretched, sailing in rings round
and round in the sunlight glare, impatient and athirst,
its glittering eyes fixed on him—the watcher and the
harbinger of death.

By the sheer force of animal instinct, strength for

the moment was restored; he sprang up to drive from off him the murderous beak that would seek his life-blood, the carrion-greed that would wrench out his eyes whilst yet they saw the day! He leapt forward, striking wildly and blindly at the black shadow of the hovering bird;—at the action the wound opened, the hemorrhage broke out afresh—he fell back senseless.

CHAPTER IV.

"N'êtes vous pas du Paradis?"

Even in the silent heart of the Carpathian woods two had heard that shout of mortal extremity.

They were but a woman and a wolf-hound, resting together under the shade of the pines higher up, where the head of the torrent tumbled and splashed from rock to rock, its sheet of foam glittering in the warmth of the risen day. They heard it;—and the woman rose with a stag-like grace of terror, blent with a haughty challenge of such weakness, and the dog, with his bristling mane erect, and his head lifted in the air, woke the echoes with a deep-mouthed bay. Both listened —all was still;—then she laid her hand on the hound's shaggy coat, and gave him a single word of command. He waited, sniffing the scent borne to him on the wind, then, with his muzzle to the earth, sprang off: she followed him; the lights and shadows from the pine boughs above flung, flickering and golden, on her uncovered hair; a woman fair as the morning, with the free imperial step of the forest deer, and the beauty of the classic and glorious south; the beauty of Aspasia of Athens, of Lucrezia of Rome.

A few short seconds, and the hound plunged down
into the pass, baying loud in fear and fury, as though
he tracked the trail of the crime. The birds flew up
with whirling tumult from their meal, and wheeled
aloft, scared and scattered; the vulture that had her
talons tangled in the hair of the fallen man, and was
stretching her plumed throat to deal her first aim at
his sightless eyes, taking wing slowly, leaving her prey
reluctantly. The woman fell on her knees beside him
where he lay across the body of his slaughtered mare,
as lifeless to all semblance as the animal.

She knew that she was in the presence of crime,
and she believed herself in that of death; this man
had been slain foully in the heart of the forest, and she
was alone, in the mountain ravine that had seen the
guilt done and the blow dealt, alone with one whom
his enemies had left to perish and lie unburied for the
hawks and crows to tear. The night had witnessed
the sin and shrouded it; she and the sunny light of
day had tracked and found it. And the sickness of its
guilt was on her in all its ghastliness, in all its secret
craven vileness.

One thought alone seemed left her; was she too
late, or could this human life, even in its last hour, be
saved, be called back even though it ebbed away?

She felt for the beating of his heart; a quick shudder ran through all her frame—her hand was wet
with the blood that had soaked through linen and
velvet, and flowed in its deep stream from his breast.
Yet she did not shrink, but pressed it there, seeking
for the throbbing of the life; the pulse beat slowly,
faintly still, beneath her touch—he lived even now.
The carrion birds were poised on the boughs, or settled

on the rocky ledges, waiting for the prey which soon
or late must come to them; the hound was tearing up
the moss with his muzzle to the earth; she called him
to her; the dog was her friend, her guard, her slave—
he came, reluctantly, looking backward at the mosses
he had uprooted in his thirst for the scent they gave;
she drew him to her, and signed him to look at the
dying man where he was stretched across his horse;
then pointed to the westward with some words in Silesian. The hound looked upward an instant with
earnest, eloquent eyes, trying to read her will—then,
at his full speed, obeyed her, and went down the
ravine; she had sent from her her sole defender, while,
for aught she knew, the murderers of the man she
sought to save might return to the scene of their outrage, and deal with her as they had dealt with him.
But cowardice was scarcely more in her blood than in
his to whose succour she had come with the light of
the morning, and whose face was turned upward white
and rigid, in mute appeal, in voiceless witness, stern,
as one who has fallen in fierce contest, but calm as
though he lay in the tranquillity of sleep. She gazed
at him thus, till hot tears gathered in her eyes, and
fell upon his forehead; he was a stranger, and not of
her land; she knew not how his death had been dealt,
nor in what cause he had fallen, whence he came, nor
what his life had been; but his face touched to the
heart all of pity there was in her, where he lay blind
and unconscious in the glory of the sun, though many
had said that pity was a thing unknown to her. The
falling of her tears upon his brow, or the touch of her
hand as it swept back the hair from his temples, and
fanned his temples with a fragrant bough of pine to

freshen the sultry heat of the noonday, awoke him to
some returning life; a heavy sigh heaved his chest, he
stirred wearily, and his lips moved without sound. She
knew what he must need—all of comfort or of aid
that she could give—and folding one of the broad
dock leaves cup-shape, she filled it at the bed of the
torrent, and, raising his head, held the cold water to
his parched and colourless lips.

Unconsciously, instinctively, he drank and drank,
slaking the intolerable thirst; she filled it three times
at the channel of the river, and he drained in new
existence from that green forest-cup, from that fresh
and icy water, held to him by his ministering angel.
Then his head sank back, lying against her, resting on
her arm; his eyes had not unclosed, he was senseless
still, save that he was vaguely conscious of a sense of
coolness, languor, rest, and peace; and the vultures on
the rocks above looked down with ravenous impatience,
waiting till the watcher should weary of her vigil, and
their prey be their own again.

She would not have left him now though she should
have died with him. She knew the lawless brutality
of the mountain hordes of gipsies and of plunderers,
well enough to know that in all likelihood those who
had left him for dead might return to strip him of all
that was of value on his person, and would slay her,
without remorse or mercy, lest she should bear testimony
to them and to their work; but to desert him and leave
him to the lust of the carrion-birds and the torrid heat
of the noon never passed in thought even before her
—whatever fate should come of it, she had cast in
her lot with his.

The sun fell through the tracery of firs upon the

rushing water, the mosses red with blood, the black flock of the waiting birds, and the motionless form of Erceldoune, stretched across his slaughtered horse, his head resting, as if in the serenity of sleep, upon the bosom of the woman who had saved him, while above bent the magnificence of her face, with a golden light on its mournful splendour, and the softness of compassion in the lustre of the eyes that watched him in his unconsciousness.

Time wore on, the sun rose to noon height, the heat grew more intense, and they were still alone; he lay as in a trance still, but with that vague sense of coolness and of peace, all that he knew or sought to know; once his eyes unclosed, weary and blind, and saw, as in a vision, the face as of an angel above him. He had not strength to rouse, power to wonder, consciousness to know or ask whether he slept, or dreamed, or beheld but the phantom of his own brain; but his eyes gazed upward at the loveliness that looked down on him, with the warmth of morning on it, and it pierced through the mists of death and the chaos of unconsciousness, and sank into his sight and heart, never again to be forgotten. While the sun was at its zenith and the day rolled onward, he was conscious, through all his anguish, despite all his stupor, of the fragrance of leaves that fanned his brow and stirred the heated air with soothing movement, of the gentle murmur of river-waters sounding through the stillness, and—ever when his eyes unclosed and looked upward on the radiance of the day—of the face that he saw in the luminance of the light, even as the face of a guardian angel. And he knew no more in the dulness of lulled pain, in the languor of profound exhaustion.

The loud bay of a hound broke the silence when noon had long passed, the rapid rush of the dog's feet scoured over the rocks above and down the winding path; he had known that he had been bidden to seek succour, and had left those he first met no peace till they had followed him—two Moldavian peasants, herdsmen or stable-helpers, who had understood the meaning of the hound's impatient bark and whine.

At the sound of their steps she moved from the wounded man, and rose, with the grace which made her every action beautiful as the wild antelope's; imperial as a sovereign's in her court.

The Moldavians listened with profound reverence whilst she spoke, and without pause or question hastened to obey her command; deeds of violence were not so rare at the foot of the Carpathians, in the heart of the Principalities, as to excite either the horror or the wonder of the passive serfs; they went without a word to their work, wrenched down the long boughs of the pines, stripped them, lashed the bare poles together, and covered them with lesser branches of the firs, overstrewn in turn by the yielding velvet moss of the forest, till they had formed a rude stretcher, rough in form but fragrant and easy; then they laid him on it, lifting him with kindly gentleness. At the first movement which raised him, and the sharp agony it caused, careful and not untender though it was, he fainted; they might have taken him where they would; he knew nothing. The Moldavians prepared to raise the litter on their shoulders, then looked to her:

"Home, your Excellency?"

She started, and stood silent; then over the light

and beauty of her face swept a shadow, as of bitter memory.

"No—no!" she answered them, in their own Moldavian tongue. "Go to the convent of Monastica; it is nearer, and they will tend him better there. If any can save him, the Sisters will."

"And we are to tell them——?"

"Tell them where you found this stranger, lying as one dead, and powerless to say who are his assassins; do not give my name, or speak of me; that he is wounded, and alone, and in need, will be enough to gain him care and pity at Monastica. When you have left him in safety at the convent, come back here; you shall bury the horse, it shall not be food for vultures. Now go—each moment is precious. I shall know with what fidelity you serve him, and shall reward you as you do it well."

Yet, though she had bidden them go, she stood still, looking down on the litter where Erceldoune lay; she had saved this man's life at peril of her own, yet they would probably never meet again; she had redeemed him from amidst the dead, yet he would have no memory of her, no knowledge that she had been with him in the hour of his extremity, and rescued him from his grave. Her eyes dwelt on him in a silent farewell, and a certain tenderness came over all her face as she bowed her head, while her lips moved with the words of a Greek prayer and benediction over the life of which she knew nothing, yet which in some sense had been made her own by every law of gratitude for a great deliverance.

Then she signed to the bearers to raise the litter and go onwards. They wound slowly with their burden up the narrow pass, and she sank down on the fallen trunk levelled by his assassins for their barricade, her rich dress sweeping the blood-stained mosses, her head resting on her hands that were twisted in the lustrous masses of her hair; her eyes, with their mournful brilliance, their luminance fathomless as that of tropic skies by night, gazing into the depths of the torrent foaming below in its black bed; and at her side the Silesian hound, his mane erect, his head uplifted, his feet pawing the turf, as though he scented the blood-trail, and panted for command to hunt the evil-doers to their lair.

A small antique chamber, with grey walls and snow-white draperies; an ebony crucifix with a marble Christ hanging above an altar draped with velvet, and broidered with gold, and fragrant with lilies in silver cups; a painted Gothic window through which were seen stretches of green pine-woods and golden haze beyond: and an intense stillness through which pealed, softly and subdued, the chant of the *Agnus Dei, qui tollis peccata mundi;* these were what Erceldoune opened his eyes upon, and saw, and heard, when he awoke from a long trance that had been death itself for aught he knew, and through which he had only been conscious of burning torture, of intolerable pain, of mellow strains of music floating through his brain, and of one face of divinest beauty bent above him whilst he lay bound in bonds of iron, in swathes of fire. For he had been delirious for many days in the Convent of Monastica.

His life had hung on a thread; the ball was in his breast, and the fever of his wounds, combined with the

weakness consequent on loss of blood, had kept him in
sharpest peril through all the rest of that sultry autumn.
But the bullet had missed his lungs, and the intense
vitality and resistance in him brought him through all
which would have slain at a blow a weaklier and less
hardily trained frame. The skill in leechcraft of the
Sisters of Monastica was proverbial in the Principalities;
women who loved him could not have tended him more
tenderly and unweariedly than did those high-born
recluses who had sought the solitudes of the dense
Moldavian pine-forests, in a conventual community
different to those of any other country. He was saved,
and awoke one sunlit evening, conscious and calm,
gazing dreamily and wonderingly at the dead Christ
on the altar, and the narrow arched window, with its
glimpse of plain and forest through the slit, while the
Agnus Dei pealed on the stillness of the chamber. He
thought himself dreaming still.

To his bedside came a nun, pale, gentle, with dove-
like eyes, a woman no longer young. Erceldoune
looked at her dimly; the past was a blank, yet unfamiliar as the chamber was to him, and unreal his
own personality, he vaguely desired and missed what
he had seen throughout his delirium—what he did
not behold on awakening. And the first words he
spoke were:

"Where is *she?*"

The Sister shook her head, looking on him with a
compassionate welcoming smile.

"I cannot understand, my son. I can speak a
little French, but you must not talk yet, you are too
weak."

All European languages, most of the Eastern, had

been as familiar to him as his own. He repeated his question impatiently in the nun's tongue:

"Where is she?"

"Who, my son?"

"Who? A woman—or an angel—who has been with me always."

"None have been with you, my son, save myself and those of my Order."

He made a faint intolerant sign of dissent; and his eyes wandered over the place where he lay, in weary search, missing in consciousness and in reality the face which had been ever before him in delirium.

"Where am I, then?"

"In our convent at Monastica. You were found all but lifeless in the forest by two peasants, who brought you hither. You have been in sore peril, my son, but, by the blessing of the most holy Mother of God, we have wrought your cure. But keep silence, and rest now, you are very weak."

"Weak?—*I?*"

He repeated the word in marvelling incredulity; he who had stood face to face with the lion in the sultry African night, and measured his strength with the desert king's, and prevailed,—he who from his childish years upward, through a long, and daring, and adventurous life, had never known his force to fail, his power to desert him,—was unable to realise that he could be laid low and powerless as any reed levelled by the wind! Instinctively he lifted his right arm to raise himself—that right arm which had never failed him yet in battle, in storm, in the death-grapple, or in any blow dealt in love of justice, in hatred of dishonour—it fell nerveless and broken. *Then* he realised that his strength was gone; and for the sole time in his life, Erceldoune could have turned his face to the wall and wept like a woman.

"I remember," he said, faintly. "I remember now. The cowards shot me down, and she saved me. Tell them I destroyed 'the papers;' but——"

The words died away unintelligible to the nun, his head fell back, and his eyes closed; he felt how utter was his weakness. He lay exhausted, his thoughts wandering over all that past of peril which had long been a blank to him, and which now slowly and by degrees returned to memory, striving to realise what manner of thing this could be, this calamity of stricken strength which his life had never before dreaded or conceived. Sweeping like fire through his blood, and filling his frame as with fresh life, there came with consciousness recollection of the murderous gang who had stretched him there, and fierce, natural thirst for vengeance on his cowardly foes, for the hour of reckoning when he should rise and deal with that craven womanish brute, whose gentle mellow laugh had bidden them "kill the Border Eagle," and whose shot had brought him to the earth.

A fair and open antagonist Erceldoune would honour, and forgive frankly and generously from his heart; but to the coward treachery that struck him in the dark, he swore that death itself should not be more pitiless or more inexorable than his wrath.

The shadows lengthened through the painted window, the music ceased from the convent chapel, the nun left him, and knelt before the altar lost in prayer; it was intensely still, no sound was upon the air save that from the distance the bells of one of the Moldavian

monasteries were chiming the vespers—it was a pause
as strange in his strong, rapid, varied, richly-coloured
life of action and adventure as that which we feel
when we enter the shaded silent aisles of some cathedral, and the doors close behind us, shutting out all
the accustomed crowds, the busy whirl, and the swift
press, and the hot sunlight of the city we have left
without. He had never known in all the years of his
existence that profound exhaustion, that death-like pro-
stration, in which all vitality seems suspended, and in
which a lulled, dreamy, listless meditation is all of
which we are left capable; he knew them now as he
lay gazing at the altar, with its dead Christ and its
white river-lilies, and the bowed form of the kneeling
nun, while all sense of pain, of weakness, of thirst for
the just vengeance he would rise and reach drifted
from him, merged and lost in one memory. A memory
luminous, angel-like, as are the imaginations which fill
the mind of painters with shapes divine and visions of
beauty, but such as had never entered the life or the
thoughts of this man till now, when, in the sunset stillness of the lonely oratory at Monastica he saw ever
before him, with the depths of an unspeakable compassion in her fathomless eyes, the face of the woman who
had saved him.

Where was she?

He questioned ceaselessly for many days each of
the Order who came to his bedside and tended him
with skilled care, and brought him fruits and sherbet,
and prayed for him at the altar, where the lilies were
placed fresh with every dawn, and the dead God looked
down with serene and mournful smile. He insisted

that a woman had come to him in the defile when he
lay there dying, and had given him water, and had
saved him. They thought his persistence the remembrance of some delirious hallucination, some dream
which haunted him, and which he could not sever from
reality. He saw the Moldavian serfs, who came each
day during his danger to the convent for news of him;
and, whilst he rewarded them, interrogated them as to
how and where they had discovered him. They answered that a dog had led them to where he lay, and
that they had seen that he was all but lifeless, and had
made a litter of pine-boughs and brought him to the
gates of Monastica for succour. When he pressed them,
and insisted that a woman had been the first to rescue
him, the Moldavians shook their heads; *they* had found
him, and had brought him hither. They had barely
more intelligence than that of a kindly good-humoured
animal, and adhered doggedly to their statement; it
was useless to question them; Erceldoune bade them
be given half the gold pieces in his travelling-belt, and
let them go. It was not his nature to pursue uselessly,
nor to give expression to a futile annoyance or an unavailing disappointment; he was silent from that moment on the subject.

The nuns, with their Mother Superior, thought he
had become convinced that his fancy was the phantom
of his delirium. Erceldoune remained certain that no
unreality, no mere vision fever begotten, would have
been impressed as this was upon him; he remembered
what it would have been wholly unlike him to have
imagined. And this fugitive memory of one who had
been his saviour in his extremity, yet who was lost to
him on his awakening to consciousness, filled his

thoughts unceasingly during the lull of his life in the solitudes of Monastica.

For many weeks he lay there in the antique quiet chamber, with the glimpse of hill and torrent seen through its single casement, and the cadence of the *Angelus* or the *Pro Peccatis* alone breaking the stillness at matins, mass, or vespers; the inaction, the imprisonment, the monotony, were as intolerable to him as to a fettered lion, for though solitude might be oftentimes his preference, it was ever the solitude of freedom, of action, and of the grandeur of desert wilds. He recovered slowly but surely, the science of the sisters and his own natural strength bringing him through in the teeth of imminent peril; but it was far into the autumn, and the pines were the only trees not bare in the Moldavian woods, when he rose with anything of his old power in his limbs, with anything of the old muscular force in his right arm, and breathed without pain, and was free to go back to the world of the living without danger.

Meanwhile, Europe rang for a space with his attempted assassination. A Queen's Messenger could not have been left for murdered, and English state papers of the first and most secret importance been waylaid by so singular and trained a conspiracy, without the outrage being of import, and rousing alike the wrath of his government and the speculations of all other Powers. That those who had stopped him were no ordinary assassins and marauders the object of their plunder showed; common banditti would have menaced his money, not his despatches. It seemed evident that his enemies had been men of considerable resources and power, that they had been well acquainted with his movements, and that their object had been political. Southern Europe was in the throes of revolt, and much of central and eastern Europe seething in intrigue; political gamesters would have counted one man's assassination a very little cost for the gain of political information and advantage in their unscrupulous rouge et noir.

Amidst all, the criminals remained untracked. Moldavia said she did all she could to discover and render them up to justice. Whether or not this were true, they were undiscovered; the little State was heavily mulcted for the outrage, and the perpetrators went scot free at large, the night and their masks having shrouded them, the pine-forests telling no tales, and the sole clue to their subsequent identification lying in Erceldoune's recognition by voice of their ringleader, as the vivacious and graceful bewailer for the sacrifice of crystallised violets, whom he had met at the Paris café.

The menace of England failed to track his assassins and bring them to their reckoning; but he swore that sooner or later his own vengeance should find them, and strike home to that tiger brute whose laugh he would know again though a score of years should have rolled away before they stood face to face.

"You bear no malice to your savage murderers, my son?" said the Abbess of Monastica to him, wistfully, one day, an aged woman, white-haired and venerable, gentle as a child, and unworldly as an infant, for she had taken the veil in her fourteenth year, and had never left the convent now that she had reached her seventieth, save on an occasional visit, as permitted by Moldavian rules, to the innocent festivities of Jassy.

"Malice, madam? No! I am not a woman!"

The Abbess looked at him wistfully still; the answer was affirmative, yet she was not wholly secure that this was the meek and lowly mercy which she sought to win from him.

"Then you forgive them, my son, and would remember, if you met them, the Lamb of God's injunction, 'If thy enemy smite thee on one cheek, give him the other,' and would refrain from all vengeance—would you not?"

Erceldoune's hand came down on the massive oak table standing by him with a force that shook it to its centre.

"By my honour, madam, I would remember it so, that the life should not be left in one of them. Forgive? Ay! when I have turned dastard like them."

The Mother Superior gazed at him with perplexed trouble in her eyes; the childlike innocent woman could not understand the strong unfettered nature of the man, with its deep passions and its fiery honour, which made the low serpent meanness of malice as impossible and incomprehensible to him as it made the chastisement of cowardice and the vengeance of treachery instinctive and imperative, resistless as an impulse as it was sacred as a duty.

"But forgiveness is God-like, my son."

"May-be, madam; but I am mortal."

"But it is a human duty."

"To an open, gallant foe, madam—yes! I will render it him to-morrow, and honour him from my soul the better he fights me and the harder he strikes; but the serpent that stings me in the dark I set my heel on, for the vermin he is, and serve God and man when I strangle him!"

The venerable Abbess sighed; she had ministered to him through his unconsciousness and through his suffering, she had seen him bear torture with a silent endurance that seemed to her superhuman in its heroism, and she had wept over the stately stature, levelled like a cedar felled by the axe, and the superb strength brought down to worse than a child's weakness, till she had felt for him something of a mother's tenderness, and found it hard to urge him to love and to pardon his injurers. Moreover, Mother Veronica was no casuist.

"It must be bitter, my son, I know," she murmured, "and the evil spirit is strong in us, and fearful to subdue; but one who suffered a deadlier wrong than thine forgave the traitor and the murderer, though Judas sold him to the Cross."

Erceldoune gave a movement of impatience, and the muscles of his arm straightened as though by sheer instinct of longing to "deliver from the shoulder."

"Pardon me, holy mother, I am no theologian! But I know this, that if there had been a touch of loyalty and fealty among the eleven left, that scoundrel of Iscariot would not have lived till the morrow to hang himself. If I had been in Galilee, he would have had a lunge of steel through his lungs, and died a traitor's death!"

So startling a view of apostolic duty had never penetrated the sacred walls of the convent of Monastica; the whole range of her instruction from the Church had never given her a rule by which to deal with such a novel article of creed, and she sat silent, gazing at him with a wistful bewilderment, wondering what the sainted Remigius had replied when King

Clovis gave him a similar answer in the old days of Gaul.

Erceldoune, who felt a sincere gratitude to the aged woman who had showed him a mother's tenderness and care throughout a lengthened peril, bent to her with gentle reverence, which sat well upon him.

"Pardon me, madam, I spoke something roughly, and men should not talk of these matters to women. There is one broad ground on which we can meet and understand one another, that of your goodness to a stranger, and his sincere recognition of it. Let that suffice!"

And Mother Veronica smiled wistfully on him, and after seventy years of unsullied devotion to the Supreme Church, found herself guilty of the horrible heresy of loving one whose soul was lost, and whose wild living will, and erring, wayward creeds, were the most fatal forms of tumult and revolt against which the Infallible Faith warned her!

An eagle from his native Cheviot-side fettered in a cage, would not have been less fitted for it than Erceldoune for his imprisonment at Monastica; as soon as he was strong enough to be raised in his couch, and was able to use his arm, he beguiled the time with a pastime which had often whiled away hours and days of enforced inaction, in quarantine, on board ship, becalmed in the tropics, or cooped up in Marseilles during the mistral. He painted extremely well. He was too thorough a man of action, too truly the English Effendi of the Eastern nations, ever to take art or indolence by choice; but there had come many times in his life when to paint the rare scenery, or the picturesque groupings around him, had been his only available pursuit; and he did this with singular dash and delicacy, vividness and truth. Erceldoune would never have been a creative artist; he had not the imaginative or poetic faculty which idealises, it was wholly alien to his nature and his habits; but what he *saw* he rendered with a force, a fidelity, and a brilliance of hue which painters by the score had envied him. He passed the dreary weeks now at Monastica painting what he had seen; and the picture grew into such life and loveliness that the nuns marvelled when they looked on it, as the Religieuses of Bruges marvelled when they saw the "Marriage of St. Katherine" left in legacy to them by the soldier-artist Hans Hemling, whose wounds they had dressed, and cried out that it should be the Virginal altar-piece in a world-famed cathedral. Yet the picture was but a woman's face—a face with thoughtful lustrous eyes, and hair with a golden reflex on it, and lips which wore a smile that had something more profound than sadness, and more imperial than tenderness; a face looking downward from an aureole of light, half sunlit and half shadowed.

"Now I know that I have seen it, or I could not have painted it," said Erceldoune to himself, as he cast down his brushes; and to know that, was why he had done so.

"Keep the picture, madam, as altar-piece, or what it please you, in token of my gratitude at the least for the kindness I cannot hope to return," he said to the Mother Superior; "and, if you ever see a woman whose likeness you recognise in it, she will be the one to whom I first owed the rescue of my life. Tell her Fulke Erceldoune waits to pay his debt."

And Mother Veronica heard him with as much pain

in his last words as she had had pleasure in his first, for she saw that the phantom of his delirium was still strong on him, and feared that his mind must wander, to be so haunted by this mere hallucination of the lady of his dreams.

A few days later on, Erceldoune, able at last to endure the return journey through the mountains and across Hungary, attended a Te Deum to gratify the Abbess, in celebration and thanksgiving for his own restoration from death to life; left his three months' pay to the almsgiving of the Order; bowed his lofty head for the tearful benediction of the Mother Superior; and quitted the innocent community of religious women, in whose convent he had found asylum; the *Angelus* chiming him a soft and solemn farewell, as, in the late leafless autumn, while the black Danube was swelling with the first rains of winter, and the forests were strewn with the yellow leaves that covered the grave of his dead sorrel, he went out from the solitudes of Monastica back to the living world.

CHAPTER V.
"An Ignis Fatuus Gleam of Love."

"IT was a superb thing—magnificent!"

The most popular personage in the English Cabinet was standing on the hearth-rug of his own library of his wife's château of Liramar, South Italy, where he had snatched a brief autumn holiday, nothing altered and little aged since some twenty years before when the beggared Border-lord, in the pride and liberty of his youth and his ruin, had won the great Minister's liking for life, by—a defiance.

Erceldoune laughed, a little impatiently.

"Nothing of the kind! Any other man in the service would have done the same; simplest duty possible."

"Simple duties get done in this world, do they? Humph! I didn't know it. I suppose you expected, when you gave the word to fire, that the brutes would kill you—eh?"

"Of course! I can't think now how they missed it. I ought to have been riddled with bullets, if they had aimed properly."

"I believe he's half disgusted he wasn't wholly dead, now!" said his lordship, plaintively. "It was a superb thing, I tell you; but don't you do it again, Erceldoune. The trash we write, to bully and blind one another, isn't worth the loss of a gallant man's life. *We* know that! A terrible fellow went and said so too, in the Commons, last session; he was up, and nobody could stop him. He told us, point blank to our faces, that though we *posed* very successfully for the innocent public, we might as well drop the toga and show the sock and buskin before each other, as the attitudinising didn't take in the initiated, and must be a fearful bore always for us! Clever fellow. Tremendous hard hitter; but he wants training. By-the-way, the Principalities paid us down a heavy fine as indemnity for that outrage; half the money comes to you, clearly."

"I thank you, my dear lord, I have no need of it."

"Eh? What? I thought you were poor, Erceldoune?"

"I am; but I have never been in debt, and I want

nothing. Besides, if you will pardon my saying so, I don't admire that system of 'indemnification,'" pursued Erceldoune, giving himself a shake like a staghound where he leaned against the marble mantlepiece. "A single scoundrel, or a gang of scoundrels, commits an insult, as in this case, on England, or any other great power, through the person of her representative, or perhaps merely through the person of one of her nation; the state to which the rascals belong is heavily mulcted, by way of penalty. Who suffers? Not the guilty, but the unhappy multitudes, peasants, traders, farmers, citizens, gentlemen—all innocent—who pay the taxes and the imposts! With an outrage from a great Power, if accidentally committed on a traveller by a horde of thieves, you would take no notice whatever; if one were obviously done as a political insult, you would declare war. But when the thing happens in a small state, she is punished by an enormous fine, which half ruins her, for a crime which she could no more prevent than you can help in Downing-street the last wreckers' murder that took place in Cornwall. Pardon me, but I fail to see the justice or the dignity of the system; and for myself, when my own conviction is that the assassins who stopped me were not Moldavians at all, what compensation would it be to me to have the money wrung from a million or two guiltless people, whose country the cowards chose to select as their field? If you wish to avenge me, track the dastards, and give *them* into my power."

The statesman listened as they stood alone in the library, and looked at his guest, with humour lighting up his blue eyes.

"Erceldoune, if you hadn't that stiff-necked Scottish

pride, which would make you knock me down, in all probability, if I offered it, I would give you three thousand a-year to live with me and speak your mind," laughed his lordship, meaning his words too. "You are a miracle in your generation; you're not a bit like this age, sir; not a whit more than the Napiers; you speak rarely, and never speak but the truth; you have to choose between your life and your trust, and, as a matter of course, give up your life; you are moneyless, and refuse money the state would tender you, because you think it gained 'neither by justice nor dignity;' you have dined at my house in town, you have stayed in my house in the country; you know that I like you, and yet you are the only man of my acquaintance who has never asked me for anything! On my life, sir, you don't do for this century."

"Unfit for my century, my lord, because I value your friendship, and honour your esteem too highly to regard both only as ladders to 'place?'"

The minister stretched his hand out to him with one of those warm silent gestures of acknowledgment, very uncommon with him, but very eloquent. Too sweet and sunny a temper to be a "good hater," he was a cordial friend; how true and steadfast a friend those only knew who knew him in private life.

"Well, the State at least owes you something," he said, after a pause. "You must let us pay our debt. Messengerships never do lead to anything, but that is no reason why they should not in your person. There are many half civil half military appointments for which your life has fitted you, and which you yourself would fill better than any man I know; the governorship of some good island, for instance."

Erceldoune was silent a moment, leaning against the marble.

"I thank you sincerely, but I want nothing, and I have too much, of the nomad in me to care to relinquish my wandering life in saddle. Give me no credit for asceticism, or renunciation; it is nothing of the kind. I should have been born a desert chief, I have never been happier than in the Kabyles' 'houses of hair,' living on couscoussou and camel-flesh, and waiting for the lions through the night with the Zouaves and the Arabs. If you think, however, that I have really done enough to have earned any preference from England, I will ask you to send me on service, as soon as I am myself again, to South and East Europe, with your authorisation to take leisure in returning if I desire it, and full powers from the government to go to any expenses, or impress any assistance I require, if I should be able to discover the persons, or the track of the assassins."

"Certainly, you shall have both to the fullest extent. You shall have the authorisation of the Crown to act precisely as you see fit; and spare no cost, if you can get on the villains' trail, in bringing them to justice. I fear you will be baffled: we don't know enough to identify them; they seconded us well in France, and everything was tried, but failed. It was in Paris you had seen the man whose voice you recognised, wasn't it? Would you know him again?"

Erceldoune ground his heel into the tiger-skin of the hearth-rug as though his tiger-foe were under his feet: he longed to have his hand on the throat of the silky murderous brute.

"I would swear to his voice and his laugh any-

where a score of years hence; and I should know him,
again, too: he was as beautiful as a woman, though I
did not take his measure as I should have done had I
guessed where we should meet."

"The object, of course, was purely political, and
there are thousands of men—Carlists, Ultramontanists,
Carbonarists, Reactionists, Socialists, and all the rest of
the Continentalists—who would have held that they
only obeyed their chiefs, and acted like patriots in
shooting you down, for the sake of your papers. Well,
you shall have your own way, Erceldoune, and all
you ask—it is little enough! Lady George!" broke
off his lordship, vivaciously, as a party from the billiard-
room entered the library, "here is Erceldoune so en-
amoured of the country he was murdered in, that he
is asking me to have him sent off there again! These
Messenger fellows are never quiet: he says he ought
to be an Arab chief, and so he should be."

"He only wants the white haick to look like one,"
smiled Lady George, a lovely blonde, dropping her
azure eyes on him with an effective side glance—
wholly wasted.

Erceldoune, to his own infinite annoyance, had
found himself an object of hero-worship to all the
brilliant beauties down at Liramar, where he had been
bidden by the great Minister as soon as he was able
to leave Monastica, and where that unworn octogenarian
was himself taking a rare short rest in the November
of the year. His lordship was imperative in his summons to his favourite courier, to whom the southern
air was likely to give back the lost strength which
was still only returning slowly and wearily to muscles

and limbs whose force had been "even as the lions of Libya."

The story of his single-handed peril, his choice of death rather than disloyalty to his trust, in the silent ravine of the Moldavian pine-woods, had sent a thrill of its own chivalry through the languid, *nil admirari*, egotistic, listless pulses of high-bred society. Erceldoune was the hero of the hour if he chose; and the Border Eagle might have folded his strong pinions under the soft caress of a thousand white hands. But he did not choose: he had never cared for women — they had never gained any hold on him. Steeped in vice in his earliest years, sensuality had little power over his manhood; and the languid intrigues, the hollow homage, the "love" of the drawing-rooms — pulseless, insipid, artificial, frivolous, *paré à la mode* — were still more contemptible, and absolutely impossible to him. Nor was fashionable life to his taste: its wheels within wheels ill suited the singleness of his own character; the feverish puerility of its envies and ambitions woke no chord of sympathy in him; and its hot-pressed atmosphere was too narrow, and too rarefied with heat and perfume, for the lungs which only breathed freely on the moorland and the prairie, on the ocean and the mountain-side. A man once bound to the great world is a slave till the day of his death, and Erceldoune could not have lived in chains.

"You are very like one of the eagles of your own Border, Sir Fulke," said a French Duchesse at Liramar to him. She had been a beauty, and now, at forty, was a power — the customary development of a Frenchwoman.

"In love of liberty, madame, and solitude? Well, yes."

He thought how he and the golden eagle had fallen, much alike, and the thought crossed him vaguely, should he ever live to wish that the shot, like the eagle's, had told home?

"Yes, and if I were twenty years younger, I would tame you!" said the Duchesse, with a malicious smile. "Ah! how you would suffer, how you would beat your strong wings against the chains, how you would hate and worship, in one breath, your captor, and how you would pant out your great life in torture till you sank down at last in slavery as intense as your resistance!"

"*I!* You do not know me much, Miladi."

The Duchesse gave him a perfumy touch with her fan as she swept away.

"Bah! M. Erceldoune, I know your tribe and I know their tamers. You will find a worse foe than a bullet, soon or late. Your assassins were merciful to what your love will be—*when* you love. See if I am wrong!"

And with a laugh of compassion and of mocking prescience the prophetess of dark omen went to her whist-table, where she played as well as Prince Metternich; and Erceldoune passed on his way to the smoking-room, a contemptuous disdain working in him;— "love!" he had never known it, he had never believed in it, the frank boldness of his nature had been proof against most of its seductions, and he only recognised in it a sophistical synonym for women's vanity and men's sensuality, or *vice versâ;* and, take it in the long run, he was undoubtedly right.

His passions were great; but they had never been

fairly aroused; and he had, or thought he had, them under an iron bridle, like some Knight of St. John, half priest, half soldier, stern warrior and ascetic monk in one, his soul, like his body, mailed in steel, and wrestling with the vile tempters of the flesh, as with twining serpents that sought to wreathe round and stifle out his martial strength, and drag it downwards into voluptuous fumes, and enervating shame, and weakness, that would disgrace his manhood and his pride, his order and his oath.

Yet vague, dreamy, half soft, half stormy thoughts swept over him of some love that this world might hold, with all the delight of passion, whilst loftier, richer, holier, than mere passion alone, which wakes and desires, pursues, possesses,—and dies. He believed it a fable; he was incredulous of its dominion; it was, he fancied, alien to his nature; he neither needed nor accredited it; yet the dim glory of some such light that "never yet was upon sea or land," half touched his life in fancy for a second. For, where he sat in the lonely smoking-room, with the smoke curling up from the meerschaum bowl which had turned the bullet from his heart in Moldavia, and floating away to the far recesses of Rembrandtesque shade,—out from the shadow there seemed to rise, with the lustre in the eyes and the unspoken tenderness upon the lips, the face of the one who had saved him.

The face of a temptress or an angel?

Erceldoune did not ask, as he sat and dreamt of that memory called up from the depths of thought and shade; then he rose with an impatient disdain of himself, and strode out into the white, warm, Mediterranean night.

Had he refused to surrender his life to any living woman, only to have it haunted by a mere phantom-shape, a hallucination wrought from the fever-fancies of a past delirium?

The great Minister went home; the gathering at Liramar remained with the hostess—Erceldoune with them; the sea breezes were bringing him back their old force into his limbs, and the mellow air was driving away the danger which for a time had threatened his lungs from the deep chest-wound where the ball had lodged. In physics he did not believe—he never touched them; air and sea-water were his sole physicians, and under them the fallen Titan rose again.

"I took too much killing!" he laughed to one of the men as they drifted down the waters lapping the sunny Sicilian shores, in the brief space which severs the day from the night. He had reported himself ready for fresh service, and the Messenger who was to bring the Italian bag to Palermo would deliver him despatches for the Principalities and Asiatic Turkey. Erceldoune was impatient to be on the move, and feel himself in saddle once more; while in action, too, he was no nearer on his quest—of those who had attacked his life, and of the one who had saved it. Phantom, hallucination, delirious memory, be it what it would, the remembrance which haunted him, and which he had no single proof was anything more tangible than a fever-born fancy, was strong on him—the stronger the more he thrust it away. The woman who had rescued him, and who had since been lost to him in the darkness of mystery and the wide wilderness of the world, he could not recall, save by such intangible unsubstantiated recollection as had remained to him from unconsciousness; common reason told him that it could be but a folly which haunted the brain from the visions of his long peril, but reason failed to drive it out, or shake the first impression which had ever wakened or seized his imagination. The idea which pursued him, the face he had painted in the monastic solitude of the convent, had become to him a living reality; he resisted it, he trampled it out; not unfrequently he recoiled and shuddered from it, as from the phantasia of impending insanity: but it remained there. Her face rose before him from the sea depths, when he plunged down into the dark violet waves, and let them close above his head; he saw it with every gorgeous sunset that flushed the skies with fire; he remembered it with every hour he spent alone lying on the sands, or steering through the waters, or waiting with his rifle for the sea-birds on the pine-crowned rocks. He could not banish it; and he used no sophism or half-truths with himself; he knew that, vision or reality, whichever it was, it had dominion over him, and that the search he so thirsted to make for his assassins was not more closely woven with his thoughts than the quest of what was but "un ombre, un rêve, un rien"—a phantom and a shadow.

The boat dropped down the Mediterranean that night, while the sun was setting, drifting gently through the blue stretch of the waves, while the striped sails were filled by a west wind that brought over the sea a thousand odours from the far Levant, and the voices of the women idly chaunted the "Ave Maria, Stella Virgine!" Erceldoune was stretched in the bottom of the boat, at the feet of a fair aristocrat, who leaned her hand over the leeward side playing with the water,

and letting the drops fall, diamond bright as her
rings, glancing at him now and then the while, and
wondering, as she had wondered long at Liramar, what
manner of man this was, who confessed himself poor
and a mere courier, yet bore himself like a noble; who
had the blood of an ancient race, and the habits of a
desert chief; who was indifferent and insensible to all
women, yet had, for all, a grave and gentle courtesy,
for the grape-girl among the vineyards yonder, as for
her, the patrician and the queen of coquettes, leaning
here. He was unlike anything in *her* world—and
Lady George would fain have roused in him the forbidden love which she, proud empress though she
was, had learned, in her own despite, as her own
chastisement.

But Erceldoune lay looking eastward at a lateen-
boat cutting its swift track through the waters; so little
had her beauty ever caught his eyes, that he never
even knew that he had roused her interest. Vanity he
had absolutely none; and as for pride in such uncared-
for, unsought victories, he would have as soon thought
of being proud that a bright Sicilian butterfly had flown
beneath his foot, and been crushed by it.

"How beautifully she cuts her way!" he said to
the man beside him. "Look how she dips, and lifts
herself again—light as a bird! She will be past us
like lightning."

Lady George glanced at her rival across the sea;
how strange it was, she thought, that any man should
live who could look at a lateen-boat rather than at her!

> "As with a bound
> Into the rosy and golden half
> Of the sky,

I suppose," she quoted listlessly.

Their own vessel floated lazily and slowly; the lateen-craft came on after them, as he had said, turned into a pleasure-boat, and draped with costliness, and laden with a fragrant load of violets gathered for distilling, piled high, and filling the air with odour. The skiff passed them swiftly;—half-screened by the rich draperies, the tawny sails, and the purple mound of the violets, and turned half from them, and towards the western skies, as the boat flashed past in the haze of light, he saw a woman.

With a loud cry he sprang to his feet, the vessel rocking and lurching under the sudden impetus;—he had seen the face of his dreams, the face of his saviour. And the lateen-boat was cutting its swift way through the waves, away into the misty purple shadow out of reach, out of sight!

"Neuralgia?" said one of the men. "Ah! that is always the worst of shot-wounds."

"You are ill?—you are in pain?" asked Lady George; and her voice was hurried and tremulous.

Erceldoune set his teeth hard, his eyes straining into the warm haze where the lateen-boat was winging her rapid way, out of reach, while their own lay idly rocking on the waves.

"Pardon me—no," he said, in answer to them, for the man's nature was too integrally true to seek shelter under even a tacit acceptance of an untruth. "I saw one whom I recognised as having last seen in Moldavia the day the brigands shot me down. I fear that I foolishly startled you all?"

They thought it nothing strange that any link with the memory of his attempted assassination should have roused him; and he leaned over the boat's side following the now distant track of the light lateen-skiff with his eyes,—silent in the wild reasonless joy, and the bitter baffled regret, which swept together through his veins. The face that he had dreamed had bent over him in his anguish and extremity, was then a truth, a living loveliness, a life to be found on earth—no fever-born ideal of his own disordered brain; he had seen again, and seen now in the clearness of reason, the face of the woman who had been his ministering angel. Yet, as she had been lost to him then, so she was lost to him now; and as the sun sunk down below the waves, and the sudden southern night fell shrouding the Sicilian boat in its shadows, the phosphor light left in its track and the odour of its violet freight dying off from the sea and the air, he could have believed he had but been dreaming afresh.

Was he mad? Erceldoune almost asked himself the question as he leaned over the vessel's side looking down into the purple shadows of the water. High-born, by the beauty of her face, and by the luxury with which that little skiff was decked, how should she have been in the wild solitudes of the Moldavian forest? Compassionate to his peril and extremity, would she have cared nothing to know whether death or life had been at last his portion?—and could an act of such noble and pitying humanity have needed the veil of mystery and denial in which it had been shrouded by the serfs' repudiation of all knowledge that any save themselves had found him?

Yet, the face of which he had dreamed, he had seen now in the evening light of the Mediterranean—the mere phantom of a delirium could not have become vivid and living thus. A heavy oath was stifled in his teeth, as he stood with his eyes strained to pierce the cloudy offing. Why had he not been alone, that—a few yards more sail flung out to the winds, and his own hand upon the helm—his boat could have given chase down the luminous sea, and have swept away with hers, no matter at what cost of sand-reef or of shipwreck, into that golden mist, that twilight darkness!

CHAPTER VI.

The Wisdom of Mother Veronica.

THE pines were tipped with their lightest green, the torrents were swollen with the winter rains, the rafts were rushing, lightning-like, down the rivers in the impetus that the spring lends to nature and to labour, to the earth and the human swarm it bears; primroses strewed every inch of ground under the boughs of the pine-woods; and the light of the young year was on the solitary hills and ravines as Ercoldoune rode once more into Moldavia, through the same defile where his assassins had waylaid him.

He checked his horse, and wondered if the horrors of that wild night had been all a dream, as he looked down: the tumbling water glistened in the sunlight, the grass had grown in ranker luxuriance where the good bay was laid in her last resting-place; over the place where he had fallen, bright clusters of spring-flowers blossomed among the moss; two records of the night's work alone remained: the black and broken pine-trunk that had been flung across the road, and had only been now lifted to one side, and a dark crimsoned stain, where the granite rock had been soaked and crusted with his life-blood, too deeply for even the snows of winter wholly to wash out the shade it left. The most thoughtless man would have felt some shadow of earnestness steal on him in such a place, with such a memory; Erceldoune, though used to meet death in every shape, and too habituated to danger to ever feel its terror, let the bridle slacken on his stallion's neck, and gazed down on the wild ravine round him, with something of solemnity upon him—had the shot been one hair's breadth nearer his heart, he had now been rotting there with his dead horse; had she who had come as his guardian angel been one instant later, his eyes had now been blind to the light of the sun, and his life numbered with the vast nameless multitudes of the grave.

It was a strange unreal knowledge to the man in whose veins life swept with such eager vivid force, and in whose every breath and every limb strength was so vital, that life and strength both seemed eternal.

It was very still, here in the depths of the Danubian defile; and in the flood of sunset light he seemed to see the face of the woman he had lost. His heart went out to her with a futile, passionate longing; the pine-boughs that bent over him had shadowed her, the water that foamed at his feet had been touched by her hand; here his head had rested on her bosom, here his eyes had looked upward through the mists of agony to hers. The very grasses whispered of her; the very rocks were witness of his debt to her!

In madness with himself, in passionate thought of her, he dashed the spurs into his horse's flanks, and swept, full gallop, down the steep incline. Was *this* Love?

For a woman seen but twice, for a mere memory, for a loveliness, fugitive, nameless, dreamlike, mourned and lost!

In the first spring-time of the year, Holy Mother Veronica sat in her pleasant little chamber, which was panelled with maple wood, and filled with early flowers, and delicate carvings, and the soft-hued heads of saints, and had as little of conventual gloom as though it had been a boudoir in a château rather than an Abbess's "cell" in Monastica; for they are no ascetics, but enjoy life in their way, those innocent, child-like, sunny-natured nuns of Moldavian Monastica.

Mother Veronica sat in deep thought, the sun upon her silvered hair, primroses and an antique vellum "Horæ" lying together in her lap—the fresh gifts of Nature with the worn manual of Superstition—venerable and happy in her serene old age. The primroses were untouched, the missal lay unread, Mother Veronica was looking out at the blue mountain line, and thinking of the stranger to whom she had felt almost that mother's tenderness which her life had not known, though in her eyes he was godless and a lost soul, a grand Pagan whom it was hopeless to save; thinking wistfully, for she believed that on earth she would never see him again. Suddenly she heard in the convent aisle without, the iron ring of a tread more like that of the Knights Templar, who had once held Monastica, than like the subdued slow step of her order;—she started and listened; could it be that the Virgin, had heard her prayers, and allowed her to see the heathen who was, perchance, so wrongly dear to her? She hardly hoped it; yet she listened with longing anxiety. It was very sinful to so wish to behold the mere mortal life of a heretic!

But that he was such an infidel Mother Veronica wholly forgot when the door unclosed, and a sister ushered in Erceldoune.

"Ah, my son, the blessing of Heaven rest on you!" cried the Abbess, stretching out her hands with fervent welcome. "I never thought to see you here again. It is good—very good—to have remembered us, and come back from your great world to Monastica!"

"Far from it, madam," answered Erceldoune, bending lower to the simple venerable woman than he had ever bent to the patrician coquettes of Liramar. "It would be sorely ungrateful if I could enter Moldavia without seeing those to whom I owe it that I am not now rotting in its pine-woods."

"And you are recovered—entirely?"

"Entirely. My strength is wholly returned."

Her hands still holding his, Mother Veronica drew him nearer to the light, looking upward at him with as much pride and tenderness as though he had been her son by blood instead of by the mere title of the Church; then a sudden remembrance lightened her aged face and sunken eyes with all the innocent eagerness of a life which lives in solitude, where each chance trifle is a rare and wondrous event.

"Ah! my son—I forgot—I have so much to tell you. I have seen the woman of your picture!"

"*You have!* And she—?"

"She saved your life,—yes; but it is all so strange! Listen—I will tell you—"

"Do, for God's sake! And she—?"

"Oh, my son, do not take a holy name in vain for a woman's perishable beauty!" said Mother Veronica, with plaintive reproof, while Erceldoune crushed his heel into the maple-wood floor in a sore effort to contain his soul in patience. "It was about a month ago that at a Salutation to the Virgin, to which, as you know, strangers come sometimes from Piatra, even sometimes as far as from Ronan and Jassy, I lifted my eyes during the service—I cannot tell how I came to do so wicked a thing—and I saw—ah! I thought I should have fainted!—in the shadow of another aisle, living before me, the glorious beauty that you painted in our altar-piece! I never sinned so deeply in my life before, but, though I never raised my eyes again, I thought of nothing but her all through the mass. If she tempted me so, how must she have tempted the souls of men! She is more lovely even than your portrait—"

"But her name—her country?" broke in Erceldoune, impatiently. "Why have withheld from me that she—"

"My son, I will tell all I know if you do not hasten me," pleaded Mother Veronica. "When the Salutation was over, Sister Eunice came and told me that a lady sought to see me; I bade her bring her here, and it was here I saw her—the woman of your picture, with those deep marvellous eyes, and that hair which is like light. Ah! how wicked it is that a mere earthly beauty of form can touch us and win us as can never all the spiritual beauty of the saints. One sees at once that she is of noble rank, and young, but she is a woman of the world—too much a woman of the world! She apologised to me with a proud grace

that the base born never can have, my son (though we
ought to believe that the Father has made all equal),
and said she came to ask about a stranger who had
been succoured by us in the autumn, and been cured
of dangerous wounds; had he suffered much—had he
been wholly restored? Then I knew that what we
had deemed delirium had been the truth, and that this
was she who had saved you; but I said nothing of
that, only answered her fully of your illness and of
your cure, and then added to her, as it were carelessly, that in your convalescence you had painted an
altar-piece for Monastica—would she like to see it?
She assented—she has a voice as low and rich as
music—and I led her to the chapel, and pointed to
the Virgin's altar, where it hangs. She went forward
—and I saw her start; she gave a stifled cry, and
then stood silent. She could not but see that it was
her own beauty. I let her stand awhile, for I thought
she was agitated; then I went forward, and said to her,
'He who painted that picture, my daughter, when he
left it with me, said, "If you ever see a woman whose
portrait you recognise in it, she will be the woman to
whom I first owed the rescue of my life. Tell her
Fulke Erceldoune waits to pay his debt." My daughter, you are she.' Her lips quivered a little though
she answered me coldly. 'He said that? How could
he have known? how could he have remembered?'
'How well he remembered, my daughter,' I answered
her, 'his painting says. Your words confess that you
first saved this stranger's life; why conceal so noble
an act of mercy?' She turned her eyes on mine, half
mournfully, half haughtily. 'I had due reason. It
was little that I did for this English traveller. My

hound led me to him, and I found him, as I supposed, dying—left for dead, doubtless, by some forest brigands. I did what I could to revive him—it was scarce anything to name—and stayed with him while I sent my dog to bring assistance. That was all; it merited no gratitude, and I had no thought that he would ever know it, since he was unconscious all the time I watched him.' 'But you were in peril, my daughter? If the brigands had returned—' Ah, my son, if you could have seen the proud beauty of her face as she smiled on me! 'Is life so beloved a thing, that we must be too great cowards to chance its loss when another is in extremity, and needs us?' The words were so courageous, and yet so mournful! She is as beautiful as the morning, but I fear she is not happy."

Erceldoune paced the little chamber to and fro for a second, his arms folded, his head bent, his heart moved to a strange softness and pain that his life had never known; then he paused abruptly before the Abbess.

"Her name! Tell me her name!"

"Alas, my son! I cannot."

"*Cannot?* Great Heaven! you never let her go unknown?"

"Do not be angered, my son. It was not in my power to prevent it; she chose it to remain secret. All I know is, that she let fall a gold perfume-box as she left my cell, and that as I lifted it, and sent Daughter Virginia with it after her, I saw engraven on the lid one word only—'Idalia.'"

"Idalia!"

He repeated the word with passionate tremulous

eagerness; it seemed to him the sweetest poem poets could ever dream, the fairest echo that ever the world heard, the treasury of all that womanhood could give of beauty, grace, and love, that single Greek name of the woman he pursued; yet,—it could serve him in nothing.

"Idalia!—Idalia! That will do nothing to find her? Oh, my God! she is lost to me as she was lost in Sicily."

The words were more full of bitterness than any she had ever heard wrung from him by his physical anguish, while he paced up and down the narrow chamber.

"It is very strange; but indeed it was no fault of mine," pleaded the Abbess, a little piteously, for she saw that it was a heavy blow to him, and she dreaded alike to see the pain or the wrath of that unchastened Pagan nature before which the Mother Superior, used only to deal with and chasten or solace the untroubled souls of guileless women, whose heaviest sin was an omitted prayer, felt helpless. "And perhaps it is for the best that you should not know where to seek her, for hers is a wondrous sorcery, and it might be a fatal snare: if it is such a delight of the eyes to me, what might it be to you? It is not well to see anything of a mere human earthly charm so glorious as that."

Erceldoune stretched his hand out with an irrepressible gesture.

"But surely you told her, at the least, how great I held the debt I owe to her?—how deeply I felt her humanity, her heroism, her self-devotion to a stranger? How—"

"I told her, my son, that in all your delirium you spoke but of her, and that on awaking to consciousness your first question was for her, even as the first effort of your strength was to paint her own loveliness upon the canvas; and she heard me silently, and seemed profoundly moved that you should have thus remembered her," pursued innocent Mother Veronica, placidly, unwitting in her serenity that she was but "heaping fuel to the burning," while where Erceldoune leaned in the shadow his face flushed hotly again. Spoken out in the calm words of the Superior, his passionate memory of an unknown woman looked more wild and more tender than he liked that anything of his should look. "I spoke of you as I felt," went on Mother Veronica; "and she seemed to like to hear all, which was but natural, since she saved your life, and found you so cruelly injured in the forest; though she said that you owed her little, and that the dog had done more for you than she had. She looked long at the painting. 'The English stranger has honoured me too much,' she said at last; 'and so, holy mother, have you. The portrait—*my* portrait—should not be chosen for any altar-piece. Hang it, rather, in the shadow, with that Guido's Magdalen.' And with those words, my son, she bade me farewell; and I felt, all sinful though it was to feel such a thing for a mere mortal creature, as though the light had sunk out of Monastica when she was gone. Ah! just such beauty must have been the beauty of the glorified Dorothëa, when she brought the summer-roses and the golden fruit of Paradise at midnight to the stricken unbeliever!"

Erceldoune stood long silent, leaning against the embrasure, with his head bent; except under the immediate impulse of passion, many words were not natural to him.

"Is she married?" he said, suddenly, after a lengthened pause.

"I cannot tell, my son. She said nothing of herself. Her dress is rich, her manners noble. I know no more. She had many rings upon her left hand; one of them might be her marriage-ring. That she is not happy, I am certain."

Erceldoune crushed a bitter oath to silence. Not even to know *this* of her!

"Can I see the picture in the chapel?"

"Surely, my son. Do we not owe it to your art and your gift?"

His step woke the hollow echoes of the arched aisles as it rang on the stone pavements, and he passed into the chapel, far famed through all the Danubian Principalities for its antiquity, its riches, and its architecture, which closely resembled that of the Bohemian Chancery at Vienna. It was cool and dark and still, the glass stained with deep and glowing hues, the lofty arches stretching on till they were lost in gloom; and the face of his own painting, with its brilliant light, looked down like that of an angel from out the depths of shade. Thus had he seen her,—and seen only to lose her once more,—in the violet shadows and the falling night of the Sicilian seas.

Erceldoune stood there long, and in silence, as before him a Templar, leal to his monastic oath through half a lifetime, might have stood before the same altar, seeing in the virginal beauty of some sacred artist's painted thought only the loveliness of the woman before whom the asceticism of the soldier, priest, and anchorite had flung down sword and shield and cross, and bowed and fallen.

The Abbess Veronica looked at him with an earnest sadness, then went and laid her hand on his arm:

"Do not think so much of her, my son; it may be she is not worthy of it. A beauty divine she has; but it is not always in those of fairest form that the divine spirit rests. There is mystery with her; and where there is mystery, my son, all is not well. I doubt me if she be what you deem her. The belladonna is beautiful, but living in darkness, and loving the shade, it brings only poison and death. Take to your bosom that flower alone, which lives in the clearness of light, and folds no leaves unopened from your eyes."

He gave a movement of impatience, but he answered nothing: it was not in him to take shelter beneath denial, when to give the lie would have been to lie, and he turned and walked up and down the aisle, where, a few months before, the living presence of the woman he sought had been, his tread re-echoing through the silent chapel, in which the step of man had never been heard since the days of the Temple Knights. And as he went, pacing slowly to and fro in the religious solitudes, he saw nothing but the face above the Virgin's altar—the face of the woman on whose heart he had rested, from whose hand he had drunk the living waters of life, and yet who was lost to him—a stranger and untracked—in the wide wilderness of the world.

He stayed that night at Monastica.

The nuns were innocent as children, and though reluctant to receive a male guest, entertained him cheerfully, once admitted. He was reluctant to leave the place where at least one could speak to him of the woman whose memory was so dear, where at least her

presence once had been, and still seemed to him to
sanctify the very stones that she had trodden. Mother
Veronica made him welcome with almost a mother's
devotedness: this strong, fiery, lawless heathen, as she
held him, had grown very dear to her, and having
eased her conscience by warning him, she could no
longer resist the temptation, so strong in a monotonous
and one-idea'd life, of dwelling on the romance and
mystery of the single episode which had broken the
even tenor of her days. He listened over and over
again to the same words, never wearying of them, for
he was in love with his own ideal as utterly as any
lad of twenty. In the pause between her religious
services, in the hush of the spring-tide, while she walked
with him in the still convent gardens, and at the supper
she shared with him in her pretty little cell, with its
maple wood, its sunny pictures, and its fresh primroses,
that had nothing of the recluse, as the meal had nothing of the ascetic in its frothing chocolate, golden
honey, milk-white cakes, dainty river fish, and newly
laid eggs, the Abbess spoke incessantly and garrulously
of but one theme. She did penance for the indulgence
every ten minutes, it is true, by a gentle little pleading
sermon against the desire of the eye, the perishableness
of earthly beauty, and the danger of erring idolatry;
but the penance done, she perpetually nullified it by
dwelling, in all her innocent unwisdom, on every grace,
on every word, on every charm of the woman against
whom, nevertheless, she tenderly warned him. Every
syllable she uttered heightened a hundred-fold the
sorcery which his lost saviour's memory had for him,
and all her simple warnings drifted past his thoughts
unheard. A child's hand will sooner stop the seas,

when they rise in their wrath, than counsels of caution
or of prudence arrest the growth of a great passion.

"Idalia!"

That solitary word seemed all he could see or hear
as he sat in the twilight, while the mist slowly stole
over the bright primroses, the sculptured ivory Passion,
and the silver I.H.S. that glistened on the draperies of
the Mother Superior's peaceful altar, as it had once
done on the *labarum* of the Constantines.

"Idalia!"

It seemed to fill the night, that single name of the
shadow he pursued, as Erceldoune stood on the balcony
that ran round the convent, alone, while all around
him slept, while the great forests stretched away on
every side into the darkness, burying in them the little
Swiss-like châlets, in each of which there dwelt, accord-
ing to Moldavian custom, one nun alone; safe in that
lonely wilderness, though with no guardian but her own
sanctity.

The stars were bright, the murmurs of innumerable
torrents filled the silence, the heavy odours of a million
pines rose up from below, and over the far Danubian
plains the woods trembled as though stirred by the
shadowy hosts of Persian myriads and of Scythian
chiefs, of Roman legions and of Avar hordes, whose
bones had whitened in their eternal sands, and whose
graves were locked in their funereal depths. It was
profoundly still, while from the convent tower the midnight strokes fell slowly, beating out the flight of Time,
that in its merciless eternal movement had left of the
Great King but the writing on the wall, but the mute
story of Assyrian stones; and that had swept down,
like insects of a summer day, the mailed and mighty

cohorts who once had passed the windings of the Ister, with the shouts of "Ave Cæsar Imperator!" proudly heralding the passage of the Last Constantine. Where were they—the innumerable Peoples of the Past?

Where were they?—bright Greek and delicate Persian, ravening Hun and haughty Latin, swift Scythian and black-browed Tartar, brute Mogul and patrician Roman, whose bones lay buried there, unmarked, unparted, in the community of the grave?

The Danube rolled along its majestic waters, while centuries and cycles passed; sweeping onward under the same sun that once flashed on the diadem of Darius; flowing in solemn melody through the night under the same stars which the wistful eyes of Julian once studied in the still lonely watches of his tent. The river was living still, dark and changeless, rushing ever onward to the sea; but they, the fleeting and innumerable phantoms, the Generations of the Dead, were gone for evermore.

As he stood there in the midnight solitude, it seemed to him as if, in the midst of his virile and adventurous life, he suddenly paused for the first time, and thought itself paused with him; it was because he was, for the first time, a dreamer—for the first time a lover.

Something of melancholy, of foreboding, were on him; the world for once seemed weary to him; he wondered why men lived only to suffer and to die. In all his years before he had never felt this; they had been filled with rapid action and vigorous strength, finding their joys in the close conflict of peril, in the mere sense of abundant and powerful life, in the victories of an athlete wrestling breast to breast with the lion or bear, and in the swift sweep of a wild gallop through jungles of the tropics, or cold crisp dawns of northern moorlands. Now he knew that his life was no longer under his own governance; now he knew that the vague fantasy of a baseless dream was dearer to him than anything which the earth held. It had its sweetness and its bitterness both: she lived; she had remembered him; she was not happy; this was all he knew, but it was enough to fill the night with her memory, and from those brief words to build a world.

His imagination had never awakened before, but now his fancies thronged with dreams, wild as a youth's, vague as a poet's, and dazzling as

Fireflies tangled in a silver braid.

Thus, before him, in the Danubian solitudes, once the battle-field of nations, the Persian of the Immortal Guard had thought of some gazelle-eyed Lydian, seen once, never to be forgot, in the Temple of the Sun; the wild Bulgarian had felt his savage eyes grow dim with tears of blood when the Byzantine arrow pierced his breast, and he remembered some Greek captive, loved as tigers love, who never again would lie within his arms, and to whose feet he would never bring again the pillage of the palace and the trophies of the hunt; the Roman Legionary leaning on his spear, on guard, while the cohorts slept in their black frozen camp, had dreamed of a gold-haired barbarian far away in the utmost limits of the western isles; whom he had loved under the green shadows of fresh Britannic woods, as he had never loved the haughty Roman matron who bore his name where tawny Tiber rolled.

Thus, before him, men had mused, in those forsaken
solitudes, of the light of a woman's smile, of the softness of a woman's memory, where, standing in the
silence of the night, he heard the fall of the torrents
thunder through the stillness, and watched the black
pines tower upward into the starlighted gloom. Nations
had perished on those shadowy battle-plains; but the
same river rolled unchanged, and unchanged the same
dreams of passion dreamed themselves away.

CHAPTER VII.
The Badge of the Silver Ivy.

It was midnight and mid-winter in Paris, snow
lying thick on the ground; dead lying thick in the
Morgue; outcasts gnawing the bones dogs had left, and
shivering on church-steps built by pious crowds, who
glorified God and starved their brethren; aristocrates
skimming over the ice, flashing their diamonds in the
torchlight, warm in their swansdown and ermine;
wretches who dared be both poor and honest sleeping,
famine-stricken, under bridge-arches, as such a twin-
insult to a wise world deserved; philosophers, male and
female, who were vile, and got gold, and *joliment
jouaient leurs mondes*, drinking Côte and Rhine wines,
and laughing at life from velvet couches. It was a
bitter icy night, and the contrasts of a great city were
at their widest and sharpest, as the chiffonnier searched
in the snow for offal as treasure, and the Princess lost
in the snow, as a mere bagatelle, wealth in an emerald
that would have bought bread for a million; as a young
child, half naked, sobbed, homeless, under the pitiless
cold, and a State Messenger, wrapped in furs, was

rolled in his travelling carriage through the bright gaslit streets. The Royal Courier was lying, stretched nearly at length on his carriage-bed, while he dashed through the capital full speed, not losing a moment to get through to Persia.

There was plenty of time to sleep while the train tore through the night to Marseilles, and he raised himself on his arm and looked out at the old familiar, welcome streets of Paris; a mistress for every new-comer, a friend to every well-worn returning traveller, a syren ever fresh, ever dear, ever unrivalled. As he did so, the carriage was passing down the Rue Lépelletier and before the Opéra, where the doors had just opened for one of those balls to which all Paris proper (or improper) flocks. The throng was great; the wheel of his carriage nearly locked in another, whose gas-lamps, flashing off the snow, lighted up the face of a woman within, with the azure of sapphires glancing above her brow. The Queen's Messenger started up from his carriage-couch and threw himself forward; his postboy saved the collision, his horses dashed on without a pause.

He flung himself back among his furs, with a fierce bitterness in his soul:

"Good God, again!—and *there!*"

The carriage whirled on, leaving the masked throngs to flock to the wild Rigolboche of the Opéra.

That night under the glitter of a chandelier in the Hôtel Mirabeau, before a fire which shed its warmth over the green velvet and walnut wood, the ormolu and silver, the mirrors and consoles of the chamber, two men sat smoking over claret and olives, having dined alone, by a miracle, in the midst of the laughing, dazzling, contagious gaieties of peopled Paris. In these days confederates meet over liqueurs and cigarettes, instead of in subterranean caverns; and conspirators plan their checkmates in a coffee-room, an opera-box, or a drive to an imperial stag-hunt, instead of by midnight, under masks, and with rapiers drawn.

One of the men was Victor Vane, the other that dashing Free Lance, that Monodist of the Sugared Violet, that political brigand of the Carpathian Pass, to whom the telegram had been addressed as to the Count Conrad Constantine Phaulcon: a man in physical beauty, physical prowess, talent, wit, and bearing, far the superior of the Englishman, yet whom the latter dominated and held in check, simply by that fine and priceless quality, which is colourless because inscrutable, and irresistible because prévoyant—Acumen. It crowns genius, and dethrones kings.

Socially, there was the same anomaly between them. Vane, of whose antecedents none knew very much (except that his mother had been a Venetian, wedded, but not of very fair fame, and his father a decayed English gentleman, chiefly resident in Naples, both of whom had been dead long ago), with no title, with no connections, with a somewhat notorious association with the ultra parties of Southern Europe, and with no particular quality of social distinction beyond his perfect breeding, his scientific whist, and his inimitable tact, was, nevertheless, seen at all courts save those of Vienna and the Vatican, and had made himself not only received, but welcomed in many of the best families and highest sets in all countries. Phaulcon, on the other hand, in whose veins ran blood of purest Hellenic breed, who could trace his chain of descent unbroken, who had a marvellous beauty, a marvellous grace, and a marvellous tact, with many other gifts of fortune and nature, was contraband of courts, had long since been exiled from "good society;" and was considered, rightly or wrongly, to belong to the Bohemian class of Free Lances, the Chevaliers d'Industrie of politics, the wild lawless Reiters of plot and counterplot, of liberalism and intrigue, who are the abomination of the English mind (which commonly understands not one whit about them), and are the arch disturbers of continental empires, where the people recognise at the bottom of all their schemes and crimes the germ and memory of one great, precious, living truth and treasure—Liberty. At the core, both these men were as deeply dyed, and as utterly unscrupulous, the one as the other, the only difference being that the one was the more wilily dangerous, the other the more visibly lawless; both deserved equally to be out of the presence-chamber of princes and the pale of aristocratic cliques, yet Vane was accepted as a man of fashion by the most fastidious, Phaulcon was excluded by the least fastidious, as among the "equivocal." What made the difference?

Victor would have told again, with his charming low laugh, that when quiet on his lips was always in his sunny eyes, which dazzled women and never met men fairly—"Acumen!"

"I cannot imagine how you could miss him!" he was saying now, breaking a macaroon, with a slight superb disdain in his tone, as of a man who never missed anything.

"How should I know?" cried Phaulcon, with petulant impatience. "We fired half a dozen balls at him, the man fell dead, never stirred, never breathed; who on the face of the earth could imagine he was going to get up again?"

"Carissimo," said Vane, with soft persuasion, "why *will* you persist in that most deleterious habit of trusting to chance, and satisfying yourself with 'appearances' and with 'beliefs?' Nothing more fatal. Always make sure. Just a farewell plunge of an inch of steel into the aorta, and you are always certain."

The picture-like beauty of Phaulcon's face reddened with a momentary flush, and he tossed back his long hair.

"Parbleu! one is not an assassin?"

"Since when have you discovered that?"

The flush grew darker on Count Conrad's forehead; he moved restlessly under the irony, and drank down a draught of red fiery Roussillon without tasting it more than if it had been water. Then he laughed; the same careless musical laughter with which he had made the requiem over a violet—a laugh which belonged at once to the most careless and the most evil side of his character.

"Since sophism came in, which was with Monsieur Cain, when he asked, 'Am I my brother's keeper?' It was ingenious that reply; creditable to a beginner, without social advantages. 'An assassin!' Take the word boldly by the beard, and look at it. What is there objectionable?"

"Nothing—except to the assassinated."

"It has had an apotheosis ever since the world began," pursued Phaulcon, unheeding, in his bright vivacity. "Who are celebrated in scripture? Judith, Samuel, David, Moses, Joab. Who is a patriot. Brutus.

Who is an immortal? Harmodius and Aristogiton. Who is a philosopher? Cicero, while he murmurs ' *Vixerunt!*' after slaying Lentulus. Who is a hero? Marius, who nails the senator's heads to the rostra. Who is a martyr? Charles who murders Strafford. What is religion? Christianity, that has burnt and slain millions. Who is a priest? Calvin, who destroys Servetus; or Pole, who kills Latimer, which you like. Who is a saint? George of Cappadocia, who slaughters right and left. Who is a ruler? Sulla, who slays Ofella. Who is a queen? Christina, who stabs Monaldeschi; Catherine, who strangles Peter; Isabella, who slays Moors and Jews by the thousand. Murderers all! Assassination has always been deified; and before it is objected to, the world must change its creeds, its celebrities, and its chronicles. 'Monsieur, you are an assassin,' says an impolite world. 'Messieurs,' says the polite logician, 'I found my warrant in your Bible, and my precedent in your Brutus. What you deify in Aristogiton and Jael, you mustn't damn in Ankarström and me.' Voilà! What could the world say?"

"That you would outwit Belial with words, and beguile Beelzebub out of his kingdom with sophistry," laughed Vane, with a quiet lazy enjoyment. "Caro, caro! with such 'exquisite subtleties in speech, how is it that you are so uncertain in acts, so rash even occasionally, and so—just now and then—so weak?"

Phaulcon laughed too.

"Because, intellectually, I am quite a devil, but morally, perhaps, keep a pin's point of humanity still. I am ashamed of it, but what would you have? Achilles could be shot in the heel."

And there was the very slightest shadow of bittreness in the words, which showed that there was a "pin's point," too, of truth in them. Vane looked at him with his quiet amusement undisturbed.

"And your delicate susceptibilities will let you shoot a man but not stab him? What an artist's eyes for imperceptible shades of colour?"

And it was with that gentle mocking banter that he had killed—perseveringly and remorselessly killed—any lingering touches of nobler things, any stray instincts towards holier impulses, that he had found in that unscrupulous, brilliant, lawless Free Lance, who laughed now with an evil glitter in his eyes, and a sense of ridicule and shame for the single impulse that had moved him with something true and human.

"Madre di Christo! shot or steel, I would have given him either willingly enough when he outwitted us. Curse him! if ever we come across each other, it shall go worse with him for that trick."

"Oh no," interposed Victor, languidly. "No, certainly not; let him alone. Never *kill* save when there is necessity; besides, any row between him and you might draw attention to that little affair, and though we must make the sacrifice of those unpleasant trifles to *la haute politique*, it does not do for them to get wind. They do not dream we were in it. They have plenty of toy-terriers, and yapping puppies, and truffle-dogs with a good nose for a perquisite at the English Foreign Office, but they have no bloodhounds in the bureau—they can't *track*. A propos of tracking—I tell you who I wish were more completely pledged to us—"

"Lilmarc, of course. So do I, but he is caution itself; and I believe, on my faith, that a white wand at

Vienna would buy up what little Magyar spirit there is
in him. He is a fox, with the heart of an ape!"

Lilmarc was the Graf von Lilmarc, au Hungarian
noble of splendid possessions, and of wavering allegiance
—now to Austria, and now to his Fatherland. Vane
trifled gravely with his olives.

"But Lilmarc has one weakness—women. Cannot
the Countess Vassalis seduce him?"

Phaulcon gave a despairing shrug of his shoulders.

"'There is no reliance on women! I don't know
what has come to Idalia of late; she is not herself, and
is oftener dead against us now than anything else. I
have asked her to make play with Lilmarc; she might
have him in her hands like wax in no time, but she
will not; she is wayward, cold, haughty—"

"Perhaps she has taken a lover you know nothing
about," said Victor, with a smile in his eyes. He liked
his friend and confederate as well perhaps as any
one in the world, but he liked better still tormenting
him.

The blood flushed Phaulcon's forehead.

"If I thought that—" Then he laughed the melodious laugh which was in harmony with the reckless
poetic grace of the man's beauty. "Oh, no! She only
sees through us, and has found out that our sublime
statue of Liberty has very clay feet. *Moitié marbre et
moitié boue*, as Voltaire said of the Encyclopédie."

"Why do you let her see the clay feet, then?"

"Why? Idalia is not a woman that you can blind.
You have not seen her."

"Unhappily, no! I have heard men rave of her, as
they never raved of anything, I think; and I know how
madly they have lost their heads for her—to our

advantage. Miladi's loveliness has done more for the cause than half our intrigues. She is now at Naples?"

"She was; to-night she is in Paris."

"In Paris?"

"Yes; I thought you knew it? In half an hour I am going back to take her to the Opéra ball Lilmarc is sure to be there, and she must beguile him out of his reticence and caution if she can; there is not a better place for enticing Tannhäuser into the Venusberg than *en domino* in an opera box, while all the world is going mad below."

"*D'avance*, I am jealous both of Lilmarc and of you!" cried Vane, with that easy worldly serenity to which such a normal and barbaric passion as jealousy seems wholly antagonistic and impossible. "At last I shall see her, then —your beautiful Vassalis! Shall I come with you?"

"No; better come up to the box when Lilmarc is not there. If he saw you with her he might take fright and cry off; if you have an ivy spray at your buttonhole she will understand and admit you, whether I be there or not. Here!" With the words he opened a small, long bonbon-box he took from his coat, and tossed Vane one of the little sprays of silver ivy that it held—the badge which all those who would be recognised by Idalia, Countess Vassalis, must wear on their dominoes that night.

"Thanks," said Victor, as he slipped it in his waistcoat-pocket. "I shall be there by one o'clock at latest. Idalia—this wonderful Idalia!—how often I have missed her, how often I have longed to see her; the fairest conspirator in Europe!"

The Bal de l'Opéra was brilliant, crowded, dizzy, mad with the very insouciant and reckless gaiety of the

Prince who invented it, as though the spirit of Philippe
d'Orléans still presided over the revelries. Dominoes
here, dominoes there; gold spangles, silver spangles,
rose and white, blue and amber, violet and grey, scarlet
and black, mock jewels flashing like suns and glancing
like stars, "*débardeurs*" and "*grands bébés*," Pierrots and
Scaramouches, white shoulders and black masks, fluttering rosettes and dainty signal-roses, were all pell-mell
in glittering tumult and contagious riot; and Vane in
a domino of imperial blue, with the silver ivy spray
fastened on his shoulder, made his way through the
crowd, not dancing, not heeding much the invitations,
mockeries, and whispers of a score of charming masks,
but looking incessantly upward at the boxes.

He did not see what he looked for; but he did see
every now and then, till they had numbered more than
a dozen, on an Ottoman, on a Knight of Malta, on a
Pharaoh, on a Poissarde, on a black domino, on a scarlet,
on a purple, on a violet, the little spray of ivy like his
own, that had come out of Phaulcon's bonbon-box.

"Che, che, ch-e-e!" murmured Victor, with the
southern expletive. "Miladi Idalia will have a large
gathering. Is she as beautiful as they say?—one would
think so, to judge by her power."

He got as much out of the press as he could, and
moved on in silence, heeding nothing of the *cancan
d'enfer* and *chaîne du diable* dancing round him. He
was not a man who cared for noisy dissipations; they
had no sort of attraction for him; indeed, dissipation
at all had not much, unless it were associated with the
intricacies of intrigue. He cared for nothing that was
not *rusé:* his own life was emphatically so; he had
begun it with serious disadvantages: first of birth,

which, though gentle on one side, was not distinguished; of fortunes which were very impoverished; of a world in which he had no place, and which had no want of him; of a temperament that was intensely ambitious, intensely dissatisfied, and intensely speculative. Despite all these drawbacks, by dint of tact and finesse, he had now, when he was but thirty, moved for many years in some of the best society of Europe; he lived expensively, though he was very poor; and he was deferred to, though no one could have said why they gave him such a preference. He had the spirit of the gambler, with the talent of the statesman, and he found the world one great gaming-table. He could not be a statesman in his own country; England will not accept as statesmen what she is pleased to term "adventurers," whereby she loses all men of genius, and gets only trained men of business: hence he had thrown himself, partly in pique, more in ambition, into the interests of a certain *ultra* political party abroad. Bred in Venetia, he hated Austria with a cold but very virulent hatred. Rash only in the height and unscrupulousness of his ambitions, he adopted politics—or, perhaps, to give them their true and naked name, conspiracies—as the scaling-ladder for his own advancement. If all the waters round him were lashed into a tempest, he knew so cautious and tried a swimmer as himself would have a fair chance to come uppermost while other men went down. He loved intrigue for mere intrigue's sake, and power for the simple pleasure of holding it. Serene, sunny, impassive, and even indifferent in bearing, and, indeed, in temperament, he could seize savagely, and hold pitilessly. In deceiving any one, Vane had no sort of scruple—it was only an artistic kind of exercise; but kill anybody, or provoke anybody, he would not think of doing—it was a barbaric, blundering style of warfare. He never went out of his way in wrath; but all the same, he never missed his way to revenge. He had a good deal of ice in his nature; but it was, perhaps, the most dangerous of ice—that which smiles in the sun, and breaks, to drop you into the grave. In the world of fashion, Victor was *but* a man of fashion—popular, very successful with women, an admirable tactician, and a guest who brought his own welcome everywhere by his easy social accomplishments, and his languid gentle temper, which had over and over again smoothed a quarrel, prevented an embarrassment, hushed a provocation unuttered, and arranged a misunderstanding before it grew to a rupture. In that world unseen, which revolves under the rose, he was very much more than this, and had a sway and a place of considerable influence in a society of politicians whose members are in all classes and orders, and whose network spreads more widely and finely beneath society than society dreams, stretching from Paris to Caucasus, and from the Quadrilateral to the Carpathians, in their restless scheming for the future, and their plans for the alteration of the map of Europe. It was not, however, of the French in Rome, the White Coats in Venice, the Muscovites in Warsaw, or the state of siege in Galicia, that he was thinking now, as he went through the wild, panting, crushed crowd of dancers at the French Opera; it was of something far fairer, if equally dangerous—a woman.

"Is she here?" he asked a violet domino, who wore, like himself, the badge of silver ivy.

"No. Perhaps she will not come, after all!"

"Oh yes, she will."

"How do you know? Have you seen her?"

"No, I never saw her. But Conrad has been dining with me, and left me to go and fetch her."

The violet domino went on, without a word.

"He's in love with her, too; he can't speak of her without a tremor in his voice; and by his voice he is nobody less than Prince Carlo himself," thought Vane, glancing back at his silver ivy, in apprehension lest it should be torn off or stolen in the press. "What can her power be? Ah, bah! What was that of the L'Enclos? Nobody knew, but nobody resisted."

And he went on, humming to himself Scarron's quatrain:

> "Elle avait au bout de ses manches,
> Une paire de mains si blanches;
> Que je voudrais en vérité,
> En avoir été soufflété!"

"Ah! there she is!"

The stifled exclamation fell on his ear, low spoken but impulsively passionate, as only a lover's entranced recognition is. He turned, and saw a mask in Venetian costume, to whose shoulder was also fastened the little badge of ivy.

"One of us! Who, I wonder? He, too, cannot speak of her without betraying himself," thought Victor, as he swung round quickly, and glanced over the boxes. In one of them he saw what he sought: with black laces and azure silks sweeping about her, caught here and there with sprays of silver ivy, a woman masked, who, leaning her arm on the front of the box, and her cheek upon her hand, gazed down into the tumult of colour and of movement that made up the ball below. Her face was unseen, but the lips, exquisite as the lips of a Greuze painting, had a certain proud weariness on them; and in the bright richness of her hair, in the elegance of her hand and arm, in the languor and grace of her attitude and her form, there were sufficient sureties of the beauty that would be seen if the black mask that veiled it were removed.

The Venetian domino looked at her long, then, with a stifled sigh, turned away.

"You have loved her?" whispered Vane.

The domino started, and glanced at the ivy branch on Victor's arm.

"To my cost," he said bitterly, as he plunged among the whirling dancers, and was lost in the spangled and riotous multitude.

His hearer smiled. A woman who owned a limitless power, and was unscrupulous, and without pity in its use, was, perhaps, the only woman he was capable of respecting. Cold as he was, and but little accessible to anything of passion, for which his blood ran too suavely and too tranquilly, he felt something of warm, eager curiosity sweep over him, and his pulse beat a shade quicker with a new expectation. He had long heard of this sorceress—he had never seen her; and he threaded his way with impatience through the Arléquins, Pierrots, masks, and costumés, till he reached the stairs, and mounted them lightly and rapidly towards the box, opened the door, and entered.

It was filled with dominoes, all decorated with the silver spray, and all bending towards her with eyes

that told their admiration through their masks, and
voices that murmured flatteries, homage, and wit—to
an inattentive ear. She lifted her head, and turned
slightly as the door unclosed; her eyes dwelt on him
through her mask, noting the badge he wore. She
bowed languidly.

"Enter, monsieur."

And Victor Vane, all impassive diplomatist, all-
rusé man of the world though he was, felt a thrill run
through him, and a hot breath seemed to pass, sirocco-
like, over his life, as he heard the nameless magic of
that melodious lingering voice, and found himself, for
the first time, in the presence of that Queen of the Silver Ivy, who was known as—Idalia.

Could Erceldoune have seen afar as Surrey saw
his mistress, the magic glass would not have brought
him such secure and happy peace as came with the
vision of Geraldine. Late into the dawn as the night
express plunged through the heart of France downward
to where Marseilles lay beside the southern sea, through
the cold clear night, the plains white with sheeted
snow, the black and spectral woods, and the sleeping
hamlets, with the pointed towers of châteaux and ma-
noirs rising against the leaden clouds, behind him the
City that Julian loved sparkled under a million lights;
strangely altered since the days when Julian wrote in
adoring phrase of the studious and tranquil retirement
of his austere and beloved Lutetia. The bright tide of
Parisian life was at its gayest in the first hours of the
midwinter morning; and in one of its richest quarters
an opera-supper was at the height of its wit and of
its brilliancy. The guests had come from the Opera
ball, the dominoes powdered with silver violets, gold

bees, diamond clusters, and glittering stars, were tossed down on the couches with the Venetian masks; being no tinsel costumes of the Passage des Panoramas, hired for a night, but the silk and satin elegancies of a court costumier, for men who wore these trifles at the masked fêtes of the Tuileries, in the Colonna palace in Carnival, and at the Veglione with noble masquers of Florence. The supper-room was a long and handsome chamber, hung with rose silk, flowered with silver, with crystal chandeliers flashing globes of light, and with a meal of the choicest extravagance on the table, about which half a dozen men and but one woman were gathered.

She—alone there at the head of her table, with her bouquet lying idly by her little army of deep claret-glasses, broad champagne goblets, and tiny spiral mousselines for liqueurs—was well worth a host of women less fair. Marie de Rohan, when Buckingham and Holland and Lorraine, and all that glittered greatest at two Courts were at her feet, and even the Iron Cardinal, in the censure of his blackest enmity, could not wholly keep his eyes from being dazzled by the shine of the arch-intriguer's golden hair,—was not more beautiful than she. Many would have added, also, that the Duchesse de Chevreuse was not more dangerous.

That her form and her face were perfect, was not half nor a tithe of her resistless charm; it lay in still more than these, in every glance of her eyes, blue-black like the gazelle's, in every slight smile that crossed her proud lips, in all the sunlit lustre on her hair, in all the attitudes of her southern grace, in every movement, accent, and gesture of one who

knew to its uttermost the spells of her power, and was
used to have that power courted, flattered, and obeyed.
Her loveliness was very great; but, great as it was, it
was comparatively forgotten beside so much that was
of still rarer fascination; the patrician ease, the silver
wit, the languor and the laughter, the dignity and the
nonchalance, the brilliance and the eloquence which
turn by turn gave their changing sorcery to her. The
innocence and fawn-like shyness of a young girl in
her earliest spring may be charming in a pastoral; but
in real life they are but awkward and tame beside the
exquisite witchery, the polished insouciance, the careless disdain, the cultured fascination of a woman of
the world. And these were hers in their utmost
perfection; a woman of the world she was in the
utmost meaning of the words, and all of victory,
of power, and of beguilement that the world could
give were added to the beauty of Idalia, Countess
Vassalis.

Men passing her in the open air gazed after her,
and felt a sudden giddy worship for what they only
saw one moment to lose the next; men who held themselves, by age or coldness, steeled to all the glamour
of her sex, fell before her; a few low lingering words
from her lips, a breath of fragrance from her laces,
the disdain of her delicate scorn, the caress of her
soft persuasion, the challenge of her haughty indifference, the sorcery of her sovereign smile,—these
at her will did with men as they would; intoxicated
them, blinded them, wooed them, bound them, subdued their will, their honour, and their pride, fettered
their senses, broke their peace, gave them heaven, gave
them hell, won from them their closest secret, and

drew them down into the darkest path. A power wide and fatal—a power that she was said, and justly, to have used with little scruple. Who was she—what was she, this beautiful enchantress?

In one word she was—"Idalia."

Her supper-room, perfumed, mellowly lighted, the supper served without ostentation, yet, in truth, as extravagantly as any Court banquet, with summer fruits though it was mid-winter, with wines Imperial palaces could not have eclipsed, with hookah-tubes curled through the arms of the lounging chairs, and lazily floating in their great bowls of rose-water, was sought with that eagerness for the entrée which is only found when—for far different attractions—men seek either the salons of a Princess of the Ton or of an Empress of the Demi-Monde, the legitimate leader of the Aristocracies, or the yet more potent law-giver, Anonyma. There was a cosmopolite gathering about her table; the Prince of Viana, a Neapolitan; the Count Phauleon, a Greek; the Graf von Lilmarc, a Hungarian; the Marquis de Beltran and the Maréchal d'Ivôre both of Paris; and one Englishman, Victor Vane. Here, at three o'clock in the morning, with the wine just flushing their thoughts with its warmth, and the scented smoke of the narghilis curling out in languid aërial clouds, they supped à la Regénce with one of the fairest women of her time; and she—lying back, with her Titian-like draperies, floating out like the deep-hued plumage of some tropic bird, toying with her bouquet of rose japonicas, stooping her lips to the purple depths of her Rousillon or the light sparkles of her Moselle, giving her smile to one, her wit to another, letting the wine steal the caution from their speech and the fragrant vapour charm the secrets from their heart—knew that her beauty drew them down into its charm and chain, her creatures and her captives, and let the revelry flash on around her, brilliant as the aiglettes in the discarded dominoes; and, while they supped with her in the dawn of the Paris morning, weighed them each and all—at their worth.

Like the jewels that glistened above her fair forehead, they had no value in her eyes save this—what they were worth.

Yet, if ever there were on any face, there were in hers, a haughty power in the arch of the classic brows, a generous grace in the smile of the proud lips, a fearless dignity in the gaze of the long lustrous eyes: looking on her, he who should have had force to resist her beauty would have still said, "If this star have fallen from heaven, it is great still even in its fall."

The Lost Pleyad of fable may sink downwards through the darkness of an eternal night, and become one of the women of earth, earth-stained, earth-debased; but the light of forgotten suns, the glory of forsaken worlds, will be upon her still. It might be so here.

CHAPTER VIII.
"Passion born of a Glance!"

WITH his rifle resting against his knee, its butt bedded in the moss, Erceldoune sat alone a few months later on, in the warm Turkish night, on the Bosphorus shores. He had been shooting sea-gulls, jackals, or a stray hill deer, if such came within range, through the last half of the day, whilst waiting for return despatches in Constantinople, and was now resting on a boulder of rock under a cypress, in his white burnous and sun-helmet, the Monarch, a fine English chestnut, straying loose at his side, a pile of dead game at his feet, and the starlight full on his face, as his eyes looked seaward thoughtfully.

A year had gone by since he had stood before the altar-piece in Monastica, and he was no nearer to either aim of his twofold quest. Power, patience, vigilance, inquiry—all had failed to bring him on the track of his assassins; masked nobles, reckless adventurers, political secret agents, whichever they were, they had had wit and wisdom to organise their plot so that no trace was left of it and them, and they were beyond all reach of justice, as it seemed, for ever. And of the woman, to whom his only clue was the fairness of her face, he had learned nothing. Shadowy, fugitive, lost in mystery, fantastic as a madman's dream, the hold she had gained upon his thoughts was so utterly foreign to them, that it was the stronger once admitted there. Speculation was wholly antagonistic to him—his nature was forcible, single, vigorous; that he acted greatly when great occasions arose, was due to the mould in which his character was naturally cast, not to any premeditation or previous contest and sifting of principles; he lived, as all bold men do, meeting accident or emergency as it came, content with the activity of the present, looking very rarely to anything past, never to anything future. To sift moral problems, to torture himself with theoretical questions, was what would no more have occurred to Erceldoune than to have sat twisting ropes of the Bosphorus sand; hence

the poetic unreality of the memory which possessed
him was so abhorrent and antagonistic to his whole temperament that it gave a deeper colouring to his life,
once received, than it would have done to any other
to which it had been less alien. Mental disquietude,
moral tumult, were unknown to him; a shadowy pursuit, a speculative meditation, were no more in con-
sonance with his character than it would have been to
study the stars for Chaldean knowledge of things
obscure. Therefore it was with the stronger force and
the more unbelief that Erceldoune felt that a well-nigh
mythical mystery had power over him, and touched his
heart, and stirred his thoughts, as no living woman had
ever done through the varied course of his life.

So sacred had the vision of his ministering angel
become to him, so intimately interwoven with holiness,
loftiness, purity, with the compassion of the luminous
eyes, and the hush of the convent solitudes where her
picture hung, that to have seen her at the entrance of
the Opera had given him a sharp and unwelcome recall
to the fact of how utterly he followed—a phantom;
how utterly he knew nothing of the woman who had
wound herself into his thoughts.

The face which he had seen in the haze of golden
light in what he had deemed his dying hour, the loveliness that he had found afresh, only afresh to lose it,
in the softness of the Sicilian seas, among the heat,
the noise, the maskers, the false brilliants, false flowers,
false laces, false beauty of the Rigolbochade!—it
gave Erceldoune a bitter revulsion. True, there might
be nothing in it to do so; she might go thither, not to
the lawless whirl of the stage, but simply to the boxes
as a spectator of the scene below; he knew this was

common enough with the proudest and purest of
women. Still, it revolted him; his memory of her, his
belief in her, was as of a life as unlike, and as above
the world, as the stars that shone now across the sea
above the classic shores where old Olympus rose. It
was an instinct, an impulse, a folly, never analysed,
only felt; but to think of her in the gas and throngs
of the masked midnight gathering, had given him
much such a shock as an artist, soul-devoted to his
art, would feel if he could come suddenly on a Raphael
or Correggio Madonna made the sign and centre of a
riotous casino, or flung by a drunken soldier as worthless loot into the flames of a bivouac fire. This
woman, all unknown though she was, had become the
single poetic faith, the single haunting weakness of a
passionate and earnest temperament, of a changeful
and self-sustained life; to have seen her at the Bal de
l'Opéra grated jarringly on both.

He thought of it now—and the thought was full
of tempestuous pain to him; to find in her a leader of
the artificial worlds of fashion; a coquette, worn,
brilliant and chill as her own diamonds, with every
smile a beautiful lie, with every glance a demand for
accustomed homage, would be scarce better than to
find in her one of the *cancan* worshippers of the Opera
throng, a *débardeur* in rose and silver, laughing through
her velvet mask of Venice! Of all places, of all hours,
were there none in the width of the world, in the
vastness of time, to have found her in at the last than
at midnight in the Rue Lepelletier! Who was she?
What was she?—this phantom which pursued him?
He wondered restlessly, as he did often in lonely moments like these, while he sat looking down the Bos-

phorus as the lights gleamed in the distance among the cypress and orange groves of the city of the Moslem, and the far-off cry of the Imaum wailed deep and mournful through the silence, chanting the evening prayer of the Faithful.

As he sat thus he did not notice or hear a man approach him on horseback, riding slowly along the sea-shore, unarmed, and lightly chanting a little French air—a handsome, careless, graceful Greek, whose saddle reveries seemed of the lightest and brightest as he swayed a bunch of Turkish lilies idly in his hand. His roan mare's hoofs—she was a Barbary—sank noiselessly in the sands; and Erceldoune did not lift his head; he sat motionless under the cypress, resting on his rifle, with the starlight falling fitfully on the white folds of the Arab cloak and the Rembrandt darkness of his face, as his head was bent down and his eyes gazed seaward. The rider came nearer, the hoofs still noiseless on the loose soil; and the hummed song on his lips broke louder, till he sang the words clearly and mellowly on the air, in the mischievous truth of Dufresny's chanson:

> "Deux époux dit un grand oracle,
> Tout d'un coup deviendront heureux,
> Quand deux époux, pas un miracle,
> Pourront devenir veufs tous deux!"

The voice fell on Erceldoune's ear, rich, harmonious, soft as a woman's contralto—the voice that had given the word to "kill the Border Eagle." He started to his feet, flinging back his burnous; in the silvery silent Eastern night they met once more—and knew each other at a glance: there is no instinct so rapid and so unerring as the instinct of a foe. With an oath that rang over the silent seas, Erceldoune sprang forward, as lions spring, and covered him with his rifle; swift as an unconsidered thought, Phaulcon wheeled and dashed his spurs into his mare's flanks, which sprang off at a headlong gallop a hundred paces in advance by that second's start; in an instant the other caught at the loose rein of his English horse, flung himself into saddle at a leap, and tore down the Bosphorus shore, his rifle levelled, the bridle between his teeth, the Monarch racing at full speed. They were in chase—the pursuer and the pursued.

"Halt!—or you are a dead man."

The challenge rolled through the night out and away to the Bosphorus;—the sole answer of the Greek was to dash the rowels again into his roan's sides, and tear on without other thought than flight, tasting all the long bitterness of death with every time that the beat of the gallop grew closer behind him, with every moment that the shriek of the bullet might whistle down on the wind and the shot pierce his heart from the hand he had once thought picked bare to the bone by the vultures, and buried safe in Moldavian snows.

The blood coursed like fire through Erceldoune's veins, every muscle in him strained like those of a gallant hound in chase; he longed, as the hound longs, to be at the throat of his flying foe: he had a mortal debt to pay, and a deadly wrath to pay it with; the life of his murderer lay at his mercy, and he panted— with brute thirst, perhaps—to take it, and trample it out on the sands in a just and pitiless vengeance. Yet—he did not fire.

All that was boldest and truest in him refused to

let him do as he had been done by;—forbade him to
shoot down an unarmed man.

With the hoofs now thundering loud on barren
rock, now scattering in clouds the loosened sand, now
trampling out the fragrance from acres of wild myrtles
and basilica, he rode on in close hot chase, the bridle
held in the grip of his teeth, his rifle covering his assassin, while Conrad Phaulcon fled for his life. A
single shot, from an aim which never missed, and the
coward would be slain as he would have slain, would
die the death that he would have dealt; a single ball
sent screaming, with its shrill hiss, crash through his
spine, and he would drop from the saddle dead as a
dog. The Greek knew that as well as the man who
held his life in his hands, to take it when he would;
and the sweat of his agony gathered in great drops
on his brow, the horror of his death-blow seemed to
him to quiver already through all his limbs, and as he
turned in his saddle once—once only—he saw the
stretching head of the Monarch within fifty paces, the
face of his pursuer stern and dark as though cast in
bronze, and the long lean barrel of steel glistening
bright in the moonlight, lifted to deal him the fate he
had dealt.

Onward, while the chant of the Muezzin grew
fainter and fainter, and the lighted mosques of Stamboul were left distant behind; onward, through the
night lit with a million stars, and all on fire with
glittering fire-flies; onward, down the beach of the
luminous phosphor-radiant sea, along stretches of yellow sand, under beetling brows of granite, over rocky
strips foam-splashed with spray, through fields of sweet
wild lavender and roses blowing rich with dew, and

tangled withes of tamarind tendrils, and myrtle thickets sloping to the shore, and netted screens of drooping orange-boughs, all white with bloom; onward they swept—hunter and hunted—in a race for life and death.

The Greek was always before him; now and again they well-nigh touched, and the foam from his horse's bit was flung on the steaming flanks of the mare he chased; now and again the dull thud of the hoofs thundered almost side by side as they scattered sand and surf, or trampled out the odorous dews from trodden roses. His enemy's life lay in the hollow of his hand; he saw the womanish beauty of Phaulcon's face, white and ghastly with a craven terror, turned backward one instant in the light of the moon, and a fierce delight, a just vengeance, heated his senses and throbbed in his veins. He panted for his foe's life, as he hunted him on through the hot night, as the lion in chase may pant for the tiger's; all the passions in him, rare to rise, but wild as the wildest tempest when once roused, were at their darkest; and the creed which chained them, and forbade him to fire on a man unarmed, served but to make each fibre strain, each nerve strengthen, with the fiercer thirst to race his injurer down, and—side to side, man to man—hurl him from his saddle and fling him to earth, held under his heel as he would have held the venomous coil of a snake, imprisoned and powerless, till its poisonous breath was trodden out on the sands.

They rode in hard and fearful chase, as men ride only for life and death.

The surf flashed its salt spray in their eyes as they splashed through the sea-pools girth-deep in water;

startled nest-birds flew with a rush from bud and bough, as they crashed through the wild pomegranates; white-winged gulls rose up with a shrill scream in the light of the moon, as the tramp of horses rang out on the rocks, or scattered the sands in a whirling cloud. There was savage delight to him in the breathless ride, in the intoxication of the odours trampled out from trodden roses and crushed citrons, in the fierce vivid sense of *living*, as he swept down the lonely shore by the side of the luminous sea, hunting his murderer into his lair;—the wolf in its own steppes, the boar in its own pine-forests, the tiger in the hot Indian night, the lion in the palm-plains of Libya; he had hunted them all in their turn, but he had known no chase like that he rode now, when the quarry was not brute, but man.

The snorting nostrils of the Monarch touched the flanks of the straining Barbary, the hot steam of the one blent with the blood-flaked foam of the other. They raced together almost side by side, dashing down a precipitous ridge of shore, entangled with a riotous growth of aloes and oleander: Erceldoune saw that his assassin was making for some known and near lair, as a fox hard-pressed heads for covert, and he thundered on in hotter and hotter pursuit, till the steel of the rifle glittered close in Count Conrad's sight as he turned again, his face livid and the breath of the horse that was scorching and noxious against his cheek, like the breath of the bloodhound on the murderer's. There were barely six paces between them, going headlong thus down the sloping ridge, and through the cactus thickets; as he turned backward, with that dastard gesture of pitiful despair, they looked on one another by the light of the moon, and the fairness of the Greek's face was ghastly with a coward's prayer, and the dark bronze of his pursuer's was set in deadly menace, in fierce lust of blood. Phaulcon knew why, with that lean tube flashing in the starlight, he was till spared; he knew, too, that once side by side in fair struggle, he would be hurled from his saddle, and crushed out under a just retribution, till all life was dead, as pitilessly as righteously as men crush out the snake whose fangs have bit them.

And the pursuit gained on him. Erceldoune rode him down, dashing through the wilderness of vegetation, with the surf of the sea thundering loudly below, and a loathing hate, a riotous joy seething through his veins. The horses ran almost neck by neck now, nothing between them and the billows lashing below but a span's breadth of rock and a frail fence of cactus. One effort more and he would be beside him; the bloodshot eyes of the mare were blinded with the foam flung off the Monarch's curb, and his own arm was stretched to seize his assassin and hurl him out to the waters boiling beneath, or tread him down on the rock under his feet, while he wrung out his confession in the terror of death. He leaned from his saddle; his hand all but grasped his enemy in a hold Phaulcon could no more have shaken off than he could have loosened the grip of an eagle, or the fangs of a lion: he was even with him, and had run him to earth in that wild night race. Then—suddenly, with a swerve and a plunge as the spurs tore her reeking flanks— the mare was lifted to a mad leap, a wall of marble gleaming white in the starlight, and rising straight in face of the sea; she cleared it with a bound of agony, and the dull crash that smote the silence as she fell, told the price with which she paid that gallant effort of brute life.

His foe was lost.

A fierce oath broke from his lips and rang over the seas. As he put the Monarch at the leap, he reared and refused it; a second was already lost, an eternity in value to him whom he pursued. His face grew dark—all that was worst in him was roused and at its height; he wheeled the hunter and rode him back, then turned again and put him full gallop at the barrier, nursing him for the leap; the marble wall rose before them, clothed with the foliage of fig and tamarisk trees; he lifted the horse in the air, cleared the structure, and came down on the yielding bed of wild geranium that broke the sheer descent.

On the ground lay the Barbary mare, panting and quivering on her side: the saddle was empty.

A darkness like the night came upon Erceldoune's face as he saw that his enemy had escaped him— a darkness closely and terribly like crime on his souL

Wolf, and boar, and lion, he had chased them all to their lair, and brought them down, now and again, a thousand times over, by the surety of his shot, by the victory of his strength. His secret assassin, hunted and run to earth, at his mercy and given up to his will through the whole length of that race down the Bosphorus waters, had outstripped his speed, had baffled his vengeance, and was let loose again on the world with his name unconfessed, with his brute guilt unavenged, lost once more in the solitudes of the night, in the vastness of the Ottoman empire. A second more,

and his hand would have been at the throat of this
man: he would have hurled under his feet the dainty
silken beauty of the coward who was thief and murderer
in one, and would have crushed the truth from his
throat and the craven life from his limbs under the
iron grind of his heel, giving back vengeance as great
as his wrongs. A second more, and the traitor who
had laughed with him in good fellowship in the Parisian café, and butchered him in cold blood in the
Danubian solitudes, would have answered to him for
that work. Now, the Barbary mare lay riderless at
his feet, and before him, around him, stretching dim in
the distance, were thickets of myrtle, labyrinths of cactus,
dense groups of oleander, of palm, of pomegranate,
where his quarry had headed for a known covert, or
had found one by chance, and from which it was as
hopeless to draw him again as to unearth a fox once
outrun the hounds' scent, or pursue a stag that had
once swam the loch.

A curse broke again from Erceldoune's lips, that
the distant wail of the Imanm seemed to mock and
fling back, as he rode the Monarch headlong down
into the wilderness of shrubs and flowers, trampling
the boughs asunder, crushing luscious fruit and odorous
blossom under the horse's hoofs, searching beneath the
shadows and under the tangled aisles of foliage for the
dastard who must be refuged there; one dusky glimpse
of a crouching form, one flash of the starlight on a
hidden face, and he would have fired on him now
without a moment's check; his blood was up, his passions were let loose, and the Greek might as well have
sought for leniency from the jaws of a panther as for
mercy from Erceldoune then, had he ridden him down

in his cover and dragged him out in the still Eastern night.

He rode furiously, hither and thither, through the thickest glades and where the shadows were deepest, searching for that to which he had no clue, in chase of a quarry which every turn he missed, every clump of shrubs he passed, every screen of aloes whose spines his horse refused to breast, might hide and shelter from his vengeance. Nothing met his eye or ear but the frightened birds that flew from their sleep among the piles of blossom, and the shrill hiss of the cicala, scared from its bed in the grasses. In the leafy recesses and the winding aisles of those hanging gardens overlooking the Bosphorus, a hundred men might have been secreted, and defied the search of one who was a stranger to the ground; and he was cheated at every turn by the fantastic shadows of the moonlight and the palms. His foe had escaped him; before the dawn broke he might have slipped down to the shore and be far out at sea beyond the Dardanelles; or if the gardens were the known lair for which he had purposely headed in the race along the beach, he would be safe beyond pursuit wherever he made his den.

Erceldoune dropped the bridle on the chesnut's neck, and let him take his own pace; a terrible bitterness of baffled effort, of foiled wrath, was on him—a passion, like a weapon which recoils, and hits the one who holds it hard. This man's life had been in his hands, and had escaped him!—and the unexpiated vengeance rolled back on his own heart, fierce, heavy, dark, almost as though it were twin crime with what it had hitherto failed to punish. A night-assassin, only of the viler stamp because of the gentler breed, went through the world unbranded and unpunished, whilst honest men died by the score of cold and famine in the snows of Caucasus and the streets of cities! Erceldoune's teeth ground together; when they met again, he swore it should be for shorter shrive and deadlier work.

The Monarch, with his dead drooped and the steam reeking from his hot flanks, took his own course over the unknown ground, and turning out of the thickets, paced down a long winding aisle of cedars: the night was perfectly still, nothing was heard but the surging of the Bosphorus waters, nothing was stirring save the incessant motion of the fire-flies, that sparkled over all the boughs with starry points of light. Erceldoune had no knowledge where he was, except that the sea was still beside him, and he let his horse take his own way. Suddenly, through the dark masses of the cedars, a light gleamed, which came neither from the fire-flies nor from the moon, but from the Turkish lattice-work of a distant casement.

Was that where his foe had found covert? He raised the Monarch's drooping head with the curb, and urged him at a canter down the cedar-aisle, the noise of the hoofs muffled in the grass, that grew untrimmed, as though the wild luxuriance of the gardens had long been left untouched. Sultan's palace, Queen's serail, sacred Mosque, or Moslem harem, he swore to himself that he would break down its gates, with the menace of England, and have his murderer delivered up to him, though he were surrounded by an Emir's eunuchs, or harboured in the sanctuary of the Odà itself. For anything that he knew, the light might glitter from the dwelling where his enemy and all his gang had made stronghold, or the place might swarm with Mussulmans, who would think there was no holier service to Allah than to smite down the life of a Frank, or the latticed window might be that of a seraglio, into whose anderūn it was death for a man and a Giaour to enter. But these memories never weighed with Erceldoune: he was armed, his blood was up, and if his foe were sheltered there, he vowed that all the might of Mahmoud, all the yataghans of Islam, should not serve to shield him.

A flight of steps ending the cedar-walk stopped the chestnut's passage: above ran a terrace, and on that terrace looked the few lattice casements allowed to a Turkish dwelling, whose light from within had caught his eyes. He threw himself out of saddle, passed the bridle over a bough, and went on foot up the stairs. Erceldoune's rifle was loaded; he had on him, too, the hunting-knife with which he had grallocked the hill deer; and he went straight on—into the den of the assassins, as he believed. Foolhardy he was not; but he had found sinew and coolness serve him too well in many an *avatar*, east and west, not to have learned to trust to them, and he had resolved, moreover, to go through with this thing cost what it might, bring what it would.

He hurried on the terrace, laden with the scarlet blossoms of the trumpet-flower and japonica, and heavy with odours from the nyctanthus and musk-roses trailing over the stone; a door stood open on to it, leading into the large court which forms the customary entrance of a Turkish house; he paused a moment and looked through; there was only a dim light thrown on its walls and floor, and there was no sound but of the falling of the water into the central fountain. He passed the threshold, and entered, the clang of his step resounding on the variegated mosaic of the pavement: its own echo was the only sound which answered—for its stillness the place might have been deserted. But the court opened into a chamber beyond, flooded with warm, mellow light, its dome-like ceiling wreathed with carved pomegranates, while another fountain was flinging its shower upward in the centre, and the fragrance of aloe-wood filled the air from where it burned, like incense, in a brazier;—a picture, full of oriental colouring. With his rifle in his hand, his white burnous flung behind him, and his single thought the longing which possessed him to unearth his foe, and have his hand upon his throat, he swept aside the purple draperies, that partially shadowed the portico, and passed within the entrance.

A woman rose from her couch in the distance, startled, yet with the look of one who disdains to give its reins to fear—as a sovereign would rise were her solitude desecrated;—and he paused, his steps arrested and his passions silenced, as in ancient days he who came to slay in the deadliness of wrath, uncovered his head, and dropped his unsheathed sword, entering the holy shrine at whose altar his foe had taken sanctuary. His enemy was forgotten;—he stood before Idalia.

He saw her in the flood of amber light that fell upon the lustre of her hair, on the white folds of her dress with its hem of gold, on the scarlet blossom of the roses clustering about her feet, on the aromatic mist of the aloe-wood burning near;—and in an instant he had crossed the marble that severed them, his head uncovered, his hand disarmed, his eyes blinded.

"At last!—at last!"

And he had never known how strong had become the power, how eager had grown his quest, of the memory which had pursued him, until now, when he bowed before her, when his lips were on her hand, when a hot joy that he had never known swept through his life, when in that sudden meeting his gaze looked upward to the face which had mocked him a thousand times, from the blue depths of sea waves, in the tawny stretch of eastern plains, in the stillness of starry nights and the darkness of convent aisles, and now at length was found.

She drew herself with haughty amazed anger from him:—she saw her solitude violated by the abrupt entrance of an armed man when the night was so late that the chant of the Imaum was calling to prayer: she saw a stranger, by his dress an Arab, bend before her in homage that was insult. She wrenched herself away, and signed him back with a gesture too grand in its grace for fear, and in her eyes a glance which spoke without words.

Then, as he raised his head, she saw the features which she had last beheld in what had seemed their death hour, while up to hers gazed the eyes that but for her succour the vulture's beak would have struck, and torn out for ever; then she knew him;—and over her proud loveliness came a sudden flush, a softness that changed it as by a miracle; and she looked down upon him with that glance which he had seen and remembered through the dizzy mists of delirium, and had given to his Madonna in the altar-picture at Monastica.

"*You!*"

It was but one word; but by that word he knew

that as he had never forgot, so he had not been forgotten.

He bent lower yet, till his lips touched her hand again.

"At last! I thought that we should never meet! And now—I have no words. To strive to pay my debt were hopeless; God grant the day may come when I can show you how I hold it. You saved my life; you shall command it as you will."

His words broke from his heart's depths, and in the rapid breathless tide of emotion, strongly felt and hard to utter; few women would have failed to read in them that, with his bold, keen, dauntless nature, self-reliant, danger-tested though it was, there went a faith that would be loyal to his own utter ruin, once pledged and given, and a tenderness passionate and exhaustless, through which he might be lured on to any belief, dashed down to any destruction. A dangerous knowledge; there are scarce any women to be trusted with it.

Silence fell between them for the moment, where she stood beside the scarlet roses of the fountain, with the heavy aloes perfume rising round, and at her feet, bowed low before her, the man whose life was owed to her by so vast a debt—a stranger and unknown, yet bound to her by the golden bonds of service that had loosed and freed him from his grave. All the glory of her beauty was deepened and softened as she looked on him, startled still, and hardly conscious of his words; and Erceldoune gazed upward to her face, with a dim mist before his sight, as he had never gazed before upon the face of woman:—he had forgotten all in that luminance of light, that glow of colour, that delicious dreamy fragrance.

Remembrance returned to him as she released her hands from his hold, and drew slightly from him. They could not meet as strangers, while betwixt them was the tie of a life restored, and the memory of that hour of awful peril in which she had been his saviour. But he had come, armed and alone, by violent entrance into her solitary chamber in the lateness of the night; and on her face was the look of one to whom insult was intolerable and all fear unknown—then he remembered what had brought him thither, and spoke ere she could speak.

"Pardon me for the rude abruptness with which I have broken on you; nothing can excuse it save the truth—I followed, as I thought, one of my Moldavian assassins; I hunted him down the Bosphorus, and lost his track in the gardens here. I fancied——."

"Your assassins!—here!——"

"Doubtless it was an error of mine!" he broke in hastily; that this house could be his murderer's lair was impossible, since it was hers, and he forebore to tell her how closely he had hunted his quarry to her presence, lest he should give her alarm. "I rode him down into a wilderness of palm-trees and cactus, and missed his trail in the darkness;—the coward was unarmed, I could not fire on him, and he escaped me. I saw a light gleam through the cedars; and I forced my entrance; then I forgot all—even forgot what my own violence must appear—since it led me to you!"

His voice dropped and softened as he spoke the last word; the pitiless passion which had alone possessed him as he had dashed aside the draperies and forced his way into what he had believed the covert of the man he hunted, were outweighed and forgotten; even while he spoke he had no memory but for her.

She shuddered slightly, and glanced into the dim twilight gloom of the court on to which her chamber opened.

"If you tracked him into these gardens, he may be there, or may have hidden here. Search;—have my people with you—let them take torches, and seek through the gardens. No one can have entered; but the grounds are a wilderness——"

"More likely he has escaped to the sea-shore; and all I know, or care now, is, that he has served to bring me—*here!* Oh! my God, if you knew how I have sought you!—and now that we have met, what can I say? Nothing that will not leave me deeper your debtor than before."

"Say no more. You owe me nothing. Who would not have done for you the little that I did?"

"You perilled your life to save mine, and mine is owed to you if a man's life was ever owed for angel work," broke in Erceldoune, while the force of a new and strange softness trembled through his voice as he stood alone in the stillness of the night with this woman, of whom he knew nothing—nothing, save that she filled his soul and his senses with a sweet fierce joy that had never touched them before, and that he had been rescued from his grave by her hand.

Over her face swept a look almost of pain:

"Call nothing *I* did by that name. And—why should you feel it as a debt, as a merit even? A little cold water held to a stranger's lips! It is not worth a thought."

"It was worth my life, and with my life I will pay

it, if you will take the payment, be it made in what guise it may."

They were no empty words of courteous requital; they were an oath to the death, if need be; she was silent, while her glance dwelt on him where he stood, reared now to his full stature, in the amber flood of the lamps, the snowy folds of the burnous flung back, and on his face a grandeur from the stormy passions an instant ago lashed to their height, blent with the eager light with which he looked on her. Then she held her hand out to him, with the beautiful impulse of a proud and gracious nature, touched and bending with a sovereign grace.

"I thank you for your words. There is no question of debt now; they more than pay the little I could do to serve you in your peril. We cannot meet as strangers; let us part as friends."

The words were even in their gentleness, a sign of dismissal. He had broken in on her abruptly, and the night was late. He bowed low over her hand—as we bow over that of an Empress.

"Part! True;—I come unbidden here; I have no right to linger in your presence; but we cannot part until I know that we shall meet again. I have not found to-night what I have sought so long unceasingly and hopelessly, only to-night once more to lose it."

She drew back slightly, and her face grew paler, while over its brilliance swept a troubled feverish shadow; she answered nothing.

"You can know nothing of me now, but at least you will consent to know more?" he pursued. "A name alone tells little; yet had I had one by which to seek the saviour of my life, it would not have been so long before you had heard mine."

In the hot night, in the perfumed stillness, in the sudden revulsion from the violence of vengeance to the wild sweetness of this woman's presence, words far different reeled through his thoughts and rose to his lips; but they were held back by his own sense of their madness, and by the dignity, nameless yet resistless, which surrounded her.

"You would know my name? It is Idalia Vassalis."

She uttered it almost with defiance, yet a defiance which had a profound sadness in it, like the defiance of the slave.

"And why conceal it so long? Can you not think what it was to owe so great a gratitude to you, yet to be left in such strange ignorance of my preserver that, for anything which I could tell, we might never have met on earth?"

"I had reasons for desiring my own name untold," she answered, coldly, as though interrogation were unknown to her. "Besides I never thought that you would have any remembrance of me."

"To have lost remembrance I must have lost the life you rescued."

The brief words said a volume; she knew they were no offspring of hollow courtesy, but a passionate truth broken up unbidden from a character in which a bold and noble simplicity prevailed over all that the world had taught, in motive, in purpose, in action, and in speech; to understand *her*, might for years bewilder and mislead the man; to understand *him*, the few moments of that night sufficed to the woman.

"It is few remember as you do," she said, and the soft lingering richness of her voice, with an unspoken melancholy vibrating through it, thrilled through him. "Life is no great gift given back to merit gratitude! But, while we lose time in words, your murderer will escape; if you chased him to these gardens, there is no outlet seaward. Take my people with you; some are Albanians, and will serve well and boldly under need; let the grounds be searched, for my safety if not for your own."

Whilst she spoke she rang a hand-bell; a negress obeyed the summons, an Abyssinian, clothed in scarlet and white.

"Bid Paulus and his sons take arms and torches, and wait without on the terrace," said the mistress to her slave, who gave the salaam silently, and left the chamber. "The men will be faithful to you," she resumed to Erceldoune. "Let them accompany you home; if your assassins be in Turkey, the Bosphorus shores cannot be safe for you alone. No:—you will not refuse me; you can set little store on the life you say I gave you back if you would risk it wantonly so soon."

"My life will be richer and dearer to me from tonight."

The words broke from him on impulse and almost unawares, as he bent before her in farewell: he could not linger after her dismissal; to have disputed it would have been impossible, for there was about her that nameless royalty which is its own defence, and which no man ever insulted with impunity, or insulted twice.

She avoided all notice of his words as she gave

him her adieu, speaking, as she had hitherto done, in French.

He bowed over her hand, but he held it still.

"And to-morrow I may have permission to return, and seek to say all for which I have no words to-night? The debt that you disclaim must, at least, be sufficient bond between us for us not to part as strangers?"

Looking upward he saw a certain hesitation upon her face; her eyes were suddenly darkened by a shadow it were hard to describe, and she was silent. Chivalrous in his courtesy to women, pride was too strong in him for him to sue where he was repulsed, to entreat where he was undesired. He released her, and raised his head.

"It is not for me to force my presence on you. Farewell, then, and take, once for all, my gratitude for a debt that it has pleasured you to embitter."

The words were proud, but they were also pained; they were the terse, unstudied phrases of a man who was wounded, but who could not be lowered, and would not be angered; they served him better, and touched her more keenly, than more servile or more honeyed utterances would have done. She smiled with a certain amusement, yet with a graver and a gentler feeling too.

"Nay—you need not read my silence so. Come here again—if you wish."

Just then the clang of the Albanians' arms announced their readiness on the terrace without; he bowed down once more before her, and left her standing there, with the clusters of the roses at her feet, and the colour of the rich chamber stretching away into dim distance around her as she had suddenly broken on his sight, when he had dashed back the purple draperies in pursuit of his assassin.

And he went out into the night with one thought alone upon him; he felt blind with the glow of the light, intoxicated with the incense odours, dizzy with all that lustre and maze of delicate hues, of golden arabesques, of gleaming marbles, and of scarlet blossoms; but what had blinded his sight and made his thoughts reel, was not these, but was the smile of the woman who had suddenly lit his life to a beauty which he had passed through half the years that are allotted to man, never having known or cared to know.

CHAPTER IX.
Ritter Tannhäuser.

Of his foe there was no trace.

The Monarch stood undisturbed, with the bridle flung over the cedar bough, and the Barbary mare lay motionless, with her right fore leg twisted under her and broken; of his foe there was no trace, and he rode on silently down the Bosphorus shore back into Pera, with the Albanians running by his horse's side, their torches throwing a ruddy glare over the moonlit sea and silvered sands, and on their own picturesque dresses and handsome classic faces, as they held on to his stirrup-leather.

A few moments before, and he had had no thought save of the blood-thirst with which he had ridden his enemy down the shore, and of the just vengeance of an unpardonable wrong; now he had no memory save one.

With the morning he rose, with but this one thought still—he would see her again! With the early dawn, while the sound of the drums was rolling through the mists, as they heralded the Commander of the Faithful going to prayer, he was plunging into the grey depths of the Bosphorus: sleep beyond his bidding. He knew that for hours yet he could not go to her, but he watched the sun in intolerable impatience for it to travel faster on its way; he walked alone to and fro the silent shore in a dream that was filled with her memory, and dead to all else. He did not pause to analyse what he felt, not even to wonder at it; his life was launched on the tempestuous sea of passion, and he lived in a trance of feverish intoxication, restless pain, and sweet idolatry. What avail how great had been his strength before? It only served to fling him down in more utter captivity now.

Far sooner than ceremony would have allowed him, he rode down the same path by which he had pursued the Greek the night before; but of him he had no more thought than if he were blotted from his life, when once more he looked upon her;—a woman fitted for a throne.

She did not give him her hand, but she smiled, that smile which gave its light to her eyes yet more than to her lips; and he thought that she must hear the beating of his heart—it had never throbbed so thick and fast when he had given the word for his own death-shot in the Carpathian pass. He had never felt himself stricken strengthless and powerless, blind and dizzy with a thousand new emotions, as he felt now:—so had another bold Border chief, the Night

Rider of the Marches, been conquered when Bothwell stood before his Queen.

His thoughts were full of fever, his life seemed confused yet transfigured. To have thrown himself at her feet and gazed there upward to her in silence and in worship, would have been to follow the impulse in him. She knew it; his eyes spoke all on which his lips were perforce dumb; he did not think how much they betrayed him, he did not dream how much they told—to a woman who had wakened so much love that its faintest sign was known to her—of the tumult in his heart, of the glory in his life, of the madness in his soul, which were so mingled and so nameless to himself.

In that moment, the whole heart of the man, in its brave truthfulness, its bold manhood, its headlong faith, and its awakening passions, was open before her as a book;—she knew her power over a dauntless, loyal life: how would she use it?

She let her glance dwell on him for a moment, those lustrous changeful eyes, whose hue could never be told, calmly meeting the passion of his own: calmly reading and watching the type and the worth of this life, which through her was still amongst the living.

"Have you found no trace of your assassin?" she asked him carelessly. "They told me there were no signs of him on the shore last night."

"I forgot him! I have only remembered that he brought me here."

"It is not many who would follow so generous a code as yours. You have a deathless memory for gratitude, a forgiving oblivion of injury."

"Hush! do not give me credit that is not mine.

As for gratitude—it is not *that* only which has made my life know no memory save the memory of you!"

His voice trembled, the words escaped him involuntarily: he was scarcely conscious what he said. She bowed with that dignity which repulsed without rebuking the meaning of the words.

"You do me far too much honour. The little I did in common human charity merits, as I said before, neither thanks nor memory. You stay in Constantinople, I suppose?" she continued, with that ease which was almost cold—cold, at least, compared to the tumult of impassioned impulses, unconsidered thoughts, and newly-born emotions which were warm and eager in the heart of her listener. It checked him, it stung and chilled him.

"I am waiting for home despatches," he answered her; "I am a Queen's courier, as you may have heard. You are living here?"

"Only for a while; some months, a few days, I do not know which it may be. You, who are so splendid an artist, must find constant occupation in the East?"

"I? I am little of an artist, save when my horse or my rifle are out of reach. We, of the old Border, rarely carved our names in any other fashion than by the sword."

She saw how little his thoughts were with his words, as she met again the burning gaze of eyes that told far more than he knew; their language was too familiar to her to move her as it would have moved a woman less used to its utterance; it was a tale so old to her! She sighed, a little impatiently, a little wearily;

she was unutterably tired of love. What was intoxication to him was but a thousand-times-told story to her. And yet—she saw that this man would suffer, and she foresaw that he would suffer through her. She pitied him, as it was not in her commonly to pity.

"I saw you in Sicily, surely?" he pursued. "For one moment, as you passed in a lateen-boat?"

"I was in Sicily a year ago; I dare say you might have seen me."

"You travel much?"

"Who does not in our days?" she answered, with carelessness, but carelessness that veiled a refusal to speak further of herself, which was impenetrable. She had every grace of womanhood, but beneath these she had a haughty and courtly reticence that was impassable. "Travel has one great attraction—it leaves little room for reflection. You like it yourself?"

"Yes, I like it. A courier's suits me better than any life, except a soldier's, would have done. However, it was not with me a matter of preference; I was ruined; I was glad of any post."

He said it frankly, and with the indifference which his decayed fortunes really were to him; but he saw that she was rich, he heard that she was titled, and he would not form her friendship under false colours, knowing that his own title gave him a semblance of wealth and of station he had not.

She smiled slightly, there were both wonder at his honesty, and comprehension of his motives in that smile; the candour and the integrity of his nature were very new to her, and moved her to a wonder almost kindred to reverence.

"You are rich, I think," she said, a little wearily.

"You have strength, liberty, manhood, independence, honour;—how many have forfeited or never owned those birthrights! You chose very wisely to take a wanderer's freedom rather than the slavery of the world."

Erceldoune shook himself with a restless gesture, as an eagle chained shakes his wings:

"Ich diene nicht Vasallen!"

he muttered in his beard.

She laughed, but her gaze dwelt on him in sympathy with the fiery independence of his nature.

"Never the vassal of a slave? Then never be the slave of a woman!"

He looked at her, and there was something wistful in the look; he wondered if she knew her power over him, and if she made a jest of it; he could not answer her with that badinage, that gay light homage, that subtle flattery, to which she was accustomed; he felt too earnestly, too deeply; a man of few words, save when keenly moved or much interested, he could not give himself to the utterance of those airy nothings, while all his life was stirred with passion he could not name.

At that moment the great Servian hound entered through the open window from the terrace, and stood looking at him with its wolf-crest up, its fine eyes watchful and menacing, and a low angry growl challenging him as a stranger. It was a magnificent brute, massive in build, lithe in limb, pure bred, and nearly as tall as a young deer.

Erceldoune turned to him and stretched out his hand.

"Ah! there is my gallant friend. I owe him a debt too."

The animal stood a second looking at him, then went and laid down like a lion couchant at her feet.

She laid her hand on his great head—a hand of exceeding fairness and elegance, with the sapphires and diamonds glittering there, which Mother Veronica had noted, with a recluse's quick appreciation of worldly things.

"You must forgive him if he be discourteous; he has so often been my only champion, that he is apt to be a little rash in his chivalry."

"I honour him for his fidelity. But, your only champion? Where was the chivalry of the world, to leave such a post to a dog?"

"Where! In idle vows and poets' dreams, I imagine; its only home in any time, most likely. The Ritter Tannhäuser swore his knightly homage in the Venusberg, but ere long he turned on her who gave him his delight:

"O Venus schöne Fraue mein,
Ihr seyd eine Teufelinne!"

The German legend is very typical!"

"Tannhäuser was a cur!" said Erceldoune, with an eloquent warmth in his voice rather than in his words. "What matter what she was—what matter whence she came—she was the sovereign of his life; she had given him love, and glory, and delight; she was *his*. It was enough—enough to lose a world for, and to hold it well lost!"

He paused suddenly in the passionate poetic impulse on which he spoke, which had broken up in his heart for the first time, utterly alien as he believed to his nature, to his temperament, to his will. It was of her and of himself that he thought, not of the old Teutonic Minnesinger's legend of Tannhäuser: and the rich glow of the sunlight slanting across the mosaic pavement, shone in the dark eagle lustre of his eyes, and lent its warmth to the Murillo-like bronze of his cheek.

She was a woman of the world; that noble truthfulness, that gallant faith, that knightly earnestness were new and very strange to her. They touched her.

"If Tannhäuser had loved like *that*—who knows? —even she, the Teufelinne, might have been redeemed. She could not have been faithless to such faith," she said, half musingly, rather following out her thoughts than addressing him; and in her voice there was a vague pathetic pain.

Mad words rose to his lips in reply—words that he had to hold down in silence; the room seemed dizzy round him, the odours of the flowers reeled in his brain as though they were narcotics; he watched, like a man half-blinded, her hand wander among the scarlet blossoms, and toy with the waters of the fountain. It was a delirium; and, for all its feverish pain, he would not have exchanged it to have back the happiest and most tranquil hour of his past. He had dreamed of her, till he had loved her, as utterly as ever a man loved a woman; he was in her presence—at last!—and all love that before might be but a dream became at once with giant growth a passion. She did not—with him at least—seek her power; but such power was hers in its widest magnitude of empire; and she was a little weary of it, as sovereigns are weary of their crowns.

"You give fresh air the preference,—will you come into my gardens? They are very wild, but I like them the better for that," she asked him, as she rose with that half-languid grace which bespoke something of oriental blood in her, and, moved out on to the terrace.

The gardens were, in truth, untrimmed as the neglect of years could make them, but they had been originally palace grounds, and all the colour and luxuriance of unchecked vegetation made them beautiful, with their wilderness of myrtle, cactus, and pomegranate, and their stretches of untrained roses blooming round the splashing waters of the marble and porphyry fountains.

"Little has been done here for years, and yet there is a loveliness in them not to be had in trimmed and trained château gardens," she said, as she turned so that the sun fell full on her face with its delicate haughty lustre, its richness and fairness of hue.

"Yes! there *is* a loveliness," he answered her, as his eyes looked down into hers, "greater than I ever believed in before."

She laughed a little; slightly, carelessly.

"What enthusiasm. So great a traveller cannot, surely, find anything so new and striking in a wild Turkish garden?" she said, half amusedly, half languidly, a trifle ironically, purposely misapprehending his words.

The look came on him that had been there before, when she had bade him never to be the slave of a woman; proud, and yet wistful.

"I do not know that!" he said, almost bitterly: "but I know that the gardens may be as fatal as those of Uhland's Linden-tree. You remember how the poem begins?"

The words took an undue effect on her; resentment came on her face, inquiry into her eyes, that she turned full on him in some surprise, some anger, and yet more, as it seemed to him, disquiet. Then all these faded, and a profound sadness followed them.

"Yes, I remember," she said, calmly. "Take warning by Wolfdieterich, and do not lie under the linden! Rather, to speak more plainly, and less poetically, never come where you do not see where your footsteps will lead you. You know nothing of me, save my name; leave me without knowing more. It will be best, believe me—far best."

She paused as she spoke, as they moved down the avenue, the roses strewing the grass path, and the Bosphorus waves flashing through the boughs. The singularity of the words struck him less at that moment than the injunction they gave him to leave her. Leave her!—in the very moment when his quest had been recompensed; in the first hour when, at last in her presence, at last in her home, the fugitive glory of his dreams was made real, and he had found the woman who had literally been to him the angel of life.

Beneath the sun-bronze of his face she saw the blood come and go quickly and painfully; he paused, too, and stood facing her in the cedar aisle, with that gallant and dauntless manhood which lent its kingliness to him by nature.

"Best? For which of us?"

"For you."

"Then I must refuse to obey."

"Why? Refuse, because it is for yourself that I have spoken?"

"Yes. If my presence jeopardised you, I must obey, and rid you of it; if I alone be concerned, I refuse obedience, because I would give up all I have ever prized on earth—save honour—to be near what I have sought so long, and sought so vainly."

It was all but a declaration of love, to a woman of whom he knew nothing, save her beauty and her name. She read him as she would have read a book, but she did not show her knowledge.

"You are very rash," she said, softly, without a touch of irony now. "I have said truly, I have said wisely, it will be best for you that our friendship should not continue—should barely commence. If you persist in it, the time will, in every likelihood, come when you will condemn me, and reproach yourself for it. I speak in all sincerity, even though I do not give you my reasons. You consider—very generously—that you owe me a debt; it would be best paid by obeying what I say now, and forgetting me, as if we had never met."

She spoke with the courtly ease of a woman of the world, of a woman used to speak and to be obeyed, to guide and to be followed; but there was a certain inflection of regretful bitterness in her voice, a certain shadow of troubled weariness in her eyes, as if she did not send him from her without some reluctance. They were strange words; but she had known too many of the multiform phases of life to have any feminine fear of singularity or of its imputation, and had passed through unfamiliar paths with a fearless careless grace wholly and solely her own.

His frank eyes met hers, and there was in them a passionate pain.

"You bid me pay my debt in the only coin I cannot command. Obey you, I will not. Forget you, I *could* not."

She smiled.

"Twenty-four hours' absence soon supplies any one with oblivion!"

"It is a year since I saw you in the Sicilian boat, yet I have not forgotten. I shall not while I have life."

His voice was very low; he was wounded, but he could not be offended or incensed—by her.

She bent her head with a sweet and gracious gesture of amends and of concession.

"True! Pardon me; I wronged you. Nevertheless, indeed rather *because*, you remember so well—I still say to you, Go, and let us remain as strangers!"

All that was noblest in her spoke in those words: all that lingered, best and truest, in her, prompted them. She wished, for his peace, that he should leave her, because she knew his heart better far than he himself; she wished—now, at the least—that he whom she had rescued, should be spared from all shadow from her, from all love for her; she wished—now, at least—to save him. From what? From herself.

Yet it was not without pain on her side also, though that pain was concealed, that she spoke.

He looked at her steadily, the earnest, open, loyal, unartificial nature of the man striving in vain to read the motive and the meaning of the woman, and failing, as men mostly do.

His face grew very white under the warm brown left there by Asian and Algerian suns.

"If you command it, I must obey. My presence shall be no forced burden upon you. But you cannot command on me forgetfulness, and I could wish you had been merciful *before*, and left me to die where I lay."

Unconsidered, spoken from his heart, and the more profound in pathos for their brief simplicity, the words moved her deeply, so deeply, that tears, rarest sign of emotion with her that she had never known for years, rose in her eyes as they dwelt on him; her lips parted, but without speech; she stood silent.

The day was very still; sheltered by the cedars from the heat, the golden light quivered about them; there was no sound but of the cicala among the pomegranate leaves, and of the waves breaking up against the marble palace stairs; neither ever forgot that single hour when on one word the future hung. His eyes watched her longingly; he did not ask who she was, whence she came, for what reason she thus bade him go from her; he only remembered the glory of her loveliness, and the words in which she had said, "Go, and let us remain henceforth as strangers."

"Answer me, Madame," he said, briefly, "Do you, for yourself, command me to leave you?"

"For myself? No. I cannot command you—it is only for your sake—"

She paused. What was, in truth, in her thoughts it would have been impossible to put in clear words before him; she could not tell this man that what she feared for him was the love that he would feel for herself; and what she had said sufficed to give back to his heart its restless tumult of vague joys, sufficed to make the present hour in which he lived full of sweet intoxication.

"Then, since not for yourself you command, for myself I refuse to obey; refuse, now and for ever—come what will—ever to be to you again as a stranger."

The tremor was still in his voice, but there were in it, too, the thrill of a triumphant gratitude, the reckless resolve of a tropic passion: she knew that the die was cast, that to send him from her now would serve but little to make her memory forgotten by him. She knew well enough that forgetfulness was a treasure for evermore beyond the reach of those who once had loved her.

"Be it so! We will have no more words on the matter," she said, carelessly, as she passed onward with a low, light laugh; her temperament was variable, and she did not care that he should see that new unwonted weakness which had made her eyes grow dim at the chivalry and pathos of his brief words. "The fantasies of Uhland have made us speak as poetically as themselves. My counsels were counsels of wisdom, but since Wolfdieterich will rest under the linden, he must accept the hazard! How calm the Bosphorus is, the waves are hardly curled. There is my boat at the foot of the stairs; it is not too warm yet for half an hour on the sea if you would like to take the oars."

A moment ago and she had forbade him any knowledge of her, and had sought to dismiss him from her presence; now she spoke to him familiarly and without ceremony, with the charm of those first bright sweet hours of communion when strangers glide into friends; that hour which, either in friendship or in love, is as the bloom to the fruit, as the daybreak to the day, indefinable, magical, and fleeting.

The caïque rocked on the water, half hidden under the hanging boughs of myrtles at the landing-stairs, while the sea lay calm as a sun-girded lake, nothing in sight except a far-off fleet of olive-wood feluccas. And with one stroke of the oars among the fragrant water-weeds, the little curled gilded sea-toy floated softly and slowly down the still grey waters that glistened like a lake of silver in the sun. Erceldoune was in as ecstatic a dream as any opium-eater. She had cast away whatever thoughts had weighed on her when she had bade him leave her; a step once taken, a decision once given, she was not a woman to vacillate in further doubt or in after regret, she was at once too proud and too nonchalant. She had bidden him, in all sincerity, remain a stranger to her; he had refused to obey, and had chosen to linger in her presence. She let his will take its course, and accepted the present hour. The vessel dropped down the Bosphorus in the sunlight, so smoothly, that a lazy stroke of the oars now and then sufficed to guide it along the shore, where the cypress and myrtle boughs drooped almost to the water, and the heavy odours of jessamine and roses floated to them from the gardens across the sea. Lying back among her cushions, so near him that he could feel the touch of her laces sweep across him as the breeze stirred them, and could see the breath of the wind steal among the chestnut masses of her hair that was drawn back in its own richness from her brow and fastened with gold threads scarce brighter than its own

hue, the fascination of Idalia—a danger that men far
colder and better on their guard than he, found themselves powerless against—gained its empire on him,
as the spell of the Venusberg stole on the will and the
senses of the mailed knight Tannhäuser. With a
glittering gaiety when she would; with a knowledge of
the world, varied, it seemed, almost beyond any woman's
scope; with the acquisition of most languages and of
their literature, polished and profound to scholarship;
with a disdainful, graceful, ironic wit, delicate, but
keenly barbed; and with all these a certain shadow of
sadness, half scornful, half weary, that yet gave to her
at times an exquisite gentleness and a deeper interest
yet, she would have had a fatal and resistless seduc-
tion, without that patrician grace of air and form, and
that rarity of personal attractions, which made her one
of those women whom no man looks on without homage,
few men without passion. With the ease which long
acquaintance with the world alone gives, she spoke on
all topics, lightly, brilliantly, the languor or the satire
of one moment changed the next to the poetry or the
earnestness which seemed to lie full as much in her
nature; and even while she spoke of trifles, she learnt
every trait, every touch of his life, his character, his
fortunes, and his tastes, though he never observed or
dreamt of it—though he never noted in turn that in
it all no word escaped her that could have told him
who she was, whence she came, what her past had
been, or what her present was. The frank, bold, loyal
nature of the man loved and trusted, and had nothing
to conceal. She, in penetration as keen as she was in
tact most subtle, read his life at will, while her own
was veiled.

The caïque dropped indolently down the shore, the oars scarcely parting the bright waters, the warmth of the day tempered by a low west wind, blowing gently from the Levantine isles, spice-laden with their odour. With the rise and fall of the boat, with the perfumes of rose gardens borne on the air, with the boundless freedom of cloudless skies and stretching seas, there were blent the murmur of her voice, the fragrance of her hair, the glance, whose beauty had haunted him by night and day, the fascination of a loveliness passing that even of his remembrance. It seemed to him as if they had been together for ever, drifting through the glories of an Avillion—as if, until now in all his life, he had never lived. He was like a man in enchantment; the world seemed no longer real to him, but changed into a golden and tumultuous dream.

Time, custom, ceremonies, all grew vague and indifferent; it seemed to him as if he had loved this woman for an eternity. The passion suddenly woke in him would have broken its way into hot unconsidered words, but for that light chain lying on his love and binding it to silence which only gave it more tenacity and more strength. She would not have been what she was to him could he have approached her with familiarity; could he have sought her as his mistress, she would have fallen as his ideal.

No one could have called her cold who looked on the brilliance of her beauty, on the light of her smile; but the languor with which she turned aside homage, and let words of softer meaning glide off her ear unnoted or unaccepted, gave her an impenetrability, a nonchalance, a serenity, that were as impassable as coldness.

"I may return to-morrow?" he asked her, when she at last had made him turn the caïque back, and had tacitly dismissed him.

He spoke briefly, but his voice was very low, and there was entreaty in the tone that pleaded far more than a honeyed phrase would ever have done with her. Her eyes dwelt on him a moment, once more with that profound and undefinable look of *pity*.

"Yes, since you wish. I shall be happy to see you at dinner, if you will do me the honour. Adieu!"

She bowed, and moved to leave him. Something in his look as he answered her made her pause as she swept away, and stirred by a sudden impulse (impulse was rare with her), she waited an instant and held out her hand.

He took it; and bending his head, touched it with his lips as reverently as a devotee would kiss his cross. She laughed a little as she drew it gently away.

"We are not in the days of Castilian courtesies! Farewell until to-morrow!"

And with that graceful negligent movement which gave her so languid a charm, she passed away from him into the villa; and for Erceldoune the sun died out of the heavens, and all its beauty faded off the bright earth about him.

He spent the remaining hours of the day alone—alone till long after nightfall—pushing a boat far out to sea, and letting it float at hazard, in the sunset, in the twilight, in the phosphor-brilliance of the moon, till the chant of the Muezzin rang over the waves with the dawn. His existence seemed dreamy, unreal, transfigured; he neither heeded how time went nor what he did; but lay leaning over the side of his boat gazing all through the night at the lighted lattices of her windows, where they glittered through the cypress and myrtle woods. He was in the first trance of a passion he had scorned.

CHAPTER X.
The Sovereign of the Round Table.

ALL the day Erceldoune spent aimlessly; he took his rifle and went over wild tracts of outlying country, he never asked or knew where, but he scarcely fired a shot; the hours seemed endless till they brought the evening, and he walked on and on through scar deserted valleys, and over hills thick clothed with the sombre cypress, with little object except to throw off the fever in him by exhausting exercise and bodily fatigue. The tumultuous happiness and the restless disquiet he felt were alike new to him; he was not a man easily to be the fool of his passions, or to let loose his judgment in their intoxication; he had held them down in almost as stern a curb as any of the iron knights of the Calatrava, and now, in solitude, and in the calmness of morning, he saw his own peril and his own madness as he had not in the enchantment of her presence, or in the impassioned phantasies of the night. He loved her; he did not disguise it from himself; he was not likely to mislead either his own mind or others by the veil of a specious sophistry; and in the freshness and the abandonment of those first hours there came the chillier memory of the bidding she had given him, to leave her and remain a stranger to her. Fear or doubt were alike alien to him. Yet, in calmer reason, he could not but remember that such words must have their motive in some cause he could not fathom; that their mere expression had been strange, and argued of mystery, if not of evil. She had spoken nothing of herself; there remained still unexplained, unguessed at, the cause she had had for the concealment of her name at Monastica, or of her presence at all in those barbaric Moldavian wilds. Who was she? What was her history? He could not tell. Not even did he know whether she were wedded or unwedded; whether his love could ever bring him any chance of happiness through it, or whether it were already forbidden and doomed to be its own misery, its own curse. He knew nothing. And alone on the hill-side, with the vulture wheeling above-head in the noon skies, and the cypress thickets stretching downward to the precipice beneath his feet, a quick shudder ran through his blood. Had he had the mastery of his life so long only to yield it up now to break in a woman's hands? Had he believed in and followed the ideal of his dreams only to suffer through her, and be divorced from her at the last?

He ground the butt of his rifle down into the loose black soil.

"It is too late now!" he said, unconsciously, aloud. "She saved my life; she shall claim it if she will. Come what may, I will believe in HER."

It was a loyal and gallant oath, pledged to the sunburnt solitudes and the blue cloudless skies. Was she for whose sake it was sworn worthy of it?

The world would have told him no, and, being questioned why, would have answered in three words:

"She is Idalia."

Anything of doubt, of depression, of pain, that

had mingled with the tumult of his thoughts through the day, swept far away when the hour came for him to go to her again. One of the Albanian men-servants ushered him through the hall and into the magnificent chamber, which, once the Odà of an Andertin, served now as the reception-room of the villa; the curtains were drawn back, the blaze of light dazzled his sight, and his eyes, eagerly glancing through the vastness of the space for the Countess Vassalis, met instead the eyes of Victor Vane.

His first sensation was one of intense disappointment, the next of intolerable impatience, the third of reckless hatred. He did not pause to remember how improbable it had been to think that she would have invited him alone to dine at her table; how unreasonable it was to suppose that a titled woman of so much youth and so much brilliance could live in solitude the life of a recluse; how natural it must be that she was acquainted with a man of fashionable repute and aristocratic habits, who lived chiefly abroad, and knew almost every continental family of note; he remembered none of these things; he only realised his disappointment, he only saw before him the colourless face of the guest he had once entertained, and to whom he had felt that quick contemptuous dislike which a noted rider, an untiring sportsman, a desert-hunter, and a traveller impervious to fatigue, was certain to conceive for a delicate dilettante, an idle flâneur, a rusé silken speculator and courtier, such as Vane appeared to him.

Something in the very attitude of this man, moreover, as he leant against a marble console playing with a scarlet rose, and humming a Spanish Bolero to himself, suggested the familiarity of custom, of intimacy; he looked like one in his own home—not less so from the way in which he advanced to Erceldoune with a cordial, pleasant smile of welcome. His smile was, indeed, always very sweet, and of a rarely winning promise.

"Ah, Sir Fulke!—charmed to renew our acquaintance. I was delighted to hear from the Countess that she expected the pleasure of seeing you this evening. I assure you I have never forgotten your most comforting hospitality on the moors; my only regret is that we have not come across each other before."

"You do me much honour, and have a long memory for a mere trifle."

Idalia had announced his acquaintance with her to Victor Vane: they had talked of him then! He could not—would not—have spoken *her* name to friend or stranger.

"The Countess tells me that you think you met about here one of your Moldavian assassins," pursued the other, not noticing, or not seeming to notice, the coldness with which his advances were met. "I am not surprised—so many rascals come eastwards. I hope you will be able to track the fellow?"

"My only regret is, that I did not shoot him down."

The answer was brief and stern. He could have shot down the man before him.

"Ah! great pity you didn't. Chivalry is wasted on these *condottieri;* I have seen too much of the scamps in Italy. That was a strange affair, that, in the Carpathians? Motive was political, I should suppose?"

"Probably. Politics is the hospital for broken scoundrels."

Vane laughed softly and merrily. He was a polished gentleman and a polished diplomatist, and never betrayed it if he were hit.

"True enough! *I* used to busy myself with politics once on a time; but, on my soul, I found myself in such bad company, that I was glad to throw up the cards, and leave the tables. Voilà! two of my best friends! Allow me the honour of introducing them to one who, before long, I hope, will let me claim him to make a trio! The Count Laraxa—Baron Falkenstiern—Sir Fulke Erceldoune."

Erceldoune looked at the two men—Hungarian and Thessalian. There was nothing of the adventurer or the *chevalier d'industrie*, however, about either of them; they were of courtly breeding and of genuine rank.

"Idalia is not here?" said Laraxa, after the introduction, to Victor Vane, who gave him the slightest possible silencing glance of warning as he answered:

"She will be, in a moment, I dare say."

Erceldoune crushed his heel into the softness of the carpet with a passionate oath suppressed. What was this man to her that he had title to call her by her familiar name?—what the other that he had a right to receive her guests, and speak of her actions? At that moment Diomed threw open the broad double doors. In the flood of sunshine still pouring in through the western windows there came Idalia.

She swept towards them with the dignity and grace of a woman long accustomed to homage wherever she moved, and familiar with it to weariness. She gave the same reception to all, without a shade of difference that could have flattered any, except that, when dinner was announced as served, with a slight bend of her head she signed Erceldoune to her, and laid her hand on his arm. She might have felt the quick tremor that ran through his frame at that signal of her preference, at that light touch of her hand: she did see the gladness and gratitude that shone in his eyes as they gazed on her, and a sigh unconsciously escaped her—a sigh, not for herself but for him.

They passed into a large vaulted chamber, the walls of white marble, the draperies and couches of scarlet, the matting a silken amber tissue, the ceiling in fresco with wreaths of grapes and pomegranates raised in gold, and at one end a lofty fountain flinging its spray up among flowers.

"Who is that?" muttered Laraxa. "A magnificent man, and she seems to favour him. Is he—*prey?*"

"No. He is a beggared Queen's Messenger. Besides —don't you remember the name?—he was Count Conrad's Border Eagle. Take care what you say before him."

Laraxa lifted his eyebrows:

"Why, in Heaven's name, is he here?"

"Idalia's caprice! You remember, she saved his life; but take care—he may overhear."

"But if Conrad——"

"Conrad is at Athens by now. *Chut!*"

The table was round, so that there was no place of precedence except the right hand of the hostess. The dinner was of as much sumptuousness and elegance as if it had been served in Paris; and the various Albanian, Negro, and Turkish attendants gave the entertainment an Arabian-like effect, heightened by the Eastern character of the confectionery and the Eastern fruits and flowers. The still lingering sunset glow was shut out, and the chamber was illumined with waxlights in crystal or in candelabra at every point: everything about her spoke of no ordinary wealth, and had the air, moreover, of habitual luxury, even of habitual extravagance. It might be only surface deep; but that surface, at least, was brilliant.

"My table is round, like Arthur's," said Idalia, with a smile, as she sank into her chair. "There should be no precedence at a dinner-table: equality, at least, should exist over soups and entrées!"

"Where the Countess Vassalis is, can there fail to be a place of honour?"

She laughed softly:

"You would have me say, like the O'Donoghue, 'Where *I* am, is the head of the table.' That was a truer and haughtier pride than would have lain in a struggle for precedence. The answer always pleased me."

"And yet you are for equality, Madame?" said Victor Vane, with a significance in the tone that did not lie in the words.

A certain contempt came into her eyes and a slight flush on her cheeks.

"My fancies, at least, remain patrician: a woman is never compelled to be consistent," she said, with a negligent indifference.

Yet no physiognomist who had studied the proud curve of her beautiful lips, or the firm mould of her delicate chin, would have said that inconsistency, or any need to take refuge in it, could ever be attributed to the Countess Vassalis, whatever other errors might lie at her score.

"What can that man be to her?" thought Erceldoune, while the dark colour flushed over his brow. Vane had not been named as any relative: there was no difference in her manner to him from her conduct to others, yet he had about him a nameless familiarity, graceful and polished like all his actions, which seemed to betoken in him either some sway over her or some accepted tie to her. Could he be her lover?—her husband? The blood grew like ice in Erceldoune's veins as the thought glanced across him. He felt dizzy, blinded, sick at heart, and drank down unconsciously the great goblet glass beside him that they had filled with champagne. The wine that he was used to drink like water felt now like so much fire: the fever was in his life, not in the liquid.

The dinner was as choice and seductive a one as that with which the fair intriguing Queen of Arragon subdued the senses and stole the allegiance of Villeña. There was a shadow of melancholy still on their hostess; but the dazzling glitter of her wit gained rather than lost by that certain disdainful languor—half scorn, half weariness—which was more marked in her that evening than when she had been with Erceldoune alone in the sunny silence of the Bosphorus. A woman far less conscious of her power than she was conscious of it, would have known that all these men loved her, and were, even if unknown to them, each other's rivals. But the knowledge gave her no more sort of embarrassment than if they had been guests of her own sex. She was well used to all conquest; used to men in all their moods and all their passions; used to intoxicate them with a smile, to subdue them with a glance. She took little wine, touching each variety with her lips; but once or twice she drank a single draught of hot Chartreuse—a fiery liqueur that her sex rarely choose —and with it drove away the shadow that seemed on her, and abandoned herself to the gay glitter of the hour. Watching her, he could have fancied, had not the thought been too fantastic, that she had taken the Chartreuse as men take hot wines—to shake off thought, and give their spirits recklessness. Yet what could this woman, with her splendour, her power, her youth, and her fascination, desire that she had not? What could be the canker at the core of that purple and odorous pomegranate flower of her life?

The various courses were served admirably; and he might have been dining at a palace for the lavishness of the banquet. There was great brilliance, too, in the conversation; for in her presence every one strove to shine. There was considerable freedom in the topics and in the wit—more than is customary in the presence of most women, though never actually sufficient to become licence; but now and then there were flashes of jest at which Erceldoune ground his teeth: they were a profanation to his ideal—a taint on his angel. Unconsciously he had so idealised and etherealised her in his thoughts, that a soil of earth on her would defame if it were too late to dethrone her. "That is not the tone in which men speak before a hostess they reverence," he said in his soul, with fiery bitterness, while he glanced at her to see if she resented it. She lay back with her beautiful languor, laughing softly, slightly. She was either too familiar with it to note it, or if she felt resentment did not display it.

When only the Turkish and Levantine fruits and crystallised confections remained on the table in their silver baskets, which dainty statuettes of Odalisque slaves and Greek girls held up in a shower of flowers, hookahs were brought round by a Nubian to each of the guests.

"We have permission to smoke in your presence, then, madame?" said Erceldoune, as the porcelain narghilé was set beside him.

She looked up in slight surprise, as though the solicitation were new to her.

"Oh, yes! It is as necessary to you after dinner as your cup of coffee. Is it not?"

"It is always welcome—since you have the compassion to allow it," he answered her, as he raised the long amber-tipped tube.

She smiled.

"Of course—why not? That Latakia, I believe, is good? All the rest of it, they tell me, was bought up by the French Legation."

"It is excellent, full of fragrance, but very soft. A-propos of the Chancelleries, at which of them shall I have the honour of meeting you most? As yet, you know, I am in ignorance of your nation."

He spoke with the natural carelessness of so natural a question; the Countess Vassalis must as he deemed be known by the representatives of all the great Powers. A shadow of impatience came on her face, a defiant hauteur in her eyes.

"You will meet me at none of the Embassies," she said, briefly and coldly.

And in that moment Erceldoune saw Idalia as he had never seen her before; saw in her a certain grandeur of disdainful defiance, a certain outlawed sovereignty as of one life against a world.

"The Countess Idalia has come to the East for rest," interposed Victor Vane, with his musical, gliding voice. "How is it possible to obtain it if you go *en pénitence* to those tedious travesties of little courts, his Excellency's receptions? Visiting your Ambassador is, I think, one of the severest penalties of foreign residence."

"Our Representative will consent, I dare say, to release you from it if you petition him; or, most likely, he will not notice your choice *de briller par votre absence*," said Erceldoune, curtly.

He knew the explanation was a diplomatic lie; he was tortured with bitter impatience to know why the man made himself her apologist, or had claim to explain her actions; his thoughts were in a conflict of conjecture as to the cause of her exclusion from the Embassies—for exclusion he believed it, by the look that for one instant he had seen upon her face.

The access of vivacity and abandon which a considerable amount of wine drunk, and the introduction of tobacco invariably produce, flowed into the conversation; its gaiety grew very gay, and though there was still nothing that was licentious, there was a tone in it not customary before women of rank; the anecdotes had a Bréda aroma, the epigrams had a Jockey Club flavour, the equivoques were fitted for a little gilded supper cabinet in the Maison Dorée; such a freedom in any other hour would have added to its piquance and its savour to Erceldoune as to all other men, but it now lashed him into vehement pain and incensement; it brought the breath of the world—and of a very profane world—on the woman of his dreams, it desecrated and almost dimmed the beauty of his ideal. Out of the mists of death he had once wakened to see her face in the haze of the sunlight; the face of an angel, the face of his altar-picture at Monastica: when he sat here in the perfume and lustre of the Eastern chamber, with the odours of wines and flowers, and spices and incense, with the glitter of gold and azure, of silver and scarlet, with light laughter and light wit on the air, he seemed to have lost her again—lost her more cruelly. Even while close beside him, the richness of her beauty, the glance of her eyes, the touch of her trailing dress, the gleam of the diamonds on her hair, heightened her loveliness and heightened his passion, till the night seemed full of wild tumult to him, of fierce delight, and of as fiery a pain, there was still on him that deadly nameless sense of some impending loss. She was nothing to him, worse than nothing, if she were not what he believed her. Alas, where was there ever man or woman who reached the spiritualised standard of an idealic love?

The lustre and splendour of the chamber, the artistic mingling of colour, the rich wines, the dreamy perfumes, the scented narcotics, these were all, he knew, the studied auxiliaries of a woman whose science was to beguile. But he dashed the accursed suspicion from him as quickly as it rose; he had sworn to believe in her, he *would* believe in her.

When she at last rose and left the dinner-table, her guests rose too, and followed her. A timepiece was striking twelve when they entered the salon.

"We have been long enough at dinner to satisfy

Brillat-Savarin!" said Idalia, glancing at it. "Do you like cards, Sir Fulke?"

"I think no man could say honestly he did not, though it is the most dangerous of pastimes," he answered her, with a smile. "I have seen its evils in South America, where, as in Pizarro's time, the old proverb still holds good, and they 'game away the sun before it rises.'"

"Many do that over other things than play, and before they know what their sun is worth!" she said, with that profound sadness which now and then chequered her careless brilliance with so dark a shadow. "We will have some baccarat, then. I am fond of play—when it is high enough."

"I should not have thought that."

She looked at him with a smile; she knew his reasons as well as though he had uttered them; there was something of irony, more of melancholy in the smile.

"No? But it is true all the same. Why should it not be? High play is excitement, and it whirls thought away."

"But *you* should have no thoughts that are pain."

"Those are idle words! There are few lives without pain, there are none without reproach."

She turned from him with something of impatience, and as her Albanians wheeled the card-table nearer, sank into her couch, drawing some cards to her. She looked a woman to lean over a balcony in a starlit Southern night, and listen to a poet's cancion, or a lover's whisper stealing up through the murmurs of the leaves with the reverent worship of Petrarca; not one to need the feverish excitation of the gamester's reckless hazards. Who was she? what was she? this mystery whom men called Idalia? he wondered ceaselessly in eager unrest.

The baccarat commenced.

She played with the skill of her country, if that country were Greece, as her name implied; played like one accustomed to control chance by proficiency: but also with that alternate listlessness and eagerness which marks those who seek it as a distraction from those who crave it out of avarice. It was its excitement that was grateful to her, the rapid changes and chances. When she lost, she lost with an absolute indifference, and she staked her gold with a lavish extravagance that seemed to disdain speculation. Once or twice Erceldoune almost thought that she sought to guide the success of the hazard towards himself; if so, she succeeded; he won considerably, to his own displeasure, and she did not. Over and over again, when the current of chance ran for her, she lost it, either listlessly, with that careless scornful weariness peculiar to her, or with a recklessness that made her throw large sums away while she laughed over a bon-mot. Two hours passed rapidly in the whirl of the game, leaving him winner of some heavy sums. Her eyes rested on him a moment, on the dark soldier-like grandeur of his head, which the rich colours and light of the room behind him threw up, as a noble Spanish head by Murillo might be thrown up on an illuminated background of gold and scarlet; then, at a slight pause in the game, she rose, sweeping her laces about her.

"Play on by yourselves, mes amis, as long as you will. I am constant to nothing—the privilege of a woman!—and I shall take a cup of coffee."

They all rose, as of course she knew that they

would, and gathered about her, while two Nubians
brought round trays of Mocha and bonbons. It had
been her caprice that Erceldoune should be a gainer
by the baccarat, and she had secured her point without
any semblance of effort. The expression used by more
than one to her concerning him, had impressed her
with the idea that his necessities for money were far
greater than they were.

Taking their coffee, they stood about her by the
marble basin of the fountain. As the night grew late,
as the wine and the incense and her constant presence
added heat to their mutual rivalry, the bands of courtesy
began to loosen, the instinctive jealousy that was rife
among them began to seethe up in covert words and
bitter ironies. Erceldoune resented their presence, they
resented his; even the bright soft harmony always
characteristic of Victor Vane began to show a gleam
of constraint and impatience beneath it. Any watcher
might have seen that it needed but very slight provocation, a very little more licence, to remove the curb
that lay on them, and to let their enmity break into
feud, mere strangers though they were to one another.
She saw this, but it excited in her no passing agitation
even, no thought of difficulty; she was used to see the
strongest tempests at riot, and to control them, if she
cared to do so, with a glance or a word; often she let
them destroy themselves by their own violence. Now
she left them and ran her hands over the keys of the
grand piano which stood near the fountain, and with
hardly a chord of prelude sang a rich Romaic ode, a
mountain song with the old war-fire of Hellas in it.
Her voice was of an exquisite beauty, highly cultivated
and eloquent as any Pasta's, and it rang through the

silence, throbbing on the air, and echoing far out to the night, where it was answered by the beating of the waves and the music of the nightingales among the roses. Those round her were stilled as by a sudden spell. She sang on, scarcely pausing, grand, mournful, impassioned chants, now Romaic, now Sicilian, now Venetian; songs of the nations, of the poets, of the hours of freedom, of the glories that were gone from Hellas and from Rome; songs of a profound pathos, of an eternal meaning. Neither Mozart nor Beethoven ever gave richer melodies than were those poems brought from the past, from the peoples, from the heart of dying nations, and from the treasures of their perished liberties.

Erceldoune leant against the white shaft of the marble walls, with his head bent; music always had power over him, and it gave her back all the divinity of his dreams, all the power of his lost ideal. Never, since the first moment when she had stooped to him with that one word "You!" had he seen her look as she looked now; those were the eyes that had bent above him with an angel's pity, when he had lain dying in the sunlight. Anything of her empire that had been hazarded in the past few hours she recovered tenfold; anything of abhorrent doubt that had stolen into his loyalty and faith to her, was swept away and forgotten.

He believed in her—he worshipped her! Not less so, when with a shock of surprise, and all the Borderblood warming in him, he heard her sing the Scottish sonnet, beautiful and living still as the waters of the Esk, by which it was written:

> Sleep, silence' child, sweet father of soft rest,
> Prince, whose approach peace to all mortals brings,
> Indifferent host to shepherds and to kings,
> Sole comforter of minds that are opprest,
> Lo! by thy charming rod all breathing things
> Lie slumbering with forgetfulness possest.

The words, only the sweeter for the lingering softness of the foreign accent, came to his ear like the breath of his mountain air over the heather; as they died off the air he leaned eagerly forward:

"You know our poems? You believe that beauty may come even out of our rugged glens?"

"Surely every one knows Drummond? The gentle Cavalier who died of his Master's death? You must often have seen Hawthornden, I suppose?"

"It was my favourite haunt in my boyhood, though I believe I thought more of the birds I shot in the glen, and the water-fowls of the Esk, than of Drummond himself at that time."

"And yet there was *Patria* in every line of your face when you heard his sonnet just now," she said, with a smile.

"Ah! you know that Pope says,

> 'A Scot would fight for "Christ's Kirk o' the Green."'

To hear any of the old ballads is like hearing a trumpet-call; besides—Drummond's words on *your* lips! I cannot tell you what they were to me."

He paused abruptly, the silence more eloquent than any words could have been.

"You have never heard me speak English," she said, carelessly. "In truth, if you will pardon me, it is the language I like least. Its low Dutch, with all the exotic additions that have grown on it, is too hard for my lips; and I have rarely had occasion to use what knowledge I possess of it. Apropos of Scottish poetry, are you descended from the Rhymer?"

"We believe him to have been of the same race; but what is known of him is so enveloped in legend, that it is hard to trace. Thomas himself has grown almost mythical, though 'Syr Tristam' is immortal."

"Yes! because Syr Tristam's folly is repeated by all men, through all ages."

"Folly? It merits a better name; it was, at least, fidelity?"

"Folly! Fidelity! They are synonyms for love. *L'un vaut l'autre.*"

"Would you never, then, believe in passion as enduring as Tristam's?"

"For Ysonde, who is another man's wife? Oh yes! that is a very common feature. The love is so charming because it is forbidden!"

The evening was very still; the stars shining in myriads above the cypress and ilex woods, the heavy odours of roses and basilica on the air, and through the boughs of the cedars silvery gleams and flashes of the phosphorescent water. She left her seat as she spoke, and went out on to the terrace, and leaned a moment over the marble wall.

"How cool, how tranquil! And we spend such a night over hot wines, and idle jests, and feverish play!"

To his heart, to his lips, rose words in unison with that sweetness of the night, born from the intoxication of the hour: as though she felt them ere they were uttered, and would have them remain unspoken, she leant slightly towards him.

"Go home by yourself—with none of them, if they invite you. I don't mean," she added, with a laugh, "because they will knock you down to steal your winnings! They are not so low as that—yet."

The whisper was low and very rapid; surprise was the dominant feeling that it awoke in him, joined with something of a vivid wondering delight—she thought of his welfare!

"Your wish is my law," he answered her. "Do with my life what you will—it is yours."

"No. Not mine. It is a noble trust; never give it rashly."

There was a step beside them.

"A beautiful night, indeed," said Victor Vane. "A picture of Gherardo, and a poem of Hafiz! Certainly we never know what stars are till we come to the East."

"Never," said Idalia, turning to him; "and now you may return to Stamboul by their light. After their poetry come their practical uses. I shall dismiss you all now; I am tired. Good night!"

Lightly as the words were spoken, eagerly as they longed to dispute the dismissal, unscrupulous, at least, as were some of those about her, all were constrained to obey her command—all were powerless to remain in her presence. Erceldoune was the first to accept her dismissal; he would not offer her even so much insult as would have lain in hesitation, and he took his farewell of her instantly and almost in silence.

Vane followed him with his glance.

"Why have you taken to patronise that Border moss-trooper, madame?" he asked, with a slight satirical laugh. "He is nothing but a courier, and has only an owl's roost at home that foxes burrow in, and cobwebs keep furnished. He is a rough rider and a wild shikari, nothing else; they are odd titles to your preference."

She looked him steadily in the eyes:

"He is a frank and gallant gentleman; that is, perhaps, as strange a one! It may be odd that *I* should care to see an honest man by way of variety; but—since it is my caprice, harm him at your peril."

Her guests were gone.

In solitude she sank down in the depths of a couch, with the light still playing on the diamonds in her hair, and her eyes watching the fall of the showering spray into the basin of the fountain, where scarlet roses swayed into the lily-laden waters. She gave a weary, restless sigh as she thrust back the bright masses of her hair farther from her temples, and, leaning her cheek on her hand, gazed absently into the glancing surface. There was something of release, something of regret, something of self-reproach in her attitude and in her thoughts; though these were checked by and mingled with a careless ironic triumph, and a royal habit of command and of disdain.

"Have I done more wrong?" she said, half aloud, while her proud head fell. "Greater wrong than ever! He is loyal and lion-hearted—a brave chivalrous gentleman: he should not come amongst *us!* The others can play at diamond cut diamond; the others are fairly armed, and have but their weapons turned against them. But he is of different mould: he will suffer—he will suffer terribly!"

CHAPTER XI.
Fairy-Gold.

In the full noon heat of the next day—heat that brooded on the hills and glistened on the sea, in which the leaves and the flowers drooped, and the sails of the feluccas hung stirless—Idalia moved slowly and thoughtfully up and down her reception-room, the sunlight straying in chequered rays through the chinks of the shutters, and falling fitfully across her. The wolf-hound followed her step for step; there was not a sound except the falling of the fountains and the buzzing of a little humming-bird tangled among the flowers. There was a certain shadow on her, but it was not that of grief, still less was it that of any tremulous effeminate sorrow; it was haughty, unrestful, with much of doubt, much of rebellion, much of disdain in it—the shadow that was on the Reine Blanche in the fetters of Fotheringay, on Marie Antoinette in the presence of Mirabeau. There was an intense scorn in the dark soft lustre of her eyes—the eyes of a Georgian or a Greek. She was netted closely in, in a net of partially her own past weaving: self-reproach was not the least keen of many regrets that were heavy upon her, and the world was against her; but she was not vanquished nor intimidated.

She came and paused before an open cabinet, on whose writing-stand lay a pile of letters. Her eyes rested on the one that lay uppermost, and read its lines for the second time with disdain, revulsion, pity, impatience, and loathing all mingled in her glance.

"He always wants money! He would give his soul

for money; and yet he throws it away as idly as the winds!" she thought, while her hand absently caressed the great head of the hound. "Well! he can have it. I will always give him that. I would give it him all —down to the very diamonds—if he would leave me free, if he would cut away every link of the past, if he would go and never let me see his face again."

Yet still, though there was much of profound dejection and heart-sickness at her life upon her, there was no fear in it, and no sadness that had not as much disdain. She laid both hands on the dog's broad forehead, and looked down into his eyes.

"Oh, Sulla! when one life is chosen, is there no escape into another? If we accept error in blindness once, is there no laying it down? Plutarch has written, 'When we see the dishonour of a thing, then is it time to renounce it.' But what can we do if we cannot— if it stay with us, and will not forsake us? How can *I* be free from it?"

But bondage was not submission; and she was like the Palmyran or Icenian queens—made a slave, but all a sovereign still.

A humming-bird flew against her, and, frightened, tangled itself among her lace. She put her hand over it, and caught it, stroked smooth the little ruffled wings, laid her lips gently on its bright head, and, opening one of the lattices, loosed it, and let it fly into the sunny air.

"Liberty! Liberty! It is worth any sacrifice," she said, half aloud, as she watched the bird's flight through the gardens and outward to the sea.

At that moment a Nubian slave threw open the broad double doors of jasper at the end of the cham-her, the hangings before it were flung aside, and Erceldoune entered her presence.

She had said it would be best that he should remain absent; yet he was not in error when he thought that the smile she had given him last night was scarcely so sweet as that she gave him now. He seemed half her own by title of that death-hour in which she had felt for the faint beatings of his heart, and had watched beside him in the loneliness of the Carpathians. She could not forget that this man's strong life would have perished but for her.

He owed her a debt—the debt of faith, at the least. Whatever she might be to others, to him she had been as the angel of life. Moreover, there was in Idalia, overlying the proud earnestness that was in her nature, a certain nonchalance—a certain languid carelessness—that made her look little beyond the present hour, and change her temperament as immediate influences prevailed. The tradition of birth gave her some blood of the Commneni in her veins; and the *insouciance* of an epicurean, with the haughty power of imperial pride, were blent in her as they had been in Manuel. Therefore, since he had chosen to put aside her first warning, she allowed him now to come as he would.

As for him, life was a paradise—a delirium; and he gave himself up to it. The earth had eternal summer for him, and wore an eternal smile. He sat near her in the shaded light and sweet incense of the chamber, while they spoke of things that served to veil the thoughts burning beneath his commonest words; they strolled through the cedar aisles, and through the fields of roses, as the heat of the day faded, and the breeze began to stir among the splendours of the flower-wilderness; they passed the sunset hour on the sea, watching the day die out in glory, and the fire from the west glow over the Marmora waves, and tinge the distant snow-crests of Mount Ida and Olympus.

When the little caïque floated slowly homeward down the waters, the evening star—the star of Astarte—had risen. Through the opened windows of her villa the lights of the banqueting-room glittered, and the table stood ready served, with the Albanians and Nubians waiting about it. She bade him stay, if he would, and he was her only guest. Had her wines been opium-drugged, they could not have brought him dreams more fatally fair—a lulled delight more sure to wake in bitterness—than they gave him now. The charms for every sense, the beauty of the chamber, the odours of the flowers, the oriental languor pervading the very air—all that he had felt the night before he felt tenfold now: then a passionate jealousy, a restless doubt, had haunted him; now he was alone, and on him only did her smile glance, did her eyes fall.

There was on her this night an infinite gentleness, a gracious sweetness, often tinged with sadness, though often bright, brilliant, and illumined with all the grace of talent. But at the same time there was the sovereignty which, in her solitude, guarded her as an empress is guarded in a Court, which made her as secure from words of warmer tinge than what she chose to hear, as she was carelessly disdainful of the precise customs of the world. He felt that she forbade him to approach her with any whisper of love; he knew that to take advantage of his admission to her solitude, to give any utterance to the passion in him, would be to

be banished from it then and for ever. He felt this
though she never spoke, never hinted it; and even
while the restriction galled and stung him most, he
most revered her for it, he most honoured and adored
in her the holiness of his ideal.

There was a difference in her from the evening before; while her gaiety was less, the darker shadow was also far less upon her. She had scarcely touched the wines, and of play she did not speak; it might be but the "hope which out of its own self creates the thing it longs for," but he could have believed that for the few hours of the present she had resigned herself to happiness—happiness in his presence. The thought seemed wild to him, baseless and vain even to madness; he told himself that it was a presumptuous folly, and he felt that her gentleness to him, her smile upon him, were only such feeling as a woman might well testify, in mere pity's sake, to one whom she had found in deadly peril, and whom she had restored to life on the very brink of the grave. And, indeed, there was a weary, royal grace always in her, which would have made a man, far vainer than Erceldoune could ever become, long doubt his own power ever to move her heart.

He asked nothing, heeded nothing, doubted nothing. He moved, acted, spoke, almost as mechanically as one in the unconsciousness of fever. It was love of which men have died before now; not of broken hearts, as poets say, but of its intoxication and its reaction, as in a death-draught of opium or digitalis.

She divined well enough all that was unuttered on his lips. She let his idolatry be fostered by all of scene, time, place, and the spells of her own loveliness that a studied coquette could have devised, yet she repressed any expression of that worship as a woman of the world alone can do, without any word that was cold, any glance that was rebuke, yet proudly, distinctly, and beyond resistance.

She followed the impulse, the caprice perhaps, of the moment, without definite purpose or thought at all. For the last eight years men had never approached her save to love; it was a thousand-time told tale to her. If her heart had lost its freshness, or its pity, there could be little marvel in it, even though there were much blame.

The chant of the Imaum rang up from the shore, deep and sonorous, calling on the Faithful to prayer, an hour before midnight. She listened dreamily to the echoes that seemed to linger among the dark foliage.

"I like those national calls to prayer," she said, as she leaned over the parapet, while the fire-flies glittered among the mass of leaves as the diamond sprays glistened in her hair. "The Ave Maria, the Vespers, the Imaum's chant, the salutation of the dawn or of the night, the hymn before sleep, or before the sun;—you have none of those in your chill islands? You have only weary rituals, and stuccoed churches, where the 'Pharisees for a pretence make long prayers!' As if *that* was not the best—the only—temple!"

She glanced upward at the star-studded sky, and on her face was that graver and gentler look which had come there when she sang.

"I have held it so many a time," he answered her, "lying awake at night among the long grass of the Andes, or under the palms of the desert. It was a strange delusion to build shrines to the honour of God while there are still his own—the forests and the mountains. But do not call my country cold; we are not cold; there are bold lives among us; and we can love—too well for our own peace."

His voice had a rich melody in it, and was unsteady over the last words; in his eyes, as they burned in the shadows of the night, she saw a passion as intense as ever glowed under the suns of Asia, the stronger for the rein in which it was still held.

She was silent a moment, then she laughed a little; very softly.

"Do not repudiate coldness; it is the most precious gift the fates give, if it be not the most poetic. Remember what your namesake of Ercelcloune found when the Elf-Queen granted him his prayer; where he thought he held an angel he saw a loathsome shadow. The legend covers a wise warning."

"Ay!—but even while the horror of the shadow and the treachery were on him he had faith in *her;* and his faith was justified; it gave him, in reward, his bright, immortal love."

She turned her head and looked at him, gently, pityingly, almost tenderly.

"Ah! you are too loyal for this world, far too loyal to spend your heart on any woman's love. It is only fairy gold, believe me, which, if you took it, would turn to ashes in your hand. And now,—a safe ride homeward to you, and good night."

She held her hand out to him with a sweet and gracious gesture, the more marked in her because she never gave her hand in familiar salutation; he bent over it, and touched it with his lips, a lingering kiss in which all his silenced heart spent itself.

She did not rebuke him; she had not power to speak coldly or chidingly to the man whose life was owed her, whose head had rested in his dying hour on her bosom. As he rode slowly out down the cedar avenue that passed in front of the terrace he looked up; she was leaning still over the marble parapet, her form distinct against the dark masses of myrtle foliage, the brilliance of the moonlight shining full upon her from the sea. She gave him a farewell sign of her hand as he bowed to his saddle, such as from her palace-prison Queen Ysonde might have given to her lover; and Erceldoune went on through the fragrant night, his horse's feet beating out rich odours from the trailing leaves, dizzy with that riot of hope, joy, belief, and desire, which is too tumultuous and impatient for happiness, but yet *is* happy beyond all that the world holds. She remained long in her solitude upon the terrace, gazing down into the shelving slopes of leaf and blossom, where the fire-flies made the woodland as star-studded as the skies.

"It is too late now—he would never forget *now*," she murmured. "I tried to save him, and he would not be saved!"

Saved from what? Saved from her.

A little while before, and in her own gardens at Naples, a brave boy, in the brightness of his youth, had been run through the heart in a rapier duel for her sake; and she had not felt a tithe so much pain as lay on her now, so much weary, passionate, and vain regret. Then many had called her heartless, and the mother of the dead boy had cursed her with pitiless curses; none would have called her heartless now.

For seven or eight days time came and passed away, spent thus. He sought her in the warm amber noons, stayed with her amidst the wilderness of roses, and drifted with her down the sunny sea along the Bosphorus shore, and left her only when the midnight stars rose over the minarets of the city of Constantine. He met no one in her Turkish villa, and she let him come in this familiar unbroken intercourse as though it were welcome to her; as though, indeed, their friendship had been the long-accustomed growth of years. He asked nothing, heeded nothing; he never paused to recall that there was any defiance of custom in the intercourse between them, or to note that she, with her wealth and her splendour, was as utterly alone as though she were a recluse of Mount Athos; he never observed that she kept silence on all that could have explained her presence in Moldavia, or given him account of the position and the character of her life; he never noticed, he never recollected;—he was lost in a day-dream of such magic that it lulled him to oblivion of everything save itself, and all criticism, all reason, all doubt, were as impossible in him as insult and outrage to her. His own nature was one too boldly free, too accustomed to the liberty of both action and thought, too little tolerant of the ceremonials and conventionalities of the world, to be awake to the singularity of her reception of him as others might have been. Moreover, while she allowed him this unrestrained communion with her, he would have been a vainer man far than Erceldoune who could have flattered himself that this was done because her heart was touched; or who should have brought on him his exile for ever by warmer entreaties for a softer joy than friendship. While untrammeled by any of the bonds of conventionality, while accustomed to a liberty of thought, of speech, of act that brooked no dictator, while distinguished by a careless negligence of custom and of opinion that was patrician even whilst it was bohemian, Idalia still kept the light but inexorable rein upon his passion, which forbade him to pass the bounds that she tacitly prescribed to him. He was a bold and daring man enough; in his early days he had been steeped in vice, though he had learned to loathe it; he was impassioned in his pursuit of her as any lover that the Asian suns had ever nurtured to their own heat. But he loved her as William Craven loved the Winter Queen, as George Douglas the White Queen.

One who should not have cared for her—if such there could have been—would have found an infinite variety, an endless charm in her companionship. She had travelled in most countries, she was familiar with most nations, she had knowledge of the classic and the oriental literatures, deep to a scholar's scope and warmed with the picturesque hue of an imagination naturally luxuriant, though the world had joined with it an ironic and contemptuous scepticism that gave the keenness of wit, side by side with the colour of a poet, to her thoughts and to her words; she understood men pitilessly, human nature unerringly, none could have palmed off on her a false mask or a glossed action; she had seen and known the world in all its intricacies; the variety of her acquirements was scarcely so singular as the variety of her experience; and the swift change of her mood, now grave to melancholy, now careless to caprice, now thoughtful with a profound and philosophic insight into the labyrinths of human life, now gay with the nonchalant and glittering gaiety of bohemian levity, gave her much of inconstancy, it is true, but gave her infinitely more of charm and enchantment.

Evening fell once more, closing in the eighth day that their intercourse had thus passed on since the night when he had found her as he had hunted the Greek to his death; they had lingered without moving in the banqueting-room; the wines, and flowers, and fruits still standing on the table; no light stronger than the clear vivid moonlight shining on the freshly-cut flowers that strewed the ground, the frescoes of the pomegranates that wreathed the hall, the scarlet hues melting away in the shadow, and the tall slender column of the fountain flinging its foam aloft. Idalia leant back among the cushions, the dazzling play of her words ceasing for a while; the moon's rays touching the proud arch of her brows, the clusters of her hair bound with a narrow gold band of antique workmanship, the voluptuous softness of her lips, and the dark, unfathomable lustre of her eyes that met his own — burning with the eloquence he felt forbidden to put into words,—but were not moved by them; they did not droop, as women's often do, beneath the fire in his, they passed on from him to rest dreamily on the distance, where the domes of Santa Sophia rose against the stars, and the lighted minarets glittered among the cypress groves of the Moslem city.

"It was a fair heritage to lose through a feeble vanity — that beautiful Constantinople," she said musingly. "The East and the West. What an empire! More than Alexander ever grasped at—what might not have been done with it? Asian faith and Oriental sublimity, with Roman power and Gothic force; if there had been a hand strong enough to weld all these together, what a world there might have been!"

"But to have done that would have been to attain the Impossible?" he answered her. "Oil and flame, old and new, living and dying, tradition and scepticism, iconoclast and idolater, you cannot unite and harmonise these antagonisms?"

She gave a sign of dissent.

"The prophet or the hero unites all antagonisms, because he binds them all to his own genius. The Byzantine empire had none such; the nearest was Julian, but he believed less in himself than in the gods; the nearest after him was Belisarius—the fool of a courtesan!—and he was but a good soldier, he was no teacher, no liberator, no leader for the nations. John Vatices came too late. A man must be his own convert before he can convert others. Zoroaster, Christ, Mahomet, Cromwell, Napoleon, believed intensely in their own missions; hence their influence on the peoples. How can we tell what Byzantium might have become under one mighty hand?—it was torn in pieces among courtesans, and parasites, and Christian fanatics, and Houmousians and Houmoiousians! I have the blood of the Commneni in me. I think of it with shame when I remember what they might have been."

"You come from the Roman Emperors?"

"The Roman Emperors!" she repeated. "When

the name was a travesty, an ignominy, a reproach! When Barbarians thronged the Forum, and the representative of Galilee fishermen claimed power in the Capitol! Yes; I descend—they say—from the Commneni; but I am far prouder that, on the other hand, I come from pure Athenians. I belong to two buried worlds. But the stone throne of the Areopagus was greater than the gold one of Manuel."

"You are the daughter of Emperors? you are worthy an empire."

His were the words of no flattery of the hour, but of a homage as idolatrous as was ever offered in the fair shadows of the Sacred Groves of Antioch to the goddess from whom she took her name. And there was a great pang at his heart as he spoke them; he thought of the only thing on earth he called his own, those crumbling ruins to the far westward, by the Cheviot range, where the scarlet creepers hid the jagged rents in the walls, and owls roosted where princes once had banqueted.

"An empire! *I* thought so once," she answered, with a low, slight laugh. "I had dreams—of the sceptre of my ancestors, of the crown of the Violet City, of an Utopia here, where east and west meet one another, and nature would give us a paradise if men did not make us a hell. Dreams—dreams—youth is all a dream, and life too, some metaphysicians say. Where shall we wake, I wonder, and how—for the better? It is to be hoped so, if we ever wake at all, which is more than doubtful!"

There was an accent of sadness in the opening words, but the rest were spoken with that irony which, while it was never bitter, was more contemptuous than bitterness in its half languid levity. He looked at her with a vague and troubled pain—there was so much in the complexity of her nature that was veiled from him; seeing her life but dimly, there was so much of splendour, so much of melancholy in it, that exiled him from her, and that oppressed him; the more magnificent her lineage or her fortunes, the farther she was from him.

"You have one empire already," he said, almost abruptly, in the tumult of the suppressed thoughts in him—"a wider one than the Byzantine! You can do what you will with men's lives. I have nothing, I can lose nothing, except the life you gave me back; but if I had all the kingdoms of the earth I would throw them away for—"

The eagerness in his voice dropped suddenly, leaving the words unfinished; he crushed them into silence with a fierce effort. She glanced at him with that graceful negligence with which she silenced all she would not hear.

"No kingdom would be a tithe so peaceful as your manhood and your honour. Never peril *those* for any woman; there is not one worth the loss."

The flash of a giddy, exultant, incredulous rapture ran like lightning through his veins for a moment. She had softly repulsed, but she had not rebuked him; she had known at what his words paused, and the smile she had given him had a light in it that was almost tenderness. He did not ask, he did not think, where his hope began or ended; he did not weigh its meaning, he dared not have drawn it to the light, lest close seen it should have faded; he only felt—

> So my eyes hold her! What is worth
> The best of heaven, the best of earth?

"There it lies!" she pursued, dreamily, resting her eyes on the distant minarets and roofs of Constantinople, rising clear and dark in the lustre of the moon, undimmed by even a floating cloud. "And all its glories are dead. The Porphyry-chamber and the Tyrian dyes, the Pandects and the Labarum, the thunder of Chrysostom and the violets of child-Protus—they could not make the city live that had dared to dethrone Rome! The hordes of the Forest and the Desert avenged the wrongs of the Scipii and the Julii. It was but just?"

"As the soldiers of Islam avenged the gods of Greece. Aphrodite perished that Arians might rage, and the beautiful mythus was swept away, that hell and the devil might be believed in instead! When the Crescent glittered there, it half redressed the wrongs of your Olympus."

"And we reign still!"

She turned, as she spoke, towards the western waters, where the sea-line of the Ægean lay, while in her eyes came the look of a royal pride and of a deathless love.

"Greece cannot die! No matter what the land be now, Greece—*our* Greece—must live for ever. Her language lives; the children of Europe learn it, even if they halt it in imperfect numbers. The greater the scholar the humbler he still bends to learn the words of wisdom from her schools. The poet comes to her for all his fairest myths, his noblest mysteries, his greatest masters. The sculptor looks at the broken fragments of her statues, and throws aside his Calliope in despair before those matchless wrecks. From her, soldiers learn how to die, and nations how to conquer and to keep their liberties. No deed of heroism is done but, to crown it, it is named parallel to hers. They write of love, and who forgets the Lesbian? They dream of freedom, and to reach it they remember Salamis. They talk of progress, and while they talk, they sigh for all that they have lost in Academus. They seek truth, and while they seek, wearily long, as little children, to hear the golden speech of Socrates, that slave, and fisherman, and sailor, and stonemason, and date-seller were all once free to hear in her Agora. But for the light that shone from Greece in the breaking of the Renaissance, Europe would have perished in its Gothic darkness. They call her dead!—she can never die while her life, her soul, her genius breathe fire into the new nations, and give their youth all of greatness and of grace that they can claim. Greece dead! She reigns in every poem written, in every art pursued, in every beauty treasured, in every liberty won, in every godlike life and god-like death, in your fresh lands, which, but for her, would be barbarian now."

Where she stood, with her eyes turned westward to the far-off snows of Cithæron and Mount Ida, and the shores which the bronze spear of Pallas Athene once guarded through the night and day, the dark light in her eyes deepened, and the flush of a superb pride was on her brow—it seemed Aspasia who lived again, and who remembered Pericles.

He looked on her, with the glow of passion on his face, made nobler by the poet's thoughts that were awaking in him. He was silent, for his heart was lulled with the oppression of his love, as the great forests are silenced before the storm.

She had forgotten his presence, standing there in the hush of the midnight, with the Byzantine city to the eastward, and to the west the land that had heard

Plato—her thoughts were far away among the shadows of the past, the great past, when the Io Triumphe had been echoed up to the dim majesty of the Acropolis, and the roses had drooped their fragrant heads on the gracious gold of Alcibiades' love-locks.

He knew that he was forgotten, yet his heart did not reproach her; she was far above him in his sight, far as the stars that shone now above Athens, and his love was one that would take neglect and anguish silently, without swerving once from its loyalty. He would have laid his life down to be pressed out in agony, so that it should have given her one passing moment of pleasure, as a rose is thrown under a woman's foot to be crushed as she steps, that dying it may lend a breath of fragrance to the air she breathes.

"You are born with genius, you are made for sovereignty, and I have nothing that is worthy to bring you;" he said long after, while his voice sank very low. "Only—only—remember, if ever you need it, one man's life will be yours to be lost for you."

She started slightly where she leaned, with her musing eyes resting on the west; she had forgotten his presence, and his words, though they told her no more than she knew, startled her still with their suddenness. The look of disdainful pain that he had seen before come on her face—the disdain was not for him—but the smile that already to him was the only sun the world held, lingered on her lips a moment.

"A year's pain to a true life—a day's pain, an hour's!—were far more than mine were worth. The daughter of Emperors you called me?—the daughter of men who gamed away their birthright, and played with diadems as idiot children play with olive-stones! Is there much greatness there? Genius!—if I have it, I have sold it, shamed it, polluted it. As for you— I have had so many die for me, I am tired of the shadow of the cypress!"

Strange though the words were, no vanity of power spoke in them, but a fatal truth, a mournful earnestness, tinged by, deepened to, remorse; the shadow of the cypress seemed to fall across the brilliancy of her face as she uttered them.

"Then,—will you let me live for you?"

The words escaped him before he knew they were uttered, before he realised all they meant, before he was conscious what he offered and pledged to a stranger who, for aught he knew or could tell, might be the head of an illustrious race, the wife of one of the royal chiefs of the Levant or of the East, or—might be anything that Europe held of what was most evil, most fatal, most dangerous in her sex.

She looked at him with a long, earnest, unwavering look,

"It is well for you that I will not take you at your word. No!—your life is a noble, gallant thing; treasure its liberty, and never risk it in a woman's hands."

The calmness with which she put aside words that had been nothing less than a declaration of the love he bore her, the serenity with which her gaze had dwelt on him, were not those of a woman who did or who would give him answering tenderness; yet the tone, the glance with which she had spoken, had not been those of one to whom he was wholly indifferent, or to whom his words had been repugnant. It seemed as though she would never let him come to her as a lover, yet as though she would never let him free himself from the sway of her fascination; she refused his homage with easy and delicate grace, but she refused so that she showed that the man who had been saved by her in the depths of the Carpathian Pass had her interest and had her pity.

Noting—and for once having compassion for the deadly pain that she had dealt, she smiled on him; she talked to him of a thousand things with her rich and graphic eloquence, that charmed the ear like the flowing of music, and often sank to silence that only lent it rarer charm; she sang the chants of Bach, of Pergolesi, of Mozart; she let him stay with her till night had closed over the distant mosques and courts of Constantinople, and she bade him good night, leaning again over the marble parapet of the terrace, with the moonlight full upon her, as she gave him such a sign of adieu, just so proud, just so gentle, as Mary Stuart might have given to her Warden of the Marches while yet she knew his love and would not yield him hers.

Yet—ere many moments passed—another succeeded him; a head cooler than his felt the charm of the scene and the hour,—a pulse slower than his beat time fast, under the challenge of Idalia's eyes.

His rival was alone with her.

Erceldoune set no store on any single quality he possessed; was ignorant indeed of much of his own value; acted greatly not seldom, but never thought so by any hazard; did straightly, instinctively, and without preface or ornament that which seemed to him the need of the hour, the due of his manhood; held his course

boldly and carelessly amongst men, caring nothing for
their praise, as little for their censure; had quick, fiery
blood in him that took flame rapidly; had, on the other
hand, much earnestness, much tenacity, much tenderness, more far than he knew; had kept through his
wandering life a heart singularly unworn, a mind
singularly without guile; was naturally prone to good
faith in men and incapable of base suspicion, and was
certain whenever he did love to love to his own destruction, as such natures not seldom do. His rival was his
reverse in every quality,—cool, wary, impenetrable
under an airy semblance of nonchalance, vain, with
the pardonable if overweening vanity of unusual powers,
firmly conscious of themselves, inordinately ambitious,
but even that in a keen, critical and studiously systematic
manner, the Anglo-Venetian thought Erceldoune nothing
more than a fine animal physically, and half a fool
mentally, underrating what was dissimilar to himself
with an error not uncommon with minds of his stamp,
when their disdainful egotistic measurement has not
been corrected by the experiences of a long life. Yet,
widely diverse though they were, and utterly contrasted
in every iota, the one who never resisted his passion,
and never thought of her save with such chivalrous
trust and absolute self-abandonment as were instinctive
to his temperament, was scarcely more a prey to it
than the other, who, with his love, blended a thousand
threads of policy, design, and covetous intrigue, and
hated it for having stolen on him, hated it for halting
on his lips, hated it for levelling him with the herd he
had so contemptuously despised; hated it because, for
the first time, he had found a talent stronger, a logic
surer, and a perception keener and subtler, and courage

more daring and careless than his own; because, in fine, he had found his master, and found it in a woman.

This, a knowledge not easily to be pardoned by one like him, made a certain acrid jealousy, a certain smartened bitterness, tinge even the passion into which she had surprised him when the dark eyes of Idalia glanced over him and read thoughts he had fancied unbetrayed by speech or sign, or when her careless ironies smote him back with the polished, piercing weapons of his own sceptic indifference, his own unyielding philosophies, which were as real in her as they had been till late in him.

For many years this woman had been but a name to him; only a name, through a succession of hazards, that had time after time kept their meeting deferred; but a name that had given a personality to him, and had been interwoven with many of the more critical essays and enterprises of his career.

Moving through the gore-stained, artillery-trodden maze of Lombardic fields, where in some unrewarded skirmish, young, eager, patriotic lives had been shot down by the troops of Austria, gasping to their latest breath "Italia fara da se!" he had stood beside some shattered wreck of brightest manhood that had fallen there, down head-first into the yellowing wheat, and when he had thought all life was dead in that broken mass, above which the tangled corn-stalks nodded and met in summer winds, he had caught a last sigh, a last breath in which, the name of Idalia was blent with the name of Italy, and died together with it down the Lombard breeze. Travelling once through Russian steppes of snow in the decline of the year, when all nature was perishing, and the great bleak versts of whitened plain stretched out unbroken to Siberian desolation, he had found a prisoner working in fetters, —a haggard, blear-eyed, scarcely human thing, livid with the hue of the lead-mines, disfigured with the ravages of frost-bite, idiotic, with a strange dull stupor, that made him utter incessantly as he toiled in a gang, one word alone; and, he had known that in this wretched creature was the wreck of what once had been the finest, the most fiery, the most glittering of all the aristocratic soldiery of Poland; and that the word he muttered ever as he laboured was that which had been his ignis fatuus, his idol, his ruin,—Idalia. In his own Venice, he had once seen a terrible struggle: it was when a mere lad of Venetia, a child of seventeen years, with the clear wild noble eyes of a young eastern colt, had been brought in amongst others who were "rebels," and was given over to the rods that he might tell who his chiefs and his comrades were; the boy was frail of make, and weakened with gunshot wounds, and he reeled and fell thrice under the rain of Austrian blows, but his teeth clenched on his tongue, and bit it through, so that no speech should pass it, and when the strokes told at last more mortally than those who lashed him knew, he smiled as he murmured, though his mouth was full of blood, "Tell her I died silent!" —and he who had heard had sent the farewell message to Idalia, at whose bidding that silence was kept. Once on the brow of a steep hill, looking over the Moravian highlands, with the wide wastes of barren grasslands, mingled with jagged piles of bare rock or stunted larches, with here and there the sharp peaks of a pine belt to break the outline, and the angry lustre of a red evening fading out in the hot autumn skies, he had seen a Monarch, the centre of a little knot of Cuirassier officers, draw near, and look hardly and eagerly across to the westward, where, far as the eye could reach, a dark shadow, like a hovering bird above the stony plains, marked the place where the Uhlans rode down on a fugitive's wake; and when reeking and breathless and spent, the troopers dragged their weary horses backward without the prize they had pursued, he had heard the Kaiser mutter in the gloaming of the night, "I would give a province for that one woman!" and that woman had been Idalia. She had been long thus a name on his ear, and in his schemes, and when at last she had become known to him, he had learned to wonder no more at the name's magic.

To tell her this he had never ventured, really audacious as his temper was: circumstances united them closely in some things, but with all his tact and all his daring, he had never been able to seduce himself into the self-flattery of deeming that she would heed his love-words. She heard so many, the story had no attraction for her; and apart from his own sense of how contemptuously careless she was of how men suffered for her, was the reluctance of chafing pride to acknowledge that he also paid the life-coin of his surrender to one who could tempt like Calypso, and remain cold as Casta Diva, while her spells worked.

Yet he could not restrain one mark of the passion —jealousy—as he sat that night beside her, in the dining-hall of the Turkish villa, and stretched himself from his pile of cushions to lift from the carpet a white riding glove, that caught his eye where it lay.

"A stray waif of our beggared laird's, is it not, madame? He has been here to-day?"

"If you mean Sir Fulke Erceldoune, he only left an hour or so ago. I wonder you did not meet him."

"No; I saw nothing of him. The Moldavian bullet did him good service, since it has won him so much of your interest. He should be vastly indebted to it!"

She laughed a little.

"Surely, a shot in the lungs is not so very pleasant a matter that a man need be grateful for it."

"Are there not many who risked shots far more mortal than his in the mere hope to win what they never did, but he does—your pity?"

She shrugged her shoulders ever so slightly.

"Why should you imagine I pity him? Have you not seen him *here?*"

The emphasis spoke more than volumes could have done. Her companion bowed his head.

"'True! The real mercy would have been—exclusion! Yet pity him you do, miladi, since you bade me 'harm him at my peril!'"

She looked at him such a curiously fixed regard, that had a hundred meanings in it.

"Let us make an end of this fencing," she said, quietly. "There are none here to dupe. We can speak frankly. We have done this man quite evil enough without bringing more upon him."

"We! I fail to apprehend you—"

She gave a little gesture of impatience.

"Monsieur, you have not known me very long, or you would know me too well to attempt those tactics. Evasion answers nothing with me; and why should we attempt it? Our cause is the same, and we both are equally aware that this brave-hearted gentleman was the prey of its viler adherents."

"But—"

"Pardon me; I have said we both know it. I have grace enough to blush for it: and you—?"

For the moment a faint flush of shame kindled over his face; he was for the moment silenced, embarrassed, uncertain how to reply; he had never dreamed that his share in the Carpathian attack—which his intelligence had directed unseen, though his hand was not active, nor his complicity involved in it—had been suspected by her, and he was now almost, for the first time in his life, astray in the twilight of bewildered doubts, of intricate apprehensions.

She laughed slightly again.

"Ah! I told you you did not know me; you thought you had deceived me! Well, never seek that again. A man once did: a man of Leghorn; he was clever and vain; he said, to himself, '*Altro*, a woman! and they obey her? I, for one, I will not; I will blind her.' And he thought he was strong enough. He stole away, like the fool that he was, and carried his scheme with him—his scheme to treat with Austria unknown to us; unknown, he thought, to the very walls of the room he slumbered in, to the very river reeds he walked by, he thought himself so strong. But I learnt it."

"And then?"

"Then? Why then I taught him what such an error cost."

"And that cost was?"

"What he merited. It had been better for him that he had never been born."

A chill, of something that was almost fear, passed over her listener's cold, keen, courageous nature; he, too, held that which was concealed from her,—if she avenged treachery thus?

"Vengeance, Madame?" he said, scarcely caring what triviality of speech served to screen his thoughts. "Surely nothing so barbarous lingers amidst so much worldly wisdom, nothing so ferocious harbours amidst so much divine witchery?"

"Revengeful? No. I do not think I am that, though one knows ill one's own errors. It is easy to forgive; we scorn where we pardon, but we pardon *because* we scorn."

She spoke musingly, with a grave and weary meditation as though memory, and not his words, usurped her: then, suddenly, she shook away any darker remembrance that dwelt with her, and turned full on him brilliant, penetrating eyes of half-contemptuous questioning.

"Some one of you it was who wrought that glorious piece of honest work in the Carpathians. You see, they were afraid that I should know their scheme: they stole out to do it in darkness; they thought that I should never learn it. But it all came to me; simply enough. I found their victim and saved him; and when Marc Lassla dragged himself half dying to my lodge in the mountains, and gasped us out a lame history of a bear-play, telling that young Vlistchnau lay dead in the woods from the brute's embrace, the whole was clear enough to me. The dying man's and the dead one's injuries were both no bear's wounds, but the fruit of pistol bullets; and though Lassla breathed his last in an hour or so, saying no more, I knew well enough that they had both been shot down by the Scot, and that the planned attack had been done by my people;—by mine!"

There was a deadly bitterness in the last words, an ominous meaning: such as might have run through Catherine of Russia's speech when she found a vassal faithless.

"Your people!" His surprise was admirably feigned, but it did not deceive her.

"Never trouble yourself to assume ignorance!" she said, with a certain amusement at his discomfiture. "You knew very well of the plan—"

"On my honour—"

"Have we any of that quality amongst us to swear by?"

"Nay! as a gentleman, as a man, I declare to you I knew nothing of it."

She bowed her head; courteously, as one too highly-bred to accuse him; carelessly, as one too worldly-wise to believe him.

"Nothing!" he averred, irritably mortified by that unspoken incredulity. "You may believe me, madame; from my policies, if not my virtues, I am totally opposed to every sort of violence; deem it ill-advised, uncivilised, barbaric: invariably give my veto against it. Force is the weapon of savages; learning has done little for us if we cannot find a better, a surer, a more secret tool. To prevent the wild spirits that join us from following their brute instincts, and blundering headlong into unwise action would be impossible. You can do more than most; but I doubt very much if you have not often-times roused tigers whom even you could not tame when once they had tasted of slaughter. The evil of every national movement is that the majority, once allowed to move at all, refuse to proceed by intellectual means, and loose themselves at once to physical violence, in which every good thing is lost, every temperate voice drowned. It is this sort of fatal misconception from which such criminal essays as that which attacked Sir Fulke Erceldoune proceed: it is impossible to avoid their appearing alike expedient and pardonable to a certain class of characters."

The explanation was given with graceful ease, with eloquent address: she heard it with courtesy, also with incredulity.

"Yes; and that 'class' serve as excellent weapons for brilliant intelligences which need to use them; excellent scapegoats for such intelligences when they do not care to appear in the intrigues they suggest."

He felt the thrust, yet he parried it with seeming tranquillity.

"That is but too true, indeed, and the unscrupulousness is not, alas! on the side of the mere *mauvais sujets*. Apropos, madame, you know all things; who then was the leader of the Carpathian episode?"

A stern impatience passed for an instant over the splendour of her face, mingled with something of more wounded pain.

"You must know too well whom I supposed to be so."

The answer was very low; there was a thrill of passionate shame in it.

"Ah!" There was a whole world of gentle sympathy, of profound comprehension in the deep breath he drew. "Was he not then implicated?"

She lifted her head and looked at him long and

steadily: there was more than contemplation in the look. "You can better tell that than I."

"No. Indeed you wrong me, madame. May I hear what you think yourself now we are on the subject."

A scorn that she repressed in utterance flashed with a weary darkness in her eyes.

"I would have sworn — *Yes*. He has sworn to me by the only name I ever knew him to hold sacred, *No*."

"Why doubt him, then?"

"*Why?* Ask me rather why, even on his oath, believe him!"

The impetuous disdain that burned through the retort had scathing satire in it. He looked at her with an admiration that was the more vivid because he thought her intentionally deceiving him, and thought also the deception so magnificently wrought out.

"Ah, ma belle Comtesse," he murmured, in his liquid flowing French, that both habitually used. "That you should have to feel this; that you should have to give such passion of contempt, to one so near to you! It is 'Athene to a Satyr.' How is it that, with such an inspiration as you beside him, Conrad has never—"

She interrupted him; and with the ironical cold nonchalance of her common tone resumed,

"Count Phaulcon is at least *your* friend, monsieur; let that suffice to dismiss his name. I suspected him; I do still suspect him. Did I think that he had been on the Turkish shore last night, I should have certainty in lieu of suspicion; but in saying this to you

I say no more than I have done, or shall do, to him himself."

"And to—Monsieur Erceldoune?"

"No." The answer was rapid and peremptory. She turned her head to him with something of the goaded impatience of a stag at bay mingling with her careless dignity. "How can you ask? You have heard him say he will kill his assassin if they ever meet. And he would be justified."

"And his 'justification' would free you not a little. Ah, where is there any sophism that will curve round to its own point so deftly as a woman's!" thought her companion, while he bent forward with a gentle deference in his air, a hesitating sympathy in his tone:

"Count Phaulcon is my very good friend, it is true, madame; and yet I scarce think I deserved to be reminded of that by a rebuke, because I cannot choose but regret that——"

"Regret nothing at my score, monsieur."

"What! not even that which you yourself regret?"

"When I tell you that there is such a thing, not before."

"You are very cruel——"

"Am I? Well, I have no great liking for sympathy, and not much need for it. If one cannot stand alone, one deserves, I fancy, to fall. Poets have made an idol and a martyr of the sensitive plant; their use of it is an unwise allegory: to shrink at every touch, to droop at every stroke, to be at the mercy of every hand, strange or familiar—an odd virtue that It would not commend itself to me."

"True. Is sensitiveness much after all except vanity quick to be wounded, as the sea-dianthus that dies of a finger thrust at it? Believe me, I meant not to offer the insult of pity, scarcely dared to intend the familiarity of sympathy; I merely felt—forgive me if I say it—I have long known Conrad, I have but of late known you; can you not guess that the old and the recent friendship alike tell me that you, despite all your pride, indeed *because* of all your pride, are bitterly galled, are shamefully companioned by a life unworthy you?"

He paused; he had doubted in how far he might venture even thus much, for she was of a nature to which compassion was unendurable, a thing to be shunned far more than pain itself. He knew that already; had he never known he would have seen it in the barely perceptible quiver with which she drew away as a high-hearted and fearless hound will take its mortal wound, and refuse a sign of suffering.

"You say a fact too plain for me to give it denial," she said, chilly; "but it is also one that I must decline to discuss with you. Let us talk of other matters."

Even her companion's long-trained audacity was not bold enough to force her on a theme she thus refused.

"Forgive me," he murmured hurriedly, "it is hard sometimes not to speak out one's thoughts."

"I thought the hardship rather lay in being sometimes compelled to do so."

"You *will* jest!——"

"Well, jests are better than tragedies. Life is always jostling the two together."

"We are like enough to have one tragedy, madame, if that hotheaded courier's suspicions point the same way as yours do,"—he spoke irritably, inconsequently; for he was both checked and incensed.

"It is not likely they will ever do so."

"Why? Suppose—merely suppose—your fear aright, and that Conrad and your new friend ever meet under your roof; what then?"

She did not reply for a moment, whilst a shadow of many memories, tinged with something of a smile passed over her features.

"What then? Why then I should know the truth of this matter, which *Monsieur mon ami* here refuses to tell me."

He felt the sting; and he knew that he had better provoke no more encounters with a woman's wit. And being piqued he wronged her, as pique commonly wrongs those who have provoked it; and thought that she knew far more of this thing than even he himself.

CHAPTER XII.

"La Belle Dame sans Merci."

When he also had left her, she leaned awhile over the terrace-parapet, with her eyes musingly dropped on the shelving mass of myrtle blossom, and as she stood there in her solitude, a step hurriedly crushed the fallen leaves of pomegranate flowers; before she saw him, a man had thrown himself before her, pressing his lips on the trailing folds of her laces, kneeling there as one kneels who sues for life.

"Idalia!"

She started and looked down; and drawing herself from his clasp with the gesture of her habitual haughty grace, turned from him without a word, bending her head with a silent salutation.

"Idalia!—I have come only to look upon your face."

The vibration of intense suffering in his voice made her involuntarily pause: but when she spoke it was with a calm indifference, a pointed meaning.

"I do not receive this evening, Monsieur; did not my people inform you so?"

A quick shudder shook him; he it was who had worn the badge of the Silver Ivy, and had answered Victor Vane with three brief pregnant words—"To my cost!" To his cost, his most bitter cost, he had loved her, and he had forced his way to her here in the quiet of the night. He grasped again the hem of her dress, and held her there, looking upward to that fair and fatal face in the radiance of the full moon shining from the sea.

She had destroyed him:—but he could not look on her without growing drunk with his own idolatry as men grow drunk with wine.

"Idalia! have you no pity—no remorse? You know what you have made me, and you give me no mercy? Is your heart stone?"

No change came on her face; she smiled with a negligent disdain.

"You have studied at the Porte St. Martin! That is not the way we speak anywhere else in Paris."

There was a contemptuous languor in the words more cruel than the bitterest utterance, in earnest, would have been; with scenes and hours so vivid in his memory, in which his love had been lavished at her feet, and sunned in her smile, and welcomed by her word, they struck on him as passing all that history had ever held of women's traitorous heartlessness.

Idalia was now—what much evil done to her had made her.

His hands clenched on her dress in a convulsive wretchedness.

"Have you no heart, no soul, no conscience? I laid down all I had on earth for you; I gave you my peace, my honour, my abject slavery. And yet——"

His voice died inarticulate, while the light from the sea fell on his upturned face—a face of fair and gallant cast, of ancient race, and leonine blood, in the early prime of manhood, yet now worn, haggard, drawn, and darkened with the hopeless passions that were loosening in him beyond all strength to hold them.

She looked down on him, still without change of glance or feature. It was a tale so often told to her. She drew herself from him with her coldest indolence.

"You came here to tell me this? It was scarcely worth while. Good evening."

Like a deer stung by a shot he started to his feet, standing between her and the shafts of jasper that formed the portico into the building; the endurance that had laid him at her mercy, suffering all things for her sake, living only in the light of her smile, and knowing no law but her desire, broke its bondage now and turned against her in fierce but just rebuke, incoherent in its misery.

"It is true, then, what they say! You have a heart of bronze, a soul of marble? You have that glory of your loveliness only to draw men in your net and hurl them to perdition? It is true, then! in worshipping you we worship the fairest traitress, the most angelical lie that the world ever saw? Have you ever thought what it is you do? Have you ever asked yourself what price *we* pay for the power you hold? Have you ever thought that you may tempt us, and betray us, and destroy us once too often, till your very slaves may turn against you?"

He stood alone with her in the lateness of the night, his words incoherent and crushed between his teeth; and she knew that she had done him wrong which before now has turned men into fiends, and has made them stamp out into its grave the beauty that has beguiled them and betrayed them. But she gave no sign of fear; her dauntless nature knew fear no more than any Spartan knew it. Her conscience alone smote her, a pang of remorse wakened in her. She was silent, looking at him in the shadowy moonlight; she knew that she had ruined his life—a high-souled, patriotic life, full of bright promise and of fearless action—a life laid subject to her, and broken in her hands as a child breaks the painted butterfly.

"God!" he cried, and it was the involuntary cry of a great despair that broke his force down before the woman by whom he had been fooled and forsaken, yet whom he still worshipped but the more the more that he condemned her. "That such beauty should only veil a heart of steel! If you had ever loved—if

ever you could love—you could not do such treachery
to love as this. I know you as you are, now—now
that it is too late, and yet—and yet—"

A single sob choked his voice, he threw himself
again at her feet in the sheer blindness of an utter
misery, his hands clutching the folds of her dress, his
lips pressed in kisses on the senseless laces, conscious
alone of the woman who now had no more thought, or
need, or tenderness for him than the cold marble that
rose above him into the starry stillness of the Bosphorus
night.

"And yet there is no crime I would not take on
me at your word—there is no sin I would not sin
for you! I know you as you are—and yet, so
utterly in spite of all, I love you! I came to-night to
see your face once more. I go to die for Italy. Say
one last gentle word to me; we shall never meet again
on earth."

She stood there, above him, in the clear radiance
shining from the waters; his words had struck deep
to the core of the remorse that was slowly awaking
in her; a profound pity for him, as profound a loathing of herself, arose; all the gentler, purer, nobler
nature in her was touched, and accused her more
poignantly than the most bitter of his accusations. She
stooped slightly; her proud instincts, her habit of power,
and her world of levity and mockery, made her yield
with difficulty, made her pity with rarity; but when
she did either, she did them as no other woman could.

She stooped slightly, and her eyes were heavy as
they rested on him:

"I have but one word: Forgive me!"

And *in* that one word Idalia spoke more than could

have been uttered in the richest eloquence that could have confessed her error and his wrong. Yet while she said it, she knew that both the sin and the injury were beyond all pardon.

He looked up, hope against hope flashing in on him one moment: it was quenched as soon as born; her face had pain on it, but the light that he had once seen there was gone—there was no tenderness for him.

His head sank again:

"Forgive! I would have forgiven you death—I forgive you more than death. But if you ever meet again one who loves you as I have loved, remember me—and spare him."

The generous answer died in his throat; never again, he knew, would he look upon the loveliness that had betrayed him; he knew that he was going to his death, as surely as though he sank into the sea-depths glistening below, and that when he should lie in the darkness and decay of a forgotten soldier's grave, there would be no pang of memory for him in her heart, no thought that gave him pity or lament in the life to which his own was sacrificed.

He looked yet once again upward to her face, as dying men may look their last on what they treasure; then slowly, very slowly, as though each moment were a separate pang, he loosened his hold upon her, and turned and went through the shadows of the cypress, downward to where the waves were drearily breaking on the strand below.

Where he had left her, she stood silent, the moonlight falling on the white marble about her, till from the sea the lustre on her looked bright as day. In one thing alone had he wronged her. She knew the weariness of remorse, she knew the tenderness of pity.

Though no sign had escaped her, each word of his accusation had quivered to her heart; he did not feel its truth more bitterly than she. That upbraiding, poured out in the solitude of the night, had stirred her heart with its condemnation; it showed her what it was that she had done, it made her shudder from the fatal gift of her own dominion; how had she used it?

Again and again, till they had passed by her, no more noted than the winds that swept the air about her, the anguish of men's lives, the fire of their passions had been spent upon her, and been wasted for her; she had won love without scruple, embittered it without self-reproach. But now, her own heart for once was stirred.

"What do I do?" she asked herself. "Ruin their lives, destroy their peace, send them out to their deaths —and for what? A phantom, a falsehood, an unreality, that betrays them as utterly as I! The life I lead is but cruelty on cruelty, sin on sin. I know its crime, and yet I love its sovereignty still. I am vile enough to feel the charm of its power, while I have conscience enough to abhor its work."

The thoughts floated through her mind where she stood, looking over to where the sea lay, the dark outline of some felucca alone gliding spirit-like across the moonlit surface.

The last words of the man who had left her seemed to echo still upon the air; the summons of conscience, the reproach of the past, the duty and the demand of the present, all were spoken in them. Even as he had uttered them, she had thought of one whose fate would be the same with this which now upbraided her, and pleaded with her. She knew that he should be spared. It might not be too late to save him—to save him from herself.

He who had left her to go out and find a soldier's death on the blood-soaked plains of Lombardy, stood between her and the other life which she had once saved from such a grave, and which now was in the first flush of faith that held her rather angel than woman, and of love that had sprung up, full grown in one short night, like a flower under tropical suns.

Better one pang for him at first than for a while the sweetness of a cheated hope, to end in lifelong desolation, like that which had to-night risen before her, and arraigned her for its ruin.

"Most men in their passion love but their own indulgence; but now and then there are those who love us for ourselves; they should be spared," she thought, still standing, her face turned once more towards the sea.

They called her unscrupulous, she had been so; they called her heartless, merciless, remorseless, in all her poetic beauty; there had been too much truth in the charge, much error lay on her life, great ruin at her door; but of what this woman really was her foes knew nothing, and her lovers knew as little. With neither was she ever what she now was, looking on the white gleam of the surf where it broke up on the sands below—now, when she was musing how to save again, from herself, him whom she had once saved from the grave.

In the break of the morning Idalia rose; and thrusting back the green lattice of her casement glanced outward at the east. The loose silken folds of a Turkish robe floated round her, her face was pale with a dark shadow beneath the eyes, and her hair lay in long loose masses on her shoulders, now and then lifted by the wind. She was thinking deeply and painfully, while her eyes followed mechanically the flight of white-winged gulls, as they swept in a bright cloud above the water. The reproaches that had been uttered to her a few hours before still had their sting for her, the truths with which they had been barbed still pierced her.

Proud, fearless, negligent, superbly indifferent to the world's opinion, contemptuous of its censure as she was careless of its homage, she still was not steeled against the accusation of her own heart and conscience. She was no sophist, no coward; she could look at her own acts and condemn them with an unsparing truth; though haughtily disdainful of all censure, she tore down the mask from her own errors, and looked at them fully, face to face, as they were. Erred she had, gravely, passing on from the slighter to the deeper, in that course which is almost inevitable, since no single false step ever yet could be taken *alone*.

The brightest chivalry, the noblest impulses, the most unquestioning self-sacrifice, the most headlong devotion, these had all been wakened by her, and lavished on her; — what had she done with them? Accepted them, to turn them to her tools; excited them, to make them her slaves and her creatures; won them and wooed them with sorceress charm to weigh them with cold cruelty at their worth, and let them drift unpitied to their doom.

Those who had loved her had been no more to her than this; beguiled for the value they were, betrayed to passion that by it they might grow plastic to her purpose, bent to her command. She, who had all the superb, satiric, contemptuous disbelief in suffering of a woman of the world, still knew that, over and over again, the tide of grief had broken up vainly against the disdain of her delicate, pitiless irony; knew that over and over again a life made desolate, a life driven out to recklessness and desperation, a life laid down in the early glory of ambitious manhood, had been sacrificed through her, ruined by her, as cruelly, as carelessly as a young child destroys the brightness of the butterfly, the fragrance of the cowslip, in its sport of summer-day chase or spring-day blossom-ball. And for what? For the sake of triumphs that had palled in their gaining, for the sake of gains that were valueless now, for the sake of a sovereignty that seemed to brand her forehead with its crown, for the sake of evil things that had worn a fair mask, of freedom that had grown into slavery, of daring that had said, "Better to reign in hell than serve in heaven."

She had erred deeply; all that was noblest, tenderest, most generous in her nature—and there was much still, despite the accusers that could appeal against her—knew it, and did not seek to palliate it to herself. The career that closed her in, once entered, as the net closes round the bird it ensnares, had wearied her, had revolted her, had made her pride contemn the part she played, her conscience plead against the woe she worked, her nature, grand in its mould and fearless in its courage, revolt from much that she had once voluntarily sought and confessedly loved in the

earlier years when it was fresh to her. And she was
not happy: the simplicity of the aged recluse at Monastica had pierced to a truth that Paris, and the world,
and the men who glittered round her and adored her,
did not perceive. She was not happy. With her brilliance, her power, her enterprise, the fineness of her intricate intrigues, the daring of her constant adventures,
the excitement of her incessant changes, no morbid
sentiment, no passive pensiveness could have hold on
her or be known to her, but something deeper than this
was at her heart; it was the melancholy of a mute
remorse, the unavailing and vainly-silenced lament
of one who finds that he has bartered his gold for
stones.

Her eyes were weary in all their splendour, as they
followed the flight of the sea-gulls. She thought of
what she had been, when only sixteen seasons had
warmed the lustre of her hair, yet had made her Hellenic beauty in its early blush and sudden maturity
almost, even then, the beauty of her present womanhood; she thought of herself as she had stood one
evening at sunset leaning down over the ivy-mantled
ruins of an antique bridge in Greece, looking across
to the Ægean, flashing in the light, and thinking of
the centuries far away in the distance of the past when
those waves had broken against the prows of Miltiades'
galleys, and been crowded with the fleets of Salamis;
she remembered the vivid and decorated eloquence that
had wooed her then to her present path, murmuring
such bright words of liberty and triumph, while the
waters in their melody and the sunset in its splendour
seemed filled with the grand dead names of Gracchan
Rome and of Socratic Athens; she remembered how the

proud imagination of her dawning life had leapt to those subtle temptings as an arrow leaps from the bow into the empyrean, and had seen in its ambitious and still child-like dreams the sovereignty of Semiramis, the sway of Aspasia, the empire of Maria Theresa, waiting in the future for her.

Eight years had gone by since then, and she had known the world deeply, widely, wisely; she had been sated with homage and with victory, she had wakened love almost wherever her glance fell; her hours had been filled with vivid colour and incessant variety, with luxury and with pleasure, with the life of an adventuress in its airy nonchalance mingled with all the grace and elegance of patrician tastes, and habits, and wealth. And yet she was not happy; for the fame she had was notoriety, the power she had was used unscrupulously, in the core of the rose there was always an asp, and in the depth of her heart there were disappointment, remorse, and dishonour.

"And yet I was more sinned against than sinning," she mused. "I was so young then, and I was allured with such glorious beguilement. The regeneration of nations, the revolution of empires, the striking off of the serf's fetters, the redressing of every unjust balance, the conquest of empires and liberties, the people's homage and the monarchs' crowns,—those were what tempted me. It was the old fable of Satan and Eve: 'Eat of this fruit, and ye shall have the knowledge of heaven and earth;' 'Believe in me, follow me, and you shall have glory beside which Paradise is poor, kingdoms beside which Eden is a desert!' And I took the fruit. How could I tell then that it would be all a lie?"

The thoughts floated through her mind, leaning there wearily against the lattice, while the early wind of the warm dawn stirred the half-opened scarlet blossoms of the japonica twining round it. But she was too integrally proud to seek refuge or exculpation in self-excuses even in her solitary reverie.

"Yet that is but half the truth," she mused, while her eyes still unconsciously followed the sweep of the sea-birds out to sea. "I was sinned against then, in the first, but it has been my own wrong since. I have kept to error long since I have known it to be error. I have loved my power even while I despised its means and its ends. I have felt the intoxication of hazard till I have let it entangle me beyond recall. I have known the evil I did, yet I have not paused in it when I might. I have seen the fatal issue of so much, and I have gone on and on. I have bound them, I have blinded them, I have despoiled them, I have taken their strength and their manhood, their faith and their courage, their wealth and their genius, and ruined them all. I have spared none of them. I have betrayed so many. *That* has not been done in ignorance —*that* has not been palliated with the excuse of youth scarce conscious what it does."

Her thoughts travelled far over past years, while the sun rose higher, and while the man whose existence she had given back dreamed of her with the waking of the day, as of one so far above his love, that

> "No head save some world-genius should rest
> Above the treasures of that perfect breast."

She remained still and silent at the casement till the distant call of the drums, as the Soldan went up to the mosque for the sunrise prayers, died softly away on the air.

"I will save him at least. One sharp blow—and perhaps he will forget. Pride will aid him; and if we never meet again, I shall remain only a dream to him —a dream without pain," she said, half aloud. And, for the moment, a darker shadow swept over her face; she remembered loyal eyes that had gazed their eager passion into hers; she remembered leonine strength that would have been felled into its tomb but for her; she remembered that the man who had sought her with such untiring patience on the clue of one frail memory, would not forget in a day, in a year. But her resolve was not shaken.

"I will save him if he will be saved;—he, at least, shall have nothing with which to reproach me," she thought, while she watched the grey sea flash between the scarlet blossoms of the japonica tendrils. Then she turned away from the window, and rang a hand-bell that had once belonged to Catherina Medici: like the one whose long slender palm had before touched the spiral column of its handle, she never hesitated in any course when her resolve was taken, she never swerved when once she had decided.

The Nubian slave, who attended her wherever she travelled as her maid, answered the summons from where she stood in the ante-chamber.

"Tell Paulus that I start for Naples this morning. He knows what to do. I leave by ten."

The Nubian bowed to the ground, and withdrew. Her mistress stood beside the table where the bell was placed, thoughtful still, with the shadow that had gathered on her deepening in the purple light that fell through violet curtains near. She was not a woman to whom regret was familiar;—many would have said she was too heartless: it was rather because she had seen, and known, and penetrated too much to be lightly touched;—but a great tearless pain gathered in her eyes, and her hand closed with a gesture of impatience on the sharp metal circle of the bell.

"He will be stung to the heart—and yet, better one pang at once!" she said in her solitude. "What could it avail him to know me more except to suffer longer?"

Her resolve was not changed; vacillation was impossible to her; she had none of its weakness in her nature, but a regret poignant and almost remorseful was on her. She thought of the fearless fidelity with which he had refused ever again to become as a stranger to her, she thought of the fealty that she knew so well he bore to her, that had looked out from the ardent worship of his eyes in the calm of the eastern night a few short hours before.

And she was about to kill this at a blow, because the prayer of another had pierced her-heart and pleaded with her to spare him, if it were not too late.

A new life had dawned on Erceldoune.

All his old habits of soldier-like decision, of sportsman-like activity, were broken up; he who had used to find his greatest pleasures in the saddle and the rifle, in waiting high up in a leafy nest for the lions to come down to the spring to drink, and in riding wild races with Arabs over amber stretches of torrid sand, in spending whole days alone among the sedge-pools of the Border fowl, and in bivouacking through a scorching night with Brazilian guachos, had now changed into the veriest dreamer that ever let the long hours steal away,

> "——floating up, bright forms ideal,
> Half sense-supplied, and half unreal,
> Like music mingling with a dream."

He lived in a land of enchantment, whose sole sunlight was a woman's glance; he gave himself up without a struggle to the only passion that had ever touched his life. Now and then forebodings swept over him; now and then his own utter ignorance of the woman to whom he was yielding up his destiny, smote him with a terrible pang, but very rarely: in proportion to the length of his resistance to such a subjugation, was the reckless headlong force of his fall into its power. Moreover, his nature was essentially unsuspecting; and he had an old-world chivalry in him that would have made it seem to him the poorest poltroonery to cast doubt on the guardian-angel who had saved him from the very jaws of death. His mother, lost in his earliest childhood, had been of Spanish race; neglected by her lord, she had been left to break her spirit as she would against the grey walls of the King's Rest, longing for the perfume and the colour and the southern winds of her home in the Vega, while the Border moors stretched round her, and the Cheviots shut her in until she died, like a tropic bird, caged in cold and in twilight. A softness, inherited from the tenderness and the enthusiasm of her southern blood, was latent in her son, little as he knew it; an unworldliness and trustfulness were in his nature, though he did not perceive them; and though his career had done much to strengthen the lion-like daring and athlete's hardihood of his character, on the other hand the picturesque colouring and varied wandering in which his years had been spent had done much to preserve the vein of romance within him, unworn while unsuspected. Nothing had touched this side of his nature until now; and now, the stronger for its past suppression, it conquered him in its turn, and ruled alone.

When he left her that evening he could not sleep; he rode far and fast through the late night, dashing down into the interior, along sandy plains, and through cypress groves, across stretches of tangled vegetation, and over the rocky beds of dried-up brooks, or the foam of tumbling freshets. The swift rush through the cooled air soothed the fever in him; his thoughts and his passions kept throbbing time with the beat of the hoofs, with the sweep of the gallop.

So long ago loved his namesake the Rhymer, when under the tree of Erceldoune—the Tree of Grammarye—the sorceress-lips touched his, and the eyes brighter than mortal brightness looked into his own; lips that wooed him across the dark Border, eyes that dared him to brave the Lake of Fire for her sake. Those old, old legends!—how they repeat themselves in every age, in every life.

With the dawn he came upon a pool, lying landlocked, far and solitary, encircled with cedars and cypress and superb drooping boughs, now heavy with the white blossoms of the sweet chestnut, and while his horse drank at the brink, he threw himself in to bathe, dipping down into the clear brown waters, and striking out into the depths of green blossoming shade, while the swell of a torrent that poured into it lashed him with its foam, cold even in the east before sunrise, and hurled the mass of water against his limbs, firm-knit, sinewy, colossal as the polished limbs of a Roman bronze of Milo. As he shook the drenching spray from his hair, and swam against the current, looking upward at the sky where the dawn was just breaking, all the beauty that life might know seemed suddenly to rise on him in revelation. There is an eastern fable that tells how, when Paradise faded from earth, a single rose was saved and treasured by an angel, who gives to every mortal, sooner or later in his life, one breath of fragrance from the immortal flower—one alone. The legend came to his memory as the sunbeams deepened slanting spear-like across the azure of the skies, and he dashed down into the shock of the waters to still in him this fierce sweetness of longing for all that would never be his own.

One woman alone could bring to him that perfume of paradise; the rose of Eden could only breathe its divine fragrance on him from her lips. And he would have given all the years of his life to have it come to him one hour!

When the day was at noon he went to her, heeding no more the downpour of the scorching vertical rays than the Rhymer had heeded the leaping tongues of flame while he rode, with the golden tresses sweeping his lips, down to the glories of Faërie. Distinct thought, distinct expectance, he had none; he had but one instinct, to see her, to be with her, to lay down at her feet, the knightliest service that ever man gave to woman. He knew nothing of her, knew not whether she were wedded or unwedded, but he knew that the world had one meaning alone for him now—he loved her. That she could ever answer it, he had barely the

shadow of a hope; there was much humility in him; he
held himself but at a lowly account; though a proud
man with men, he would have felt, had he ever followed
out his thoughts, that he had nothing with which to
merit or to win the haughty and brilliant loveliness of
Idalia; he would have felt that he had no title and no
charm to gain her, and gather her into arms that would
be strong, indeed, to defend her until the last breath of
life, as they had been strong to strangle the bear in the
death grasp and to tame the young wild horse on the
prairies, but that had no gold to clasp and fling down
at her feet, no purples of state and of wealth to fold
round her, bringing their equal royalty to hers. That
he himself could attract her, he would have had little
belief; he did not see himself as others saw him; he
did not know that his vigorous magnificence of form,
his dauntless manhood, his generous unselfishness, his
untrammelled freedom of thought and deed, might
charm a woman who had been tired by all, won by
none; he was unconscious of any of these in his own
person, and he would have thought that he had nothing
on earth which could give him the right ever to hope
for her tenderness. But hope is always strong in us
till despair is forced on us, however little we may
know that hope's existence; and thought was the last
thing that was shaped in him—thought never grouped
itself before him; he was still in the opium-dream:
neither future nor past existed for him; he was drunk
with his present; his love blinded him to any other
memory than itself. It was too wholly in its early
freshness for it to forecast its fate.

His eyes eagerly swept over the building as he rode
up the avenue; the lattices were all closed; this was

usual in the noon, yet it gave him a vague disquietude and dread. The echo of his step resounded on the marble, as it had done when he had forced his entrance into what he had believed the lair of his assassin: it was the only sound, and the stillness froze his heart like ice; the rolling bay of the hound had never before failed to challenge his arrival.

The first court was deserted; in the second he saw the Abyssinian.

"The Countess Vassalis?" he asked, rapidly.

"Is not here," answered the negress.

"Not here!"

"No, most illustrious. Her Excellency left Stamboul this morning."

He staggered like a man who has received a blow.

"Left—where?—why?—for how long?"

The Abyssinian shook her head with a profound salaam; she knew nothing, or would say nothing; her mistress had left Constantinople; where she intended to travel she could not tell; her Excellency was always travelling, she believed; but a note had been given her to deliver to the English Effendi, perhaps that might tell more.

He seized it from her as she drew it from the yellow folds of her sash, and tore it open; a mist was before his sight, and his wrist shook while he held the paper as it had never done lifting the rifle to his shoulder, when one error in the bullet's flight would have been instant death to himself. The letter brought him little solace; it was but a few words of graceful courtesy, giving him the adieu that a sudden departure rendered necessary, but adding nothing of why or whither she was gone, and seeming, in their polished ceremonial, cold as ice to the storm of shattered hope, and tempestuous pain that was rife in his own heart. Instinctively as his hand closed on it he turned away from the Abyssinian, and went out of the court into the hot blaze of day, alone; he could not bear the eyes of even that African upon him in the desolation that had swept down upon his life. He went out; where, he did not see or know, passing into the scorching air and into the cooler shade of the groves, with a blind, dumb suffering on him like the suffering of a dog. For her he had no pride, against wounds from her hand he had no shield; and nothing with which she could wring his heart, nothing with which she could try his loyalty, could avail to turn his love away. They had been no idle words with which he had said that his life was hers to do with what she would; having made the vow he would keep it, no matter what the test, or what the cost.

He crushed in his grasp that pitiless letter;—her hand had touched it, her hand had written it, bitter as it was it was sacred to him; and he stood in the vertical sun, gazing blankly down on the waves below the terraces, tossing upward in the light at his feet. The blow had fallen on him with a crushing, sickening force,—again he had lost her! Again, when to the old baffled weariness with which he had so long vainly sought her was added the certainty that he who had lavished his heart's best treasure on her was no more to her than the yellow sands that the seas kissed and left.

A few hours before and her eyes had smiled on him, her presence had been with him; she had listened to him, spoken with him, let him linger beside her in all the familiar communion of a welcome friendship; he could not realise that he was forsaken by her without a word, without a regret, without an effort for them ever to meet again. He had no claim on her remembrance, no title to her confidence, it was true; his acquaintance with her was slight, as the world would have considered. But he could not realise that the tie between them of a life saved, so powerful on him, so deathless in its memory for him, could be as nothing to her. The wanton cruelty of her desertion seemed to him so merciless that he had no remembrance of how little hold he had, in reason and in fact, upon her tenderness. The knowledge of her loss alone was on him, leaving him no consciousness save of the burning misery that possessed him.

As he had never loved, so he had never suffered until now; his adventurous career in camps, and cities, and deserts, had never been touched by any grief; he had come there in the gladness of the morning, full of faith, of hope, of eager delight, and of unquestioning expectation, and he stood in the scorch of the noonday heat, stupefied, the glare of sun and sea unfelt in the fiery agony that had seized him.

The little gilded caïque was rocking at his feet, where it was moored to the landing-stairs; trifles link thought to thought, and with the memory of that first enchanted hour when he had floated with her down the water, he remembered the warning that she had given him—the warning "not to lie under the linden."

The warning had been—she had said—for his sake, not her own; was it for his that she had left him now? She had implied that some sort of peril, some threatening of danger, must await him with her friendship; was it to save him from these that she had left him thus? Then the humility that was as integrally a part of his nature, as his lofty pride of race was towards men, subdued the bitter sense of her cruelty: what was he more to her than any other to whom she gave her gracious courtesies, that he should look for recollection from her? He owed her his life;—but that debt lay on him, it left no claim to her. What was there in him that he could hope in their brief intercourse to have become any dearer to her than any other chance-met acquaintance of the hour? He could not upbraid her with having smiled on him one hour to forsake him as a stranger the next, for with the outset she had bade him leave her unknown.

Hot tears, the first that had ever come there since as a child he had sobbed over his young mother's grave, rushed into his eyes, shutting out the stretch of the sparkling seas and the rich colouring around him, where Cashmere roses and Turkish lilies bloomed in untrained luxuriance. The sea had no freedom, the flowers no fragrance, the green earth in its early summer no beauty for him;—he only felt that let him spend loyalty, fidelity, life and peace upon her as he would, he might never be one shadow nearer to her than he was now, he might never touch her to one breath of tenderness, never move her to one pang of pity. His strength was great, he had wrestled with the gaunt northern bear in the cold of a Scandinavian night, he had fought with ocean and storm in the madness of a tropical tempest, he had closed with the African lion in a fierce embrace, and wrenched the huge jaws apart as they closed on their prey; he had prevailed in these things by fearless force, by human might: but now, in his weakness and his misery, he could have flung himself down on the tawny sands and wept like a woman for the hopes that were scattered, for the glory that was dead.

Another moment, and he had crossed the labyrinth of the garden, thrown himself into saddle, and turned back towards the city. The Greeks idly lying under the shelter of their fishing or olive feluccas drawn up on the shore, and the Turks sitting on their cocoa-nut mats under the shadow of fig-tree or vine at the entrance of their huts, stared aghast at the breathless horse, thundering along the sea-road through the noon-tide heat, his flanks covered with foam, and the white burnous of his Giaour rider floating out upon the wind. Down the steep pathways, over the jagged rocks, across the flat burning levels of sand, and under the leaning grape-covered walls, Erceldoune rode, reckless of danger, unconscious of the fierce sun-fire pouring on his head.

He had sworn to follow her, whether her route were seaward to Europe, or eastwards into the wild heart of Asia. Pride, reason, wounded feeling, wavering faith, none of them availed to turn him from his course. He was true to his oath; and the madness was upon him that in the golden verse of his namesake the Rhymer makes Syr Tristam love better to go back to the risk of death and shame, to the land of his foe, to the old piercing pain and the old delicious sorcery, than to live in peace and honour and royalty without the smile of King Marc's wife, without the light of Ysonde's eyes. Let come what would, he followed Idalia.

In the love he bore her there was a strange mingling of utter humility, of most reverential chivalry, with the wildest passion and the most reckless daring; in it the two sides of his nature were blent.

He rode to the Golden Horn, where the flags of every nation were streaming from the crowded masts in the clear hot light. He knew that her departure by any one of the vessels could easily be ascertained.

To seek the guests whom he had met at her house, to inquire of her from the numerous acquaintance he had among the various chancelleries in Constantinople, and the military and naval men passing through or staying off there; to ask who she was, whence she came, how she was held in social estimation; all that might have been the natural course of most was impossible to Erceldoune. He could not have brought himself to speak of her to others; he felt that if he heard her name lightly uttered he should strike his hand on the mouth that uttered it; and intense as his longing might be to pierce the mystery that apparently shrouded her, the Quixotic code of his love and his honour would have let him ask nothing through strangers that she withheld herself. He prosecuted his search alone, and the rapidity in such investigations gained by habit soon brought him the knowledge he pursued.

Before evening he had learned among the sailors in the port that a steam yacht belonging to her, the *Io*, which had returned twenty-four hours previously from Athens, had taken its departure early in the morning; for Capri, the Greek crew had said, with no one on board but herself, her suite, and the Russian dog. The yacht was probably by now through the Dardanelles. It was well known in the Golden Horn, the sailors told him, that she usually came from Europe in it; it could be recognised anywhere on the seas, for it always carried the green white and scarlet of the Italian national colours, crossed on the Greek ensign, a fancy, it was supposed, of her Excellency's.

Erceldoune's eyes strained across the glittering expanse of water with a wistful longing as he listened; every word he gathered plunged like a knife into his heart;—no steamer went from the harbour that day to Naples; with twelve or twice twelve hours between them, how could he tell but what again she might be lost to him, how or where or when he might ever recover the clue she had rent asunder?

"If that schooner were only mine!" he muttered unconsciously aloud, as his glance fell on a yacht in the harbour, with her gold figure-head and her brass swivel-guns glistening in the sun;—his want of wealth he had never felt, his nature was too high toned, his habits too hardy, his temper too bold; but now for the first time the pang of his beggared fortunes struck heavily on him. Were wealth his own how soon the seas that severed them might be bridged!

A familiar hand was struck on his shoulder as he stood looking across at the grey arc of the Bosphorus, straining his eyes into the offing as though he could pierce the distance and follow her with his gaze.

"You want a yacht? Take *Etoile*. I am going inland on a special mission into Arabia; bring her back in a year's time, that will be soon enough for me."

Erceldoune turned and saw a man he knew well; a true and tried friend; one with whom he had gone on many a perilous expedition; a dauntless traveller, a pure Arabic scholar, and a skilled negociator with Eastern chiefs and tribes.

The *Etoile* was at his service, with her captain and
her crew, to take him where he would; there remained
but the duties of the Messenger Service to detain him,
and these, on application, let him loose. He had so
habitually abstained throughout the twenty years of
his service from any effort to shirk or shift the most
dangerous or most irksome missions, that as nothing
specially required him then, and a courier was daily
expected from Russia who could take despatches home
in his place, he easily obtained his furlough, and by
sunset he weighed anchor.

The yacht steered out of the varied fleet of mer-
chantmen that crowded the Golden Horn, steered out
to the open sea, while the scarlet glory of the after-
glow lingered in the skies and dyed the waters blood-
red in its light. To what fate did he go? he asked
himself.

Safer, wiser, better far, he thought, that he should
turn back with his familiar comrade and plunge down
into the core of Asia, into the old athletic, bracing,
vigorous, open-air life, into the pleasures that had
never palled of forest and rifle, of lake and mountain,
of the clear ringing shot and the wild day-dawn gallop,
into the pastimes that had no taint in them, the chase
that had no pang in it. That old life had been so
free, so elastic, so unshadowed, with all the liberty of
the desert, with all the zest of hardihood in it, with no
thought for the morrow, and no regret for the past,
with sleep sound as a mountaineer's, with strength exhaustless as the sea eagle's. He was leaving it. And
for what? For a love that already had cost him a
year of pain to a few short hours of hope; for a woman
of whom he knew nothing, not even whether she were

the wife or the mistress of another; for the miserable
fever of restless passion, for the haunting torment of
unattainable joys, for the intoxication of tempest-tossed
desires, for the shadows of surrounding doubt and
mystery. Better far let the strange charm that had
enthralled him be cut away at any cost, and go back
to that old life while there was yet time. The thought
crossed him for the moment as he drifted from the
quay of the Golden Horn. The next it passed as
swiftly; let him plunge into the recesses of Asia or the
green depths of Western wilds, he would carry with
him his passion and her memory; and the schooner
swept down beyond the Dardanelles in her pursuit,
through the phosphor crests of starlit waves as the night
deepened, and the distance between them grew less
and less with every dip the prow made down into the
deep-grey glistening water, like a petrel that stoops to
bathe in his passage, and shakes the spray from his
spread wings to take a freer flight.

CHAPTER XIII.

"She smiles them down imperially as Venus did the Waves."

It was evening when the schooner ran into Capri,
that Eden hung beneath the sea and sky. All its
marvellous maze of colour was in its richest glow; the
sun was sinking behind Solaro; the towering rocks of
the Salto and the Faraglioni burned through their sublimity of gloom; a lustre of gold and purple streamed over
mountainous Ischia down on the brow of Epomeneo,
and over the low hills of Procida; and the blue water
lay dazzling in the light, with the white sails of Sor-
rento skiffs scarce larger on its waves than the white

wings of fluttering monachi, while over the sea came
the odours of budding orange and citron gardens and
a world of violets that filled the woods, sloping upward
and upward into the clouds where Anacapri lay.

Erceldoune saw none of it, yet he felt it vaguely—
felt, as his vessel steered through that flood of sunlight,
coming from the rich *mezzo giorno* of the Amalfi coast
into the golden riot of this lavish loveliness, as though
he floated to a paradise. So had they thought before
him, who, sailing through those caressing seas towards
the same isles where the Syrens sang, had listened to
the enchanted song to find their grave, in tumult and
in storm.

The sun sank behind Ischia as he went ashore, and
the sudden twilight fell, quenching all the blaze of
fire, and bringing in its stead the tender night, with
the chime of the Ave Maria ringing out from church
bells over the sea.

He was known in Capri, and the men showed
their white teeth with a bright smile, and the girls
laughed all over their handsome brown faces, as they
welcomed him.

He had little doubt of soon learning what he
sought: a few brief questions brought him loquacious
answers.

"'Niursi, signore!" cried a *marinaro*, in the barbarous Capriote patois. "L'illustrissima Contessa! she
knows me well. Chiara, my wife, helped the African
carry the luggage up to her villa the day before yesterday——"

"She is here still?"

The quick Capriote caught the tremulous excitement that ran through the question, and his heart

warmed to the stranger, by whom his brother had once been brought up from the black churning waves under Tiberio in the dead of a tempestuous night.

"She is here, signor mio; she has been often here. She is at the Villa Santilla, in the Piccola Marina. I will show you the way willingly."

"No, I can find it; I know every foot of your island. But if you can get me a horse, do."

The *marinaro* put back the gold held out to him with a loving gesture, and a smile that glistened through his brown beard:

"Not from *you*, signor. We have not forgotten, in Capri here, the night after San Costanza's Day."

A while later, and Erceldoune passed up the terraced heights, through the woods, where he crushed starry cyclamen and late violets at every step, along hedges of prickly pear enclosing vineyards and fields of flax, and down rocky winding stairs shut in by walls, over which hung the white blossoms of orange-boughs.

Now and then he passed a village priest, or a contadina that was like a study for Giorgone, on a tourist party whose mules were stumbling down some narrow gorge or dense arbutus thicket; these were all; the solitude was well-nigh unbroken. He knew Capri as well as he knew the old Scottish border at home; many a time, waiting week after week at Naples for despatches, he had explored every creek, rock, and islet in that marvellous bay, from sunlit Amalfi to nestling Procida, and he made his way straight onward to the Piccola Marina, though slowly, from the steepness and vagaries of the broken Roman roads, overgrown with luxuriant vegetation, that his horse, a sturdy mountain-trained chestnut from Ischia, climbed cautiously.

A late hour was sounding from some campanile as he rode into that beautiful nook that lies turned towards Sicily, with its line of fisher-boats and white-walled cottages fringing the coast, and hidden among olives, cistus groves, and orangeries. Here and there —where strangers had made their dwelling—lights were gleaming, but the Capriotes all lay sleeping under their low-rounded roofs; he almost despaired of finding any guide to tell him which Villa was hers in that leafy nest among the sea-girt rocks.

At last he overtook a contadina heavily laden with wood, doing the work of pack-horses, as is the common custom for women in the isles of the Syrens; she knew the name; the Contessa had bought some coral of her, for pity's sake, yesterday; the villa was down there in that little gorge just hanging over the sea, where the grey plumes of olive were thickest.

If any had asked it, he could not have answered with what definite purpose he went, whether to see her, whether to break on her privacy at such an hour, whether only to look on the place where she dwelt, and watch till the day should dawn: fixed aim he had none; he was urged by an impulse as vague as it was unconquerable, unregulated either by reason or by motive. He was in that mood in which chance does its best, or its worst, for a man; when he offers no resistance to it, and may even be hurried into guilt ere he knows what he does.

The lights were shining amongst the shades of olive and arbutus woods as his horse stumbled down the narrow defile, catching in the trailing vine tendrils at every step.

The dwelling literally overhung the sea, nestled on a low ridge of rock, curved round so that the whole arc of the bay, sweeping from east to west, was commanded by its windows, that saw the sun rise over the height of St. Angelo, fall in its noonday glory full on Naples, and Vesuvius, and Baiæ, where they lie in the depth of that wondrous bow, and pass on to die in purple pomp behind wild Ischia. It was surrounded with all the profuse growth of the island; thickets of cistus, wilderness of myrtle, budding fig-trees, orangeries with their crowns of bridal blossom and their balls of amber fruit, while vast rocks rose above and shelved beneath it, with columns that towered to the clouds, and terraced ledges and broken gorges filled up with foliage. Through the leaves he saw the gleam of open windows, and the indistinct outline of the roof in the deep shade cast from the rocks above; the road he had followed ended abruptly on a narrow table of stone jutting out over a precipice whose depth he could not guess; and immediately fronting the casements from which the light streamed, divided from the terrace and strip of garden running beneath them, by a chasm perhaps some six feet wide. Thus from the rock he saw straight into the lighted chamber within, as he threw himself from his horse, and with his arm round a plane-tree to hold his footing, leaned over the edge and strained his eyes through the gloom to gaze into the interior that was before him like a picture painted on the shadow of the night. His heart stood still with a sickening pang, a deadly burning jealousy that had never touched his life before. Through the draperies of the curtains he saw her, and saw her—not alone. She sat at the head of her table, that glittered with wax-lights and fruits and wines, and with her were some six or seven men, whose voices only reached him in a low inarticulate murmur, but whose laughter now and then echoed on his ear in the silence. At the foot of the table sat one whom he recognised at once; his back was to the windows, but the slight grace of his figure, and the elegance of his throat and head, with its closely-cut blond hair, sufficed to identify him to Erceldoune. What tie could he have to her, this cold, smiling, silken politician, who seemed perpetually by her side? In the warm night he shook as with icy chillness through all his veins; a brute longing seized him to spring like a lion into that dainty group, and fell them down as men of his blood in Bothwell's days had felled their foes in Border feuds,

"when the loud corynoch rang for war
Through Lorne, Argyle, Monteith, and Braidalbane."

Her other guests were all unknown to him, and looked like gentlemen-condottieri; moreover, all he saw was Idalia: she was leaning slightly forward, her face was lighted with impassioned warmth, while her eyes, fixed upon the man nearest her, an Italian by the contour of his features, and of a careless princely bearing, that gave him greater distinction than the rest displayed, adjured him more eloquently still, than by the words with which her lips were moving.

The echo of her voice, though not the meaning of her speech, came to Erceldoune where he swung forward over the chasm in the hushed night, sweet and fatal as the Syren voices that had used to echo over those eternal seas that lapped the beach below. And as he heard it, a heart-sick misery seemed to make his life desolate: he had shaped no definite hope, his thoughts had known no actual form, but his love unconsciously had coloured both hope and thought: she so utterly filled his own life, he could not at once realise that he was nothing, not even a remembrance in hers.

He leaned nearer and nearer, regardless of the unfathomed precipice that yawned beneath him. At that instant Victor Vane rose, pushed back his chair, and approached the open glass doors; looking out from the brightly-lighted room, he could see the shadow of the man and horse upon the opposite ledge.

"The Romans hung their wreaths of roses over the doors, we in a more prosaic age must shut our windows," he said, with a light laugh, as he closed the venetian blinds, leaving only their thread-like chinks open for the passage of light outward, and the passage of air within.

A great darkness fronted Erceldoune; the moon was shining on all the silvered seas, and innumerable stars were out, but for him the blackness and blindness of night had never so utterly fallen.

Hours passed by uncounted, unheeded by him; the chimes of the campanile had chimed twelve, and one, and two, unheard by him; he was still there before the darkened windows. The Ischian horse grazed quietly off the grasses and young shoots among the rocks; Erceldoune watched the villa which sheltered her, as a lion watches the lair of his foe.

The night was absolute torture to him; intolerable suspense possessed him, and a reckless hatred of all those who were now within the chamber on which he was forbidden even to look. So near to her, and yet as far sundered as though seas divided them! His rivals with her whilst he stood without!—his imagination was filled with their looks, their words, the bold passion in their eyes, the lovely smile upon her lips. What were they, what title could they claim to her, these men, who seemed so welcome to her? Something in the familiarity, the authority, of the Englishman's action, slight though it was, bore to him a terrible significance; were her revelries such as those for which the rose was hung above the doors of Rome?—were they the revelries of a Faustina? The thought passed over him, cold, gliding, poisonous as the coil of a snake; he flung it from him with fierce loathing, true to the motto of his old race: "One loyalty, one faith"—he had given both to her. He heeded neither time nor place; purpose he had none in staying there; to watch her life with suspicion or espionage was the last thought in him, the last baseness possible to him; but he could not tear himself from the place, he was fascinated to it, even by the very torment of his pain. How utterly she must have forgotten him!—how utterly careless must she be of what suffering she had dealt him! As he thought of the look that he had seen on her face, as he thought of those men gathered about her whilst he was absent, he paced the narrow rocky ridge like a man chained to his cell, while his foes riot in all that he has loved and treasured. And the closed casements faced him like an inexorable doom, while a faint glimmer of light that here and there streamed through them seemed to mock him with fugitive tormenting glimpse, only serving to make the darkness darker still.

At last, when the greyness of dawn was breaking, there was a slight noise that stirred the stillness: the shutter unclosed, the glass door opened, he saw her—alone. There was no one now in the apartment, and she stood in the open window looking out on the sea that stretched far below, round the broken and jutting cliffs.

He leaned down scarcely breathing, till he hung half way over the chasm; was it possible that in this solitude she thought of him? Were those men anything to her, or was he more than they, or nothing?—not even a regret?

The moon at that moment strayed through on to the ledge, and she saw his shadow hanging midway down over the precipice, whose fatal depth slanted straight into the sea—which had worn a narrow way through the fissure five hundred feet below. A cry of horror broke from her that had a greater tenderness in it than lies only in a mere fear for life imperilled; for all answer he swung himself one moment on the ledge, balanced the distance with an unerring eye, and with a mountaineer's leap that the glens and hills of the Border had taught him long before, cleared the space and alighted at her feet.

"Does it matter to you whether I live or die?"

The brief prayer bore eloquence deeper than lies in ornate words; all the man's heart was spent in it; Idalia stood motionless and silent, her eyes fixed on him where he stood beside her, dropped as from the air upon the wild cliffs in the dead of night, when she believed him far distant on those eastern shores to which the sea beneath them ebbed away through league on league of starlight.

"Does it matter to you whether I live or die?" he

said afresh, while his voice quivered with a fiery piteous entreaty.

"Surely! It mattered to me when you were but a stranger."

A vivid joy thrilled through him, his eyes in the shadow burned down into hers with passionate appeal, with passionate reproach.

"Ay, but it was only a divine pity *then*, is it that only now? And with but pity in you for me, how could you deal me this last misery?"

What stirred her heart he could not tell.

"I bade you know no more of me," she said at last, while her eyes looked away from him down into the still and silvered seas. "I told you nothing but bitterness could come to you from my friendship; nothing else can. Why would you not believe me while it was time?"

There was an intense and weary mournfulness in the words; they carried a deadly meaning to him, he gave them but one significance.

"You mean that even your memory is forbidden me?—that even my worship of you dishonours you?"

"Your words are as strange as your presence here. This is the time and place for neither."

"My words are strange! God help me! I hardly know what I say. Answer me, in pity's sake, what are they to you?"

"Who?"

And as she spoke, beneath the unbent hauteur of her voice and of her glance there was something as nearly kindred to anxiety and alarm as could approach Idalia's nature.

"Those men who were with you."

"Let me pass, sir. These are not questions for which you have right, or to which I give submission."

"I swear they shall be answered! What *are* they to you?"

She glanced at him in haughty amaze, tinged with some other feeling that he could not translate.

"You dare address me thus! Are you mad?"

"I think so!"

"I think so also," she said, coldly. "And now, sir, there is an end of these unwarranted questions, which you have as little title to ask as I have inclination to answer. Leave me, or let me pass."

He stood in her path, half mad as he said:

"I will know one thing — are you any man's wife?"

Utter surprise passed over her face, and something of contemptuous annoyance.

"I reply to nothing asked in such a manner," she said briefly. "Let me pass, sir."

"No! Tell me this one thing for the love of pity!"

The anguish in his voice touched her; she paused a moment.

"It can concern you in no way," she answered him distantly. "But since you ask it—know that I cherish freedom too well to be wedded."

"I thank God,—I may love you without sin."

His voice was very low, and his words had a greater intensity because their passion was restrained in obedience to her: there was grandeur in their very simplicity. She raised her head with her old stag-like gesture—looking to the sea, and not to him.

"Sir, you have no title to speak such words. You cannot say that I have ever given you the faintest."

"Have I ever said it? No! you have given me no title, but I claim one."

"Claim!"

"I claim one. The title that every man has to love, though he go unloved—to love better than life, and only less than honour."

He spoke steadily, undauntedly, as became his own self-respect and dignity, but his voice had an accent which told her that world-wide as the love had been that she had roused, none ever had loved her as this man did. For a moment she turned and looked at him, a look fleeting, and veiled from him by the flickering shadows. The look was soon banished, and her eyes strayed backward to the sea; her face was very pale, but she moved away with her proud and languid grace:

"These words are painful to us both;—no more of them, sir. Farewell."

The word struck him as a shot strikes one of his Border deer; in the impulse of his agony he caught her trailing dress, and held it as a sentenced captive might hold the purple hem of his sovereign's robes.

"Stay! A moment ago you said you cared whether I lived or died;—as I live now I will die to-night—in that sea at your feet—if you tell me to leave you for ever."

A shudder ran through her; looking down on him she saw that fatigue, long fasting, the misery of the past hours, and the force of the feeling he bore her, had unloosed his passions and unstrung his nerves till his brain was giddy; and—his calm failing him—she saw that in every likelihood, as surely as the stars shone above them, he would keep his word and fling away his whole existence for her.

Commonly she was too careless of men's lives, as of their peace; but here she could not be so. She had saved him, she could not so soon again destroy him.

"Hush!" she said more softly. "The noblest woman would never be worth *that!* It would be better that we should part. When I tell you that it can bring you no happiness—"

"Whatever it bring, I said before, I accept it! My life is yours to save or throw away, as you will; answer me, which shall it be?"

There was a suppressed violence, a terrible suffering, in his voice, that moved her almost with such shuddering pain as though she witnessed his death before her sight; in the light falling from the opened windows she could see the burning gleam in his eyes and the red flush that darkened the bronze of his face.

"Live!" she answered him, while her own voice lost its chillness. "You do not know now what you say; with calmer hours you will see how little worth it I or any woman could be. You may meet me again,—but you must speak no more of such words as you have spoken to-night. I have your promise?"

"Till my strength shall fail me to keep it."

"When it does, we shall meet no more."

Then she left him, and passed through the chamber that was opened to the night, till, in the distance, the clustered flowers and statues veiled her among them, and the closing of a door echoed with a dull sound through the stillness.

He stood alone on the terrace, the noise of the sea

surging in his ear, his pulse beating, his brain reeling: he could not tell what to believe, what to trust, what to think.

The single-hearted nature of the man had too honest a mould, too masculine a cast, to follow or to divine the complex intricacies of a woman's life, of a woman's impulses and motives. He felt blinded, powerless, heartsick, dizzy, now crushed with reckless despair at the chill memory of her words, now touched with sweet wild hope, because he thought her free to be won if daring, fidelity, and devotion could avail to win her.

To doubt her, never—even now, even with all that he had seen and heard—occurred to him. He believed that she might only pity him with proud cold pity; he believed that it was faintly, remotely possible that by force of his own mighty love some tenderness might be at last wakened for him in her heart. But between these he saw no path. He never thought that she might be—but fooling, and destroying him.

He had comparatively seen little of women; nothing of such a woman as Idalia. His bold and sanguine nature quickly grasped at hope; even in all the humility of his love it was not in him to surrender.

Till morning broke beyond the giant mass of St. Angelo, he paced up and down the cliffs, with the waves beating music at his feet. Then he flung himself down on the moss that covered a ledge of the rock, with his saddle beneath his head, as he had lain many a night under Asiatic stars and on Andes slopes, and on yellow Libyan sand; physical fatigue brought sleep, and sleep was gentler to him than his waking life, it gave him dreams, and with his dreams Idalia.

As she passed from him through the embrasure of

the myrtle-shrouded window, and crossing her reception-room, entered an inner chamber, at the farther end stood Victor Vane—too far to have heard what had been spoken, yet near enough through the suite of apartments to have seen out on the terrace above the sea. A few minutes before he had left the villa with her other guests, whose boats were taking them across to Naples; now he had returned and awaited her, half with the familiarity of a man who shared her confidence, half with the hesitation of one who fears he may give offence.

"You are here still; and so late! I suppose you bring news of importance you could not give before them?" she said, with a shade of annoyance in the languor of her voice. He had approached with a quick step, an eager warmth upon his face; he was checked and chilled, vaguely yet irresistibly, as he met her glance. He was rarely to be daunted, still less rarely to be shamed; yet he was both now. He paused involuntarily, his eyes fell, and words died on his lips, as he bowed before her.

"And your intelligence?" she asked.

"Intelligence? Caffradali has deserted us."

Idalia lifted her eyebrows.

"He is as well lost as retained. What else?"

"You know that the Ducroses will send twenty thousand rifles into Poland, and that Falkenstein goes to take the command of the Towaricz?"

She gave a gesture of impatience.

"He will 'command' them when they are organized —*when!* It was I who sent him. This can scarcely be your intelligence—your intelligence that will not wait till to-morrow?"

He hesitated, with a strangely novel embarrassment upon him.

"I waited—to congratulate you on your conquest of the Prince to the cause."

A light of triumph gave its pride to her eyes, and its warmth to her brow; she smiled, as with the memory of victory.

"Viana! Yes—it is something to have secured him, semi-Bourbon that he is! But I still remain at a loss to imagine why you re-appear at this time of the night."

A flush of anger heated the delicate coldness of her listener's face, his silken and gentle courtesies were forgotten for the moment.

"Such an hour, madame! It is not too late for that wild wanderer yonder to be favoured with an interview!"

The moment the words escaped him he repented them; he knew how rash they were with the nature and disdainful dignity of the woman to whom he spoke. Idalia cast one glance on him of superb indifference; but she gave no betrayal of surprise, not even of disquiet, far less of embarrassment.

"If you only came to arraign my actions, I will be obliged to you to retire."

"Wait. Hear me first. I can act indifference no longer. I came back to-night for one thing only—to tell you what you know, as well as you know that the stars shine yonder—that I love you!"

She heard him with that same indifference, and ironic amusement.

"I think we are too well acquainted with each other

for this. I gave you more credit than to suppose *you* would talk in this fashion."

He looked up at her with a passionate pain; he had been heartless, and been proud of his heartlessness; he had mocked all his life through at what other men felt and suffered, and passion or tenderness had been alike the subject of his most cutting sneer; but—for the moment, at least—his creed had deserted him, his wisdom and his sarcasm had failed him; for the moment he loved, as utterly as ever a lover did, and he felt powerless to make her credit it. But eloquence was always at his bidding, and eloquence came now; every honeyed flattery, every imploring eagerness, every impassioned pleading, that could warm or shake the heart of the woman who heard him, poured from his lips. Persuasive always, he was a thousand-fold more so now that for the first time in his existence genuine passion had broken up his callousness, and a sense of hopelessness shivered his self-reliance. He loved her, if it were but a mingling of desire, of ambition, of senses intoxicated by her beauty, of pride piqued by her disdain; and he felt impotent to make her even believe this—far more impotent to make her accept it.

She heard him without interruption, smiling a little as she heard; she was half wearied, half amused, as at a comedy known and stale from custom, yet amusing because well acted.

"Monsieur, I gave you credit for better taste," she said, quietly, as he paused. "I have had so much of this so often; granted you are unusually eloquent, unusually graceful, but even with those accessories the tale is very tiresome; and it has one great drawback, you see—we neither of us believe it!"

"Believe! how can I make you believe? I tell you that ever since I saw you first I have been so changed that I have wondered if I lived or dreamed; I have felt all that once I disdained as only fit for boys and fools! What more can I tell you?—you must *know* that I speak truth."

"What a recantation! I am not a fitting hearer for it at all, nor likely to appreciate it. I will thank you far more to amuse me with your bon-mots, which are really good, than to entertain me with your efforts in Romeo's strain, which, though very pretty, are very stale!"

"Wait!—for pity's sake. Doubt what you will, mock at what you will, but believe at least that I love you!"

She laughed softly.

"We do not believe in love—*nous autres!*"

"And yet men have gone to their death only for love of you!"

"No proof of wisdom if they did."

A little while before he had thought as she thought; a few months earlier and his incredulity of every such madness and emotion was not more scornful than her own; now, intoxicated with the disdainful beauty of the only woman who had ever cost him a moment's pang, he believed in all the wildest follies of romance, and would have staked everything he owned on earth, or wagered on the future, to move her and to win her. For the only time in his life he was baffled, for the only time powerless. His hands clenched where he stood before her.

"Hear me at the least before you banish me. Listen! what is there we might not compass together?

You adore sovereignty, it should go hard if I did not give it you. You are ambitious, your ambition cannot overleap mine. We are both against the world; together we would subdue it. Empty thrones have fallen to hands bold enough to grasp them as they reel through revolutions; you and I might wear a crown if our aims and power were one. Love me, and there is no height I will not raise you to, no ordeal I will not pass through for you, no living man who shall baffle or outrun me. I have the genius that rules worlds—I would lay one at your feet."

Every word that he uttered he meant; in the excitement of the instant, sweeping down all the suave and hardened coldness of his temperament, he felt the power in him to do and to dare greatly; he felt that for her, through her, with her, there should be no limit to the ambition and the triumph of his life; he spoke wildly, blindly, exaggeratedly, but he spoke with an exaltation that for the second made him a nobler and a truer man than he had been in all the cool scorn of his wisdom and his mockery. Yet he did not move her, much less did he win her.

She looked at him with a smile in her eyes, and a haughty languor in her attitude. She—merciless from knowing the world too well, and gifted with a penetration far beyond the common range of women—saw that the gold offered her was adulterated; that the springs of his speech were as much self-love as love.

"I understand you," she said, as he paused. "I could advance your ambitions well, and you would be glad that I should do so; your vanity, your policy, your schemes, and—perhaps a little, too—your admiration, are all excited and chime in with another one; and that compound you call love. Well, it is as good a name for it as anything else. But as for thrones! I thought we called ourselves Liberalists and Redressers? Crowns scarcely hang in the air like roses, as you seem to think, for any passer-by to gather them; but if they do, how do *you* reconcile the desire for one with all your professions of political faith? I suppose, then, like most democrats, you only struggle against tyranny that you may have the right in turn to create yourself Tyrannis?"

His hands closed on a cluster of rhododendrons in the window, and tore them down with an unconscious gesture. In a measure he was wronged; he loved her enough in that moment to have renounced every ambition and every social success for her, and he could not make her even believe that any feeling was in him. In a measure, too, her satire was right, and pierced him the more bitterly because it laid bare so mercilessly all that was confused and unacknowledged to himself. In his pain in her contempt, he hated her almost as much as he loved her, and the old barbaric leaven of jealousy, that he had used to ridicule as the last insanity of fools, broke out despite all self-respect that would have crushed it into silence.

"You are very pitiless, madame!" he said in his teeth. "Do you deal as mockingly with that beggared courier whom you favour with interviews at an hour you think untimely for lovers less distinguished?"

Her glance swept over him with the grand amazement of one whom no living man ever arraigned. He could not tell whether his insult moved her one whit for sake of the man whom his jealousy seized as his rival; but he saw that it had for ever ruined all hope for himself. She looked at him calmly, with a contempt that cut him like a knife.

"I did not know that my wines were so strong or your head so weak. If you transgress the limits of courtesy, I must transgress those of hospitality, and—dismiss you."

He knew that it was as vain to seek to move or sway her from that serene indifference, as to dash himself against the Capri rocks in striving to uproot them; yet in his desperation he lost all the keen and subtle tact, the fine inscrutable ability, that had never failed him save with her. He laid his hands on the sweeping folds of her dress, with the same gesture of entreaty that Erceldoune had used in the unconscious vehemence of his prayer.

"Idalia—stay! Take heed before you refuse my love, for love it *is*, God help me."

She drew the laces from him, and moved away.

"You have as much belief in the name you invoke, monsieur, as I have in the love for which you invoke it! Come! we alike know the world too well for this comedietta not to weary both. You must end it, or I."

"No!—hear me out," he said, fiercely, almost savagely, for one whose impassive gentleness had commonly been his choicest mask and weapon. "Think twice before you refuse any toleration to my love. Take *that*, and you shall make me your slave; refuse it, and you will never have had a foe such as you shall find in me. Remember—you cannot brave me lightly, you cannot undo the links that connect us, you cannot wash out my knowledge of all that you have held most secret. Remember whose thoughts and acts and intrigues I have in my keeping. I know that you would give all your loveliness in tribute to me to bribe me from uttering to the world——"

"You try intimidation? I accredited you with better breeding and less melodrama," said Idalia, her careless negligence unruffled, as with a bow like that with which queens dismiss their courts, she passed from the chamber ere he could follow or arrest her;—it would have been a man bolder and more blinded still than he was, who should have dared to do either.

He was left there alone, in the midst of the white warm light and of the burnished leaves swaying against the marble columns; to his lips oaths never came, he was too finely polished, but an imprecation was hurled back upon his heart that cursed her with a terrible bitterness, and a hatred great as was his baffled passion. He hated her for his own folly in bending to the common weakness of men; he hated her for the disdainful truth with which she had penetrated the mixed motives in his heart; he hated her for the shame she had put upon him of offering her a rejected and despised passion; he hated her for all the numberless sorceries of her fascination, of her brilliance, of her pride, which had made him weak as water before their spell. To win her there was nothing he would have checked at; she had become the incarnation of his ambitions, as she might have been the means of their fruition; all that gave her danger to other men but gave her added intoxication for him, she would have been to him, had she but loved him, what the genius and the beauty of her whom they called Hellas Rediviva were to Tallien. And more bitter than pride

stung, or vanity pierced, or ambition shattered, was the
sense that love her as he had, love her as he would,
consume his very heart for her sake as he might, he
would never—plead, beseech, swear, or prove it as he
should—make her believe that one pulse of love beat
in him.

And all the bygone ironies and contemptuous
scoffs which he had used to cast on those who suffered
for the lost smile of a woman's eyes came back upon
him now, laughing in his ear and jibing at his weakness like fantastic devils mocking at his fall. A woman
had enthralled him; and his philosophies were dead—
corpses that lay cold and powerless before him, incapable of rallying to his rescue, things of clay without a shadow's value.

CHAPTER XIV.

The Allegory of the Pomegranate.

THE early morning broke on Capri; with the
rising of the sun the little fleet of boats all down the
shore began to flutter into motion as the birds fluttered
into song, the Angelus rang, the full daylight glittered
over the white line of towns and villages that nestled
far and wide in the bow of the bay; in the transparent
air a delicate feathery column of grey smoke curled
up from the cone of Vesuvius; the cliffs rose up in
the sunlight, vine-covered, and standing like pillars out
in the midst of the sea; while the mists were still
hanging over that deep blue western depth, stretching
out and on to the Mediterranean, farther and farther
towards the columns of Hercules and the gates of the
African and Asian worlds.

In her own chamber, a morning-room whose windows, clustering round with trained myrtle and clematis, looked out down the shelving cliff on to the sea, Idalia stood; her head was bent, her eyes were grave and filled with thought, and her lips had as much of disdain as of melancholy; she looked a woman to dare much, to reign widely, to submit rarely, to fear never. Yet she was in bondage now.

At a breakfast table, a little distance from her sat Conrad, Count Phaulcon. He was smoking, having finished with the coffee and claret, fruit and fish beside him, and was looking at her under his lashes, a look half wary, half admiring, half angered, half exultant, the look of a man foiled in holding her by intimidation, but successful in holding her by power; yet not wholly at his ease with her, nor wholly so with himself.

"If you would only hear reason," he said, impatiently; he had vanquished her in one sense, but in another she was still his victor, and he was restless under it.

"I am happy to hear reason," she answered coldly, "but of dishonour I am—a little tired!"

There was a certain listless satiric bitterness in the last words.

"Dishonour!" echoed Phaulcon, while the blood flushed over his forehead, and he moved irritably. "How strangely you phrase things! What has changed you so? For a woman of the world, a woman of your acumen, of your experience, of your brilliancy!—to pause and draw back for such puerile after-thoughts—I cannot in the least comprehend it. What a sceptre you hold! Bah! stronger than any queen's. Queens are mere *fantoccini*—marionnettes crowned for a puppet-show, and hung on wires that each minister pulls after his own fancy; but you have a kingdom that is never limited, except at your own choice; an empire that is exhaustless, for when you shall have lost your beauty, you will still keep your power. You smile, and the politician tells you his secret; you woo him, and the velvet churchman unlocks his intrigues; you use your silver eloquence, and you save a cause or free a country. It is supreme power, the power of a woman's loveliness, used as you use it, with a statesman's skill."

She smiled slightly; but the tranquil carelessness and resistance of her attitude did not change. Those persuasive, vivacious, hyperbolic words—she remembered how fatal a magic, how alluring a glamour such as they had once had for her; they had no charm now, they had long ceased to have any.

"A supreme power!" pursued Phaulcon. "In the rose-water of your hookahs you steep their minds in what colour you will. With the glance of your eyes, you unnerve their wills, and turn them which way you choose. In an opera supper you enchant their allegiance to what roads you like; in the twilight of a boudoir you wind the delicate threads that agitate nations. You are in the heart of conspiracies, in the secrets of cabinets, in the destinies of coalitions, and with Fascination conquer, where Reason would fail. It is the widest power in the world; it is that of Antonina, of Marcia, of Olympia, of Pompadour! What can be lacking in such a life?"

"Only what was wanting in theirs—honour!"

The words were spoken very calmly, but there was not the less meaning in them.

"Honour! What makes you all in a moment so in love with that word? There was a time when you saw nothing but what was triumph in your career."

"It is not for *you* to reproach me with that."

Over his changing, handsome, eloquent features a certain flush and shadow came.

"Reproach! I would rather reproach you with the change. And why should there be this continued estrangement between us, Idalia? You loved me once."

Her eyes dwelt on his musingly, very mournfully, with that lustre of disdain that was in them, mingled with a momentary wistfulness of recollection.

"Yes, I loved you once," she answered, and her voice had an excessive gentleness in it; but he knew her meaning too well to ask why it was that this was now solely and irrevocably of the past.

He was silent some moments; the dashing and reckless Free Lance felt an embarrassment and a sense of mortification in her presence. He could hold this haughty and exquisite woman in a grip of steel, and feel a savage victory in forcing the proud neck that would not bend, to lie beneath his heel; he could take a refined exultation of cruelty in seeing her pride rebel, her instincts recoil, her dignity suffer mutely; he could amuse himself with all this with a rich pleasure in it. Nevertheless, he owed her many and heavy debts; he gave her an admiration that was tinged still with a strange tyrannous wayward sort of love; he held her in an unwilling homage that made him half afraid of her, and he shrank under the sense of her censure and of her rebuke.

In one sense he was her master, but in another she

was far above him, in another she was his ruler, and escaped his power.

He rose restlessly; the glance he gave her was doubtful and embarrassed, and his tone was half appealing, half imperious.

"Well, there is one thing, I want more money."

"You always want money!"

There was a weary scorn in her words, the scorn of a proud woman forced into companionship with what has sunk too utterly in her eyes for any other feeling save that only of an almost compassionate contempt.

Phaulcon laughed; not because he was impervious to the contempt, but because the temper of the man was really lightly and idly insouciant, careless as any butterfly, except in hate.

"Of course! who doesn't? Is there anything money won't buy, from a woman's love to a priest's absolution? Tell me that! A man without money is like a man born into the world without his eyes or his legs; he exists, he doesn't *live;* he hibernates miserably, he never knows what it is to enjoy! Who are the kings of the earth? The Hopes, the Pereires, the Rothschilds, the Barings. War could not be begun, imperial crowns would never come out of pawn, nations would collapse in bankruptcies, thrones would crash down to the dust, and nobles turn crossing-sweepers, without them. Who rule Europe, kings, ministers, cabinets, troops? Faugh! not one whit of it—the CAPITALISTS! Which was the potentate, the great Emperor who owed the bond, or the great Fugger who could afford to put it in the fire? Yes, I do want money. Can you let me have any?"

Her lips moved slightly, she restrained whatever words might rise to them, but she did not repress the disgust that was spoken silently on them.

"You wish to ruin my fortune now?"

"Far from it," laughed Phaulcon. "I am not like the boy who killed his goose of the golden eggs. I would not ruin you on any account; but even if I did, you know very well that any one of your *friends* would willingly make up any breaches I caused in your wealth."

Where she stood, with one hand leaning idly on the carved ivory of a chess King, she turned with a sudden gesture. He had broken down her haughty silence, her studied contemptuous tranquillity at last. A flush rose over her brow, her lips quivered, not with fear, but with loathing; her eyes flashed fire. All the gentleness that in her moments of abandonment characterised her, and all the languor that at other hours made her so indolently and ironically indifferent, changed into a fearless defiance, the more intense from its force of contrast with the restrained serenity of her past self-control.

"One other word like that and you never enter my presence again, if to be free from you I close the gates of a convent on my own life. What! are you so vile as *that?* Is all shame lost in you?"

If it were not, there were moments when he was as bad a man as the world held, when the devil in him was alone victorious, and all conscience that had ever lingered was crushed out and forgotten. Her words, and yet far more, her look, lashed all that was evil in his nature to its height.

He laughed aloud.

"'A world of scorn looks beautiful' in you, that I grant, Eccellenza! At the same time your title to it is not quite clear. It is for the women who go to Courts to smile with that superb disdain, to answer with that proud defiance—not for the Countess Vassalis!"

There was not much in the words themselves, but in their tones there was an intolerable insolence, an intolerable insult. The fire in her eyes burned deeper still, her breath came rapidly, her whole form was instinct with a passion held in rein, rather for sake of her own dignity than for any more timorous thing. Standing in that haughty wrath, that self-enforced restraint, she looked like some superb stag, some delicate antelope, at bay, and panting to spring on its foes.

"Do you think such taunts as that—*your* taunts! have power to wound me for one instant? Where is your boasted wisdom? It has forsaken you strangely, as strangely as your memory! Whatever I have lost, the loss is due to you; whatever I have erred in, the error lies with you; whatever wreck my life has made, is wrecked through you; whatever taint is on my name, was brought there first by you. You have tried my patience long and often; you have tried it once too much. You have trusted to the tie that is between us; it is broken for ever as if it had not been. Insult through you I have continually borne. What the world has said has been as nothing to me, my life is not ruled by it, my honour is not touched by it. But insult from you I will never bear. Be my destroyer as you choose; but your accomplice again you shall never make me—nor your dupe. Stand aside, sir, I will hear no more words."

He had laid his hand upon her arm, she shook him off with an action as intense in its gesture of contempt as her words had been intense in their concentrated passion, and swept beyond him towards the doorway of her chamber.

Phaulcon sprang before her, and stood between her and the closed doors; there was a taint of cowardice in his nature, and he had forgotten all policy when he had let malice and vengeance hurry him into an open rupture with one who was beyond all others needful to him, and who, whatever her foes, whatever her faults, still never feared.

"Idalia!—wait."

"Let me pass, sir."

"No, by Heaven! not in such a mood."

"You wish to compel me to summon my household?"

"I wish to induce you to hear reason."

"Your euphuistic synonym for some new villany? I have answered you already."

"Softly, softly! It will not do for us to quarrel. You know the terms on which alone you can make such an answer final."

"Your persecution? I am indifferent to it. Allow me to pass."

"Pardon me, no. The terms I meant were—the breaking of your oath."

He spoke very gently, yet at the words she turned pale for the first time in their interview, as though he had pierced her where she was without shield; she did not reply, and he pursued his advantage.

"'Tell me,—will your new and eccentric fancy for 'honour' be greatly gratified by the deliberate rupture of your sworn word? When men and women talk much of their honour, to be sure they are always conscious of having lost it, or being just about to lose it with a more flagrant bankruptcy than common; but still, your newly-adopted principle will be ill-commenced by the repudiation of your pledged oath, of your bound engagement."

Still she said nothing, only in her eyes suppressed passion gleamed, and her hand clenched as though, but for her dignity's sake, it would have found force to strike him where he stood.

Conrad Phaulcon smiled.

"I am no tyrant, no harsh task-master, my most beautiful Countess, and I frankly admit that I admire you more in your haughty rebellion than I do in the softest smile with which you enchant all our good friends. I exact nothing. I command nothing. I merely remind you—you cannot break from me without also breaking your promise, and more than your promise—your oath. However, a woman's word, I suppose—even when it is sworn, even when it is the word of such a woman as yourself, who have none of your sex's weaknesses—is only given to *be* broken. Is it so?"

She answered nothing still; a slight quick shudder of hatred or of contempt passed over her one moment; she was torn inwardly with such a conflict as the prisoner on parole feels when he might break his fetters away, and strive, at least, for the sweet chance of liberty, were he not held back by one torturing memory —his word.

Suddenly she turned and bent rapidly towards him, her eyes looking into his with so full and brilliant a lustre of unuttered scorn, that he started and drew back.

"You sell everything—your body and your soul! What bribe would you take to give me my release?"

"What bribe? None! You are much more to me, my exquisite Idalia, than any gold, well as I love the little god. 'Bribe!' What an ugly word! Bribes are like medicines; every one takes them, but no one talks about them. Your 'release,' too! when you live as free as air!"

She said no more, but stood aloof from him again in haughty and enforced composure.

"Leave my presence, or let me pass out," she said, briefly. "One or the other."

"Either, with pleasure, if you will give me two answers. First, will you break your oath?"

The look that gave so much of heroism and of grandeur to her beauty passed across it; to stoop to supplication to him would have been as utterly impossible to her as to have put down her neck beneath his heel, and though she could not break his bonds, she was not vanquished by him. She answered with a calm endurance that obeyed, not him, but the law of her own nature:

"No."

"Ah, that is well and wise, *ma belle*. Now for the other question. You will give me the money?"

"No."

The reply was precisely the same as it had been before: the triumph in his eyes fell.

"And why not?"

"Because every sum I gave you now would seem given because I feared you. Fall as low as that, you know well enough that I shall never do. As far as you hold me by my oath, so far I will hold myself bound, no farther; for the rest I have said—all is cancelled henceforward between us."

"What? Do you mean that you deny my title to my power on you? Do you mean that it can ever be possible for your mere will to cancel such a tie as there is between us? Do you mean that, if you pretend to forget the past and all my claims on you, I shall ever allow them to be forgotten?"

"'Forgotten?' No. It is not so easy to forget. But trade on them longer, I have said, you shall never do. I have endured your exactions too many years already."

"But, by Heaven! then I insist——"

"You cannot insist. If you need money, you know the price of it: my release from you, as far as you have the power to bestow it. On other terms, you will never again live on my gold. The choice will be for you."

"But I demand——"

"You can demand nothing, sir."

And with a movement that even now did not stoop to be hurried, or lose in any sort its dignity, she swept by him before he could arrest her, passed through the door, and closed it.

He knew Idalia well enough to know that to force himself on her, or seek to intimidate her into compliance with his will, would be as utterly vain as to seek to quarry with a razor the great black heights of Tiberio towering yonder in the light. Half the victory was in his hands, half in hers. To gain the rest, he knew that he must wait.

He left her, and went out across the gardens and down the winding way that led along the rocks to the shore. He was not wholly satisfied with his morning's work; he felt the mute resistance of a proud nature against a power of which he was tyrannously and inexorably jealous, and he knew that this power did not extend over her money, of which he had often received much, of which he was always wanting to receive more. Besides, with all his evil triumph in galling and goading her to his uttermost ingenuity, a certain shame was always on him before Idalia, and a certain love for her always survived in his heart; love that was always strangely blent with something of unwilling homage, of reluctant awe, and, now and then, of absolute repentance.

He would not have undone one of the links of the fetters he had made her wear under the purple-hemmed and gold-broidered robes of her beauty, freedom, and supremacy; but at the same time, in her presence or freshly from it, he felt ashamed of having forged them. Long habit had killed almost everything in him that had once been a little better; but Conrad Phaulcon had still here and there certain flashes of conscience left.

As he went towards the beach, round a sharp point of rock abruptly jutting out with its hanging screen of ivy and myrtle, ere he looked where he went, his foot was almost against the arm of a man lying there, in the shadow, asleep.

Erceldoune lay on the grass, the horse standing motionless beside him; his limbs were stretched out in all their careless magnificence of strength, his head had fallen slightly back, his chest rose and fell with the calm breathings of a deep repose, and as the morning light slanted through a fissure of the cliffs it was full upon his face, from which in repose the dauntless light, the eagle fire, had gone, and only had left now a profound and serene melancholy.

It was yet early; sleep had only come to him as the sun had risen, after hours of intense excitement, and a night of extreme bodily fatigue. There was nothing to awaken him here, and lulled by the pleasant murmur of the seas and the warmth of the young day, he dreamt on still. The Greek started violently, and a fierce panther-like longing was the first thing that seized him, mingled with supreme amazement; a ferocious vindictiveness darkened and flushed the glory of his face; he paused, his lips a little parted, his teeth ground, his whole form quivering with the longing to spring; his temperament was intensely vivacious, and years had done nothing to chill if they had done much to harden him, and little by little he had so gathered up his hatred towards the man he had injured, that it was as great as though that injury had been received, instead of given, by him.

He stooped over the sleeper, noting the unarmed powerlessness of that slumber, while his glance wandered by sheer instinct towards a loose, weighty, mallet-like mass of granite lying near him. One blow from it in a sure hand, and the life would be still before it could waken for a struggle, a shout, a sigh.

"I might crush out his brains as easily as a fly, and, by God, I could do it, too!" he thought, in a fierce blindness of hatred that remembered only that night ride through the pomegranates, and forgot all the vileness of his own brutality towards this man who lay sleeping at his feet.

Without waking, Erceldoune stirred slightly; his right hand that lay open, clenched; he turned with a restless sigh—he was dreaming of Idalia still. At the movement his foe cowered, and drew back involuntarily; pusillanimity ran in his blood, and he had a keen dread of this "Border Eagle," who had been invulnerable under so many shots, and had had a resurrection almost from the grave; a dread nearly as strong as his hate for him. Moreover, with that action he remembered many things, policy before all, which forbade him to attempt any risk of reckoning with the man he had left for dead in the Carpathians. He took one long glance at him—the glance of hatred is as lingering as that of love, and of still surer recollection—then hastily and noiselessly turned aside over the thick grasses, and went his way down to the beach.

It was not through any sense of shame or of humanity that he left the sleeping man unharmed, it was not even that he would have shrunk from crushing the life out of him as mercilessly as out of a cicala; it was only that he remembered the danger and unwisdom of such self-indulgence, and also, in some faint emotion, he felt a sense that Idalia was near them both—too near for him to sink into such crime as this. In his own way he loved her, in his own way revered her, though he cared nothing how he tortured, almost as little how he ruined her. While under her influence he could not be his worst.

An hour later he had crossed the bay, and approached a *palazzetto* smothered in orange trees, whose terraces overhung the sea, odorous, and shaded deep with myrtle. He made his way unannounced, and passing through several chambers entered one in which he found the temporary owner of the house, who looked up wearily and listlessly;—the owner was Victor Vane.

"Well?" he asked, as the door closed.

"That Scot! That courier!" panted Phaulcon. "He is in Capri. I passed him lying asleep on the grass; I could have killed him like a dog. Does he know Idalia? Is it possible he can have learnt that it was she who saved him?"

"Know Idalia? Yes, beyond doubt, he knows her."

"He does? She never named him to me!"

"Very possibly; but you remember how she saved him, and Miladi has her caprices!—she had him with her day after day in the East."

The words were languid still; there was no irritation expressed in them, but there was a significance for which, had Erceldoune been there, the speaker would have been hurled out on to his terrace with as little ceremony as though he had been dead Border grouse.

Even his comrade and sworn ally darted a look on him savage, passionate, but withal that *better* than any look he had given, for a hot and frank wrath was in it, with something of generous challenge.

"What do you mean by that?"

"I mean what I say—no more. This gentleman —your Carpathian friend—found her out while he was chasing what he very absurdly calls his 'assassin' down the Bosphorus shore; he dined with her when we were there, and the Countess appeared to take a very flattering interest in the landless laird. He is a handsome giant, you know, and I have often noticed that your women of intellect have a wonderful eye for physical perfections!"

With every quiet word he plunged a stab of steel into his listener's heart, with every one he veiled more closely the passions that were moving in his own. The colour changed in Phaulcon's face, he writhed under every syllable, but he could resist none; the same merciless tyranny as he had exercised over Idalia was used over him now, and he had not the fearless and haughty strength which was in hers that could have enabled him to defy or to disdain it.

"In the East—in the East?" he muttered. "With *her?*—and she never told me!"

"*Caro!* Did you imagine you had your fair Countess's confidence? I can assure you you are excessively mistaken."

Phaulcon shook in all his limbs with restrained passion. Well as he knew the art of word-torturing, he was scarce so perfect an adept in it as his friend.

"Do you mean—" he began impetuously, and paused.

Vane laughed, rose, and sauntered a little way from the table.

"Have you breakfasted? Do I mean what? Just taste one of these citrons; they are the first ripe this season. Do I mean that your friend, the Border Chief, has lost his head after the Countess Vassalis? Yes, I do mean it. He is wildly in love with her, and he has eyes that say so remarkably well, considering that he had loved nothing but tiger-shooting and hard riding till that charming piece of romance in the Carpathians."

The words were easy, indifferent, a little flippant and contemptuous: they stung the Greek like so many scorpions. He flung himself out of his seat, and paced to and fro the apartment with fierce breathless oaths ground out on his lips. Vane looked at him with an admirable affectation of amused astonishment.

"*Pace, pace, caro!*" he said, softly. "Why *will* you always be so impetuous? Vesuvius yonder, who looks rather dangerous to-day by-the-by, was never more impulsive! What annoys you so much in this colossal courier being in love with Miladi Idalia? He is not the first by many a score!"

Conrad Phaulcon swung round and strode up to his tormentor.

"By Heaven, if you taunt me, or scoff at her with that—"

"Gently, gently, très cher! *We* do not quarrel. Besides, there is really no object in assuming all that with me. Just recollect how long I have known you —and how well!"

Phaulcon was silenced, and lashed into obedience: his head dropped; he turned again, and paced the chamber with fast, uneven steps.

"This idea annoys you," pursued his counsellor, leisurely. "I grant his presence is troublesome, awkward indeed for you; and Scotch patience with Spanish fire is a disagreeable combination. Besides, your own excessive impetuosity made that little affair very notorious; if he were to recognise you, I fear, do what you would, something extremely unpleasant would result. Still, with due caution this might not happen, and no danger need occur from it if Idalia do not betray you, and that she probably will not do, unless —unless—" Victor paused a moment, and let his eyes drop on his companion. "He is a magnificent man to look at, and adores her in all good faith, which might have the charm of novelty," he added, in a musing whisper.

"Damnation! I would lay her dead at my feet if I thought—"

Vane raised his hand in deprecation.

"Pray do not be so very excessive! That language was all very well in the middle ages; both you and Sir Fulke Erceldoune have dropped in on us by mistake, out of the Crusades. But your brilliant Idalia is not a woman to be murdered. In the first place, she is too beautiful; in the second, she is too notorious; in the third, a glance of her eyes would send any assassin back again unnerved and unstrung. No; you must neither kill him, nor kill her. The idea! What barbarism, and what blundering. It is only—excuse me —madmen who use force; is it not their own necks that pay the penalty?"

"But do you mean that she has any sort of feeling for this accursed Scot?"

The other smiled.

"Dear friend, is it for me to say what new caprice your fair Countess's will may indulge in? Certainly, if one might attribute such a provinciality to the most accomplished woman of her time, I should have said, by the little I saw in Constantinople, that she did feel some sort of tenderness to your Titan of an enemy. At least, she made him win at baccarat, bade me harm him 'at my peril,' and spent the hours alone with him in a very poetic manner. Though really I cannot imagine why she should smile on a penniless Queen's Messenger, except by the feminine rule of contradiction!"

Lashing him like the separate cords of a scourge, each word fell on his listener's ear. Vane watched his fury with gratified amusement; this thing had been bitter beyond all conception to him, lightly and idly as he purposely spoke of it, and it rejoiced him with a compensating satisfaction to turn its bitterness elsewhere. Furious oaths in half the tongues of Europe chased themselves one after another off the Greek's lips. Vane let this galled and futile passion spend itself in its vain wrath some moments, then he spoke again:

"The idea annoys you? Well, certainly he is an inconvenient person to be on the list of her lovers. But what can you do? As for shooting him, or doing anything of the kind, that would create a fracas,— it is not to be thought of. If you let him see you, all he will do will be to knock you down, and give you into arrest. Beside this, Idalia is in a great measure independent of you; over her wealth you have no legal control, and all moral claim to coerce her you have yourself forfeited. True, you have a hold on her by many things; but that hold could not prevent this *beau seigneur* of the barren moors from being her lover, if she choose to break her vows for him, especially if she be quite frank with him, and let him know all. Really on my honour, placed as you are through that terrible impulsiveness which you never will abandon, I do not see how you are to step between Madame de Vassalis and this modern Bothwell, if they choose to play at Love for a little while with each other."

And Vane softly finished his citron, having spoken the most stinging words he could have strung together with the gentle, persuasive accent of a woman coaxing her best friend. Phaulcon swung round and strode up to him as he had done before, his eyes glittering with fire, his face darkly flushed.

"Perdition seize you! if you dare to make a jest of—"

"*Chut!*" said Vane, with the suavest hush that ever fell from any lips. "Caro mio, if I speak a little lightly of your lovely Idalia, whose fault is it?—'is it not thine, O my friend?' *Altro!* keep that style for men who have not worn the badge of silver ivy with you at an opera ball. As regards this affair—he is certainly in love with her; she possibly encourages it. Unlikely, I know, but still — I repeat — possible. He is an excessively fine man! Therefore, since you cannot appear in the matter, owing to various little intricacies, what steps will you take? It is a delicate question, cher Conrad; the Countess Idalia is not a woman to brook open interference:—even with your title to give it. She is very proud! I am wholly with you, and I am not inclined to be very *simpatico* to that Arab-looking courier; but you must really be cautious how you touch him; that matter would look very ugly if it turned up against you. The idea of firing at him at all!—and then of not hitting him when you did fire! Will you not believe me how very mistaken all impulsiveness is?"

Phaulcon writhed under the negligent, gently-uttered phrases; all the pent passion in him was tenfold hotter and darker, because it was in so great a measure powerless; but he was blinded to all that Victor chose him to be blind to—namely, his companion's own love for her of whom they spoke—and he dreamed of nothing in his words beyond their mutual antagonism for the man they had mutually injured.

An hour went by before they parted; left alone, the master of the dainty *palazzetto* overhanging the Neapolitan waves neither peeled a citron, nor toyed lightly with this thought of Erceldoune's presence in Capri. On the contrary, admirably though he had veiled them, passions fiercer than the Greek's had lightened in him with the intelligence: the delicate colourlessness of his face flushed with a faint hot hue, his blue smiling eyes gleamed like steel, he set his teeth with a snarl like a greyhound's.

"She loves him, or she will love him;—how soft her eyes grew for him in the East! There is no assassinating him—only fools kill. There is no challenging him—that is long out of date, and, besides, he is as good a shot as any of us, or better. There is no ruining him—his fortunes are ruined already, and he is too world-wise to attempt any lies to her with a chance of success. If she choose to allow his love, who can prevent that?—Conrad cannot exert his title while the Moldavian affair hangs over his head. There is only one chance;—if he be such a fool as to take his passion seriously, if he be ignorant of her history, and give her headlong faith. But that is such a hazard!—he is in love with her beauty, what would he care though one proved to him that she were vile as Messalina? Ah, Idalia! *bellissima* Idalia! you are haughty as a queen, and beautiful as a goddess, and dangerous as a velvet-voiced cardinal, and brightly keen as the wisest statesman, but———"

And while these thoughts strayed through his mind, he thrust the knife he held up to its haft in a pomegranate amongst the citrons; and while the red juice welled out, and the purple pulp seemed to shrink as though wounded, he plunged the blade, down and down, again and again, into the heart of the fruit, as though the action were a relief to him, as though the stab to the pomegranate were an allegory.

Yet with it a nobler feeling, a melancholy that was for the moment too deep to be able to replace regret by retaliation, came on him.

"She could have made me what she would!" he thought. "I could have won a throne for *her*. Greece swings in the air for any bold hand to seize; a turn of the wheel, and Hungary may be thrown in the lottery; free Venetia, and she would give the sceptre to her deliverer. Such things have been; they will be again. Valerian was a common soldier, Themistocles was a bastard, Bonaparte an artillery officer—what has been may be again. They were once far farther off power than I. For myself, I could do all that is possible—with her, I would do the *impossible!*"

A smile crossed his face at the dreaming wildness of his own thoughts; his profound acumen could never so wholly desert him that he could be the prey to any emotion without some sense of ridicule and disdain even for himself; but there was more of pain at his heart than of self-contempt; he felt, even amidst the jealous bitterness that was turning his love into hatred, that he should have become a better and a truer man had Idalia returned his passion.

"I dream like a boy, or a madman!" he thought, while his hand crushed with a fierce gesture an odorous crown of orange-flowers, and flung the bruised petals out to the sea. "And yet,—with her,—I could have had force in me to make even such dreams real. If she had loved me, I would have slaved for her, dared for her, conquered for her. If she had loved me, there is nothing I would not have compassed."

Even where he stood in solitude, his lips quivered and his forehead contracted, as under some unbearable physical pain; hardly thirty years were over his head, all the maturity of life lay before him; he felt that he had the genius in him to rule men and to carve himself a memory in history; he had the ability that would have made him a supreme and triumphant statesman; he would have been this, he would not have failed to be it, had opportunity been his. As it was, he saw the portals of fame closed to him through the disadvantages of position, and the exercise of power denied to him because he had not the primary power of money. Impatient and bitter at his exile from legitimate fields he had thrown himself into bastard politics; and adventured his fate with the secret and uncertain gambling of intrigue and conspiracy.

He hated Austria, and would have schemed night and day to humble her; beyond this feeling he had as little unison as might be with his associates; for the grandeur of theoretic republicanism, for the regeneration of Italy, for the freedom of Hungary or Poland, for the advance of the high-flown quixotism of Garibaldians, or for such poetic partisanship as breathed in "Casa Guidi Windows," he had never a single throb of sympathy. But he loved the power that it seemed to him he might obtain through them; he loved the machinations that in their work he wove so wisely and so well; he foresaw what had not then come, the certain downfall of the Neapolitan Bourbons; he had the spirit of the gamester, and was happiest in the recklessness of chance; he had the ambition of a statesman, and he aspired, in the revival of nationalities and in the turmoil of new liberties, to seize the moment to advance himself to the prominence and the predominance which he coveted. Therefore he had embraced a party with which his temper had little akin, whose views his own mind disdained as chimerical, and whose cause only his thwarted ambitions induced him to embrace. As yet, though he held a great power in his hands over the lives of men whose projects and whose aspirations were all confided to his mercy, no substantial power had accrued to him; he had reaped but little, he had risked much, and his accumulated debts were very heavy. As he saw himself now—although in general, when in the full excitement of his life, the full complexity of its intrigues, he thought otherwise—he saw the truth: that in the flower of his manhood he was without a career, without a future; that with all his talents, graces, and fashion, he was no more than an adventurer; that bankruptcy, pecuniary and social, might any hour fall on him; that—stripped of the brilliance of his elegant world, and of the euphuisms of a political profession—he was neither more nor less in literal fact than a gamester, a spy, and a beggared speculator in the great hazards of European destinies. In such a mood he hated himself, he hated all he was allied with, he hated the world that he had the genius and the tact to rule, yet in which he absolutely owned not even a sum enough to save him from hopeless ruin whenever the fate that hung over him should fall. And a greater bitterness than even this came on him: for once he loved; for once he felt that greater, better, truer things might have been possible for him; for once a pang, almost as sharp as agony, seized him in dreaming of what he might have been.

For once he suffered.

Every disdainful word, every contemptuous glance, every cold rebuke, of the woman he coveted with the passion of ambition, as well as with the passion of love, seemed burned into his memory and perpetually before him. He could not even make her believe that he loved her!—that was the deadliest pang of all. Hate, cruel, fierce, remorseless, the most insatiate hate of all, the hate which springs from baffled love, wound its way into his thoughts again. Before now, he had been a cold tactician, an unscrupulous intriguer, a man who cared nothing at what cost his ends were gained, but still one who, from innate gentleness of temper and instinctive refinement of nature, had felt no sort of temptation towards grosser and darker evil; had, indeed, ridiculed it as the clumsy weapon of the ignorant and the fool; now he was in that mood when the heart of the man possessed by it cries thirstily, "Evil, be thou my good."

"I have all their cards in my hands," he thought, where he leaned, musingly flinging the buds of the gum-cistus into the water below. "A word from me— and her haughty head would lie on the stone floor of a dungeon."

The thought grew on him, strangely changing the character of his features as it worked out its serpent's

undulations through his mind. His clear and sunny eyes
grew cruel; his delicate lips hardened into a straight
acrid line; his smooth brow darkened and contracted;
this man, who had had before but the subtle, graceful
swoop, the bright, unerring keenness of the falcon, now
stooped lower, and had the merciless craft, the lust to
devour and to destroy, of the fox.

He drew out of his pocket a letter in a miniature
Italian hand; such a hand as a Machiavelli, a John de
Medici, or an Acquaviva, might have written. He
read it slowly, weighing every line, then put it back
into its resting-place, with a certain disdain and sneer
upon his face:—there was not the brain in Europe, he
thought, that could outwit his.

"Austria will bid higher than that," he mused,
"and the young wretch here will fall as Bourbons
always fell. Six months, and he will be driven out of
Naples—it would be much to be his 'Count d'Avalto'
and his 'Lord Chamberlain' *then!* Fools! do they think
such a bribe as that would take? If *I* make terms, it
shall be with the Hapsburg; they shall pay me in proportion to my hate. They know what my enmity has
meant!"

He leaned musingly over the marble parapet of his
terrace, the lines of cruelty and of craft sinking deeper
into his fair unworn face; even to him, free from all
such weaknesses as an unprofitable honour, and not
unwilling to sell his hate, as he would have sold his
intellect, for power, even to him there was something
bitter and shameful in the thought of treason—something that made him recoil from the desertion of those
who had been allied to him so long, and acceptance of
those who had so long had his deepest hatred; some-

thing that made the very silence of the Italian noon, the very melody of the Italian seas, the very cadence of a boat-song, that echoed dreamily over the waves from a distance, that only let its closing cadence, "Libertà! O Libertà!" come upon his ear, seem like a reproach to him by whom she—this Italy in chains, this Italy ruined through her own fatal dower of a too great beauty—was about to be betrayed.

There never yet was the man so hardened that he could play the part, and take the wage of an Iscariot, without this pang.

"She does it," he said, in his teeth, with a sophism that ere now he would have disdained. "She might have made me what she would; she chooses to make me——"

"A traitor," was not uttered even clearly in his thoughts; who thinks out clearly such thoughts as these to the last iota of their own damnable meaning? A shiver, too, ran through him as he recalled a risk that even his fertile statecraft could not avail to ward off from him, the step he meditated once being taken;—the risk of the stab-thrust in the back from the poinard of the "Brotherhood," which even in this day, even in the streets of polished European capitals, strikes soon or late, howsoever high they stand in a traitor's guilty purples, those who have broken the oath of those secret bonds.

Then he laughed; a smile in which the last instinct of his better nature died.

"Faugh! my good Italians shall believe that I join the White Coats to serve Venetia: my blind Viennese shall think I wear a fair face to Italy to entrap her confidence for them. It is so easy to dupe both. And *she*—Naples will suffice for that. A whisper of mine to Monsignor Giulio, and scorn, and wit, and statesmanship, and wealth, and all the cozenries of her loveliness, all the resources of her art, will avail her nothing. There, in the Vicaria, what will she do with her beauty, and her kingdom, and her lovers, and the insolence of her pride, *then?* Better have shared a crown with me!"

As his thoughts formed themselves into ruthless shape that dulled remorse, and stole swiftly and surely on the evil path which tempted him, the whole man in him changed: the gentleness of his nature grew into fierce lust, the unscrupulous subtlety of his intellect was merged into a deadly thirst for retaliation. On the woman who had scornfully repelled him he could have dealt a hundred deaths.

Yet for one moment more the love he had borne her vanquished him again, and he remembered nothing but its pain, its wrong, and its rejection; for one moment more he gave himself up to the misery, the weakness, the shame, as he held it, of this fool's idolatry;—it was the one thing alone, loathingly as he contemned it, that could have made him a better and a truer man.

His head dropped till it sank down on to his arms, that were folded on the marble ledge, and a sharp quiver like a woman's weeping shook him from head to foot.

"I would have forgiven her all—even her scorn," he thought, "if only she would have *believed* that I loved her!"

CHAPTER XV.
"Monsignore."

In one of the fairest nooks of the Bay of Naples stood a palace in the perfection of taste, from the frescoes on its walls within to the delicate harebell-like campanile, that threw its slim shaft aloft, looking towards Amalfi. Fronting the sea, a small oval-shaped pier ran out into the water, with a broad flight of steps terminating it; above this, the natural growth of the country had hung a self-woven screen of orange and myrtle boughs; a place of embarkation, or disembarkation, lonely, secure, and unlooked on by anything save lofty Anacapri far above, hanging like an eagle's nest among the clouds. In the shadow of the evening a boat stopped there, a man alighted, dismissed the rowers, and went on along the length of the little quay to an arched door of curious cinque-cento work; it was the private entrance of the *palazzetto*, which, despite the humility of the diminutive it was given, stretched up and around in wing on wing in stately architecture, and numbered ninety chambers.

He was admitted, and entered the house, lighted with a flood of light, crowded with a glittering suite of attendants of all grades, and seemingly endless in its vastness, with chamber and corridor opening out one on another in wearying succession of splendour, relieved from monotony, however, by the exquisite pieces of sculpture and of painting that studded the whole like a second Pitti. Some thirty of these corridors and reception-rooms ended in a little chamber, small at least by comparison, hung with purple velvet,

its furniture of silver and of ebony, its only painting
a superb Ecce Homo of Leonardo's, its windows narrow and lancet-shaped, the whole now illumined with
a soft amber light;—this was the sanctuary of Monsignore Villaflor.

Monsignore rose with affability—he was ever affable
—and advanced with courtly grace. Monsignore was
a handsome and portly man, with the beautiful Neapolitan eyes and the beautiful Neapolitan face; a little
losing the symmetry of his figure now, and over his
fiftieth year, but a very noble person still. He wore
the violet robes of a bishop, and on his hand sparkled
the bishop's amethyst ring. Looking at him, it was
hard to believe that the race of prince-bishops had
died out, for he was a very princely person. He was
not like St. Philip Neri, he was not like Reginald de
la Pole, he was not like Acacius, or François Xavier,
or the great martyred man who looked across to England with those sublime words—"Terram Anglicam video,
et favente Domino terram intrabo, sciens tamen certis-
simè quod mihi immineat passio"—and kept his oath,
and went. Monsignore was not like any of these; but
he was excessively like Cardinal Bembo, he was excessively like Cardinal Mazarin.

Victor Vane bowed before him with the grace of a
courtier and the reverence of a son of the Church;
with the Paris literati he was a Cartesian, with the
Germans a Spinozian, with the English men of science
a Rationalist, a Pantheist, a Monotheist, or a Darwinian,
with the Mountain an Atheist, as best suited; but with
the Monsignori he was always deferential to the Faith.
They met as those who have often met for the advancement of mutual aims, but they met also as those

who have to play a delicate game with each other, in which the cards must be studiously concealed. Both were perfect diplomatists. The game opened gracefully, courteously, cautiously, with a little trifling on either side; but they approached their respective points in it more quickly, less warily, than usual, for he who before had but played into the hands of Monsignore to betray him, now came to play into his hands with sincerity.

This was not the first by many audiences the brilliant Bishop, the favourite of the Vatican, had given to one who had been until the night before this the deadliest foe of his Church, of his king, of his projects, of his policies; for Giulio Villaflor had been duped despite all his finesses, and had believed the gentle and adroit Englishman his tool, while he was, in truth, the tool himself. Monsignore had his silken webs over Italy, and France, and Austria, and Spain; Monsignore had his secret *sbirri* of the ablest; Monsignore knew everything; was the lover of great ladies who played the spy in palaces, never gave a Benedicite without some diplomatic touch, never administered the Viaticum but what the Church was the richer for a legacy, never yet was compromised by a lie, yet never yet was driven to the vulgarity of the truth;—but even Monsignore had been trepanned by Victor Vane. The secret of the defeat was this; Giulio Villaflor loved power well, but he loved other things as well; the pleasures of the table, the scent of pure wines, and the gleam of almond eyes and snowy bosoms. His opponent had loved nothing but power; until now, for the first time, he loved a woman and loved a revenge. Hence, now for the first time, also, he played into Villaflor's hands.

A dusky red tinged the pale clear brown cheek of the Bishop, and in his eyes was the gleam that those who knew him had learned to tremble sorely at when too few were found for the dungeons of the Vicaria, or out of the crowds of Easter-day one face dared look a frank defiance at him while the Silver Trumpets sounded.

"All the revolutionists have not menaced us and braved us as this one woman has done!" he muttered. "All the rebels of Sardinia and Sicily have not the danger in them that Idalia has. The man is bad enough, but she—"

"Conrad can be bought," put in Vane, gently; there was, indeed, an overstrained quietude in his face and in his tone. "Name the price your Grace will give; I will purchase him for you to-morrow."

Monsignore bent his head with a slight smile.

"Promise what you will, I can confide perfectly in your discretion!" he said, with his suave dignity of grace; he reserved to himself the right to refuse ratification of the promises when the fish should be fairly baited and hooked. "*He* is but a secondary matter—can *she* be bought?"

"No!" Into the calm immutability of her betrayer's voice there glided a half sullen, half bitter, yet withal admiring savageness; he was recalling to memory the imperial disdain with which she had swept from him the night before, the indifference with which she had disregarded alike his entreaties and his threats. "What could be offered her that could eclipse what she has? She has wealth—she has dominion—she has a power wider than yours!"

The last words were almost bluntly uttered; for the

moment he felt a thrill of triumph in flinging the splendour and the influence of the woman by whom he had been rejected in the teeth of even the purples and the pomps of Eternal Rome.

The dusky red glowed slightly brighter in Monsignore's cheek, a flush of anger; he waved his delicate white hand with an expressive action.

"While they last! But if she had choice between retaining these—under *our* pleasure—and losing them—say in the casemates of the Capuano yonder; what then, my son? She would yield?"

"She would never yield."

He answered calmly, still with that restrained and impassive serenity on him; by the tone, he said as though he had spoken it that no menace, no pang, no death, would make Idalia what he was now—a renegade.

"*Altro!* she is a woman?" said Monsignore, with the mockery of the Neapolitan laugh in the protrusion of his handsome under lip.

"We waste words, Monsignore," said Victor Vane, abruptly. "She is not like other women."

"Contumacious! Then she must feel the arm of the Church." The words were spoken without any ruffle of that silken and unctuous tone in which Giulio Villaflor whispered softest trifles in the ear of Austrian and Parisian beauty, but in the lustrous eyes gleamed a glance cold as ice, fierce as lust, dangerous as steel. "My son, tell us all that you know once more."

"All that I know!" There was a smile that flickered across his features one moment, though it passed too instantaneously for it to be even caught by

Villaflor. "That would take hours. I can give you heads, and bring you proofs as you require them. I know that she arranged the escape of the two Ronaldeschi from the galleys. I know that she has effected the flight of Carradino from his prison; I know that through her twenty thousand muskets will find their way to Poland, and the same into Tuscany, by routes that all your *sbirri* will never discover; I know that it was at her salons in Paris that the war of Sicily was first organised; I know that she is the life, the soul, the core, the prophetess of every national movement. I know that she holds the threads of every insurrectionary movement from the Apennines to the Caucasus—"

Monsignore made a slight gesture of impatience; while shading his eyes with the hand on which the episcopal amethyst glittered, he narrowly watched the immutable countenance of his companion.

"We know all these, and much more," he said, with an accent of disappointed irritation. "If we can once secure her person, we have witness enough against her to consign her twenty times over to the *peine forte et dure*, to the prison, or the convent cell, for her lifetime. Idalia!—she is Satanas!—you have more to tell than these stories, *figlio mio?*"

"Or I would not have wearied your Grace tonight," assented Vane, still with that calm and undeviating air as of one who, having learnt a recitation by heart, mechanically, yet unwaveringly, repeats it out. "Yes, I know more; I know that she is—here."

"*Here!*"

Despite the perfect self-command and the trained immobility of the courtly Churchman, surprise and exultation for once escaped him, uncontrolled and unconcealed; his eyes lightened, his hand grasped the ivory and ebon elbow of his state chair, his lips moved rapidly.

"Here! She has the daring of a Cæsar!"

And there was in the words an accent of compelled admiration that was, perhaps, from such an antagonist as this great Priest of Rome, the highest homage that Idalia had ever yet extorted; for it was homage wrung out in unwilling veneration from the hatred and the cunning of an implacable foe.

Vane started, as though stung, and turned his face towards the grand dark canvas of the Ecce Homo, away from the fall of the light. When the astute Churchman, who had been his own hated enemy and duped tool so long, and whom he now used as the weapon of his vengeance—when the haughty Catholic, who pursued her with the rancour of his creed, and with the unpardoning bitterness of a mighty and unscrupulous priesthood against those who dare to defy and to disdain it—when, from the unwilling admiration of Giulio Villaflor, this tribute was wrung to the lofty and unconquerable courage of the woman whom he had come hither to betray into the unsparing hands of her foes, he—the traitor—felt for one moment sunk into depths of shame; felt for one moment the full depravity and vileness of that abyss into which thwarted ambition and covetous revenge had drawn him.

Yet if he would have repented and retracted, he could not; and would not have done so if he could. The word was spoken; he had delivered her over into the power of her adversaries, had delivered over her beautiful neck to the brand, her proud head to the cord, her wealth to the coffers of the Bourbon, her loveliness to the mercy of Rome, her life to the hell of the Dungeon. It was done; and still as he turned to the dark shadow of the Leonardo with that loathing of the light which murderers feel when every ray that touches them seems to them as though seeking out their crime, he would not have undone it if he could. For he had loved her, and now hated her with a great insatiate hate; so near these passions lie together.

"Here!" echoed Villaflor once more, while his large eyes lighted with the fire of the tiger, though that fire was subdued under the droop of his velvet lashes. "In Naples! And I not to know it?"

In that single sentence was told a terrible reckoning that waited for those of his people—of his spies—who had been thus treacherous; or for the carelessness which had withheld from him the near presence of the woman whom he had watched, waited, plotted, bribed, schemed to entrap with all the intricacies and resources of his astute intellect and far-spread meshes, for so long.

"In Capri—and without disguise," answered Vane, turning his head from a seemingly negligent glance at the Leonardo; his eyes were quite clear, his countenance quite frank, his smile gentle and delicately satirical as usual. He was now attuned to his part again, and the evil in him gaining the sole mastery upon him, made him take a Borgian pleasure in thus preparing drop on drop, with the precision and the genius of science, the poison that was to consume and wither the brilliant life of the woman he had vainly loved. "Remember!

first, she is unaware that you know all your Grace could alone have known through me—she is unaware that there are any proofs against her in the possession of the Neapolitan Court; secondly, she is one to whom the meaning of fear and submission is unknown; she claims the Greek blood of Artemisia—she has Artemisian daring; thirdly, she has so attached the Marinari to her, that, good subjects and brainless beasts though these Capriotes be, she could scarce be touched on their shore with impunity; fourthly and chiefly, so many swords would leap out of their scabbards for Idalia, despite the many dead men who have, dying, cursed her, so world-wide and so well known is the dominion of her beauty, that I believe she thinks that none of the governments dare touch her. She relies on this: that Sicily is in revolt, Naples in ferment; one public act, such as these poor, blind, contumacious mules call tyranny, done to a woman whose loveliness could excite the populace, and whose genius could command it like Idalia's, and the crisis which is, as even you confess, often so near, might come, despite you and the Palace, with a thunder you could not still by the thunder of the Vatican, Holy Father."

There was a bitter irony hidden under the gentle courtliness of the words, and of the apologetic softness of the smile with which they were uttered. He had been a foe and a traitor to Giulio Villaflor so long, that he could not at once abandon the refined pleasure of thrusting silken taunts against that silken Churchman. The words lashed the passions of the Neapolitan as was purposed; that dusky scarlet glow came again into his cheek; his nostrils dilated, his fine lips quivered haughtily; for the instant he lost the unctuousness of the Palace Priest, and had the grand arrogance of a Wolsey, a Richelieu, or a Granvella.

He moved as though to rise from his ivory chair— as though to go into the van of combat for the Church and for the Nobles, like the warrior-bishops of the past.

"Do you think I fear the people!—a beast that crouches to the whip, and kicks the fallen, that cringes when its paunch is empty, and bullies when it is bold with a full feed! *I* fear the people! By the Mother of God, I would teach them such obedience that they should never breathe, but by my will!"

For the moment there flashed out the old spirit of the Colonna and the Este in the unusual outbreak of proud passion; arrogant, cruel, and iron though the words were, Giulio Villaflor, as he spoke them, was a grander and a better man, because a truer and a bolder, than in the velvet sweetness, the courtly maskings of his palatial sanctities, of his episcopal voluptuousness, of his blending of courtier, statesman, saint, and roué. He who heard, smiled that delicate smile that meant a malice and an irony so infinite, yet never betrayed this unless it were desired to be betrayed.

"Then," he asked, softly, "you would dare arrest her in Capri?"

The eyes of Monsignore flashed upon him.

"*Dare* is not a word to use to Rome!"

It was the haughty defiance and self-deification of the Pontifical Power roused, as it had roused of old against Emperors and Kings, rebels in the Cloisters and rebels in the Courts, against the sceptre of Barbarossa as against the science of Abélard, of the Power which refuses to see that this day is not as that, which

denies that the dawn has shone because its fiat has
gone forth for darkness to endure.

"Your Grace cannot think that I used the word
save as suggestive of what is expedient. Your object
is to make the Countess Vassalis a political prisoner.
Is it advisable to allow her the halo of political martyrdom? Do you wish to give the enemies of the
Church and King the power to compare you to a second
Cyril, and her to a second Hypatia?"

Giulio Villaflor smiled a very expressive, a very
devilish smile, mellow though it was.

"No. I have no desire to deify another Greek
courtesan."

Was the word as foul slander to the living Athenian
as it was to the dead Alexandrian?

His smile was answered in his listener's eyes; in
that instant Victor almost forgave him the animosities
of lengthened years, in that instant almost loved him
and admired him; their natures were so kindred, they
could stab so well with the same weapon.

"Precisely!" he said, with that persuasive tact
which, never save once, under the contempt of Idalia,
had deserted him. "Then pardon me, Monsignore; but
will it not be well to conduct this matter with as little
publicity as may be? Where there is danger for her,
there will she remain; I know what she is. She has
all the finesse of a Greek, but she has none of a Greek's
cowardice. Moreover, it is to secure Viana that she is
here (we will come to his affair afterwards); he is all
but gained to her, and he is rash and reckless to fool-
hardiness. At his villa of Antina, in the interior, there
is, the day after to-morrow, a reunion of the 'Alpe al
Mar' confederates, and, under cover of a masquerade,

its political purpose has been kept strictly secret. Had even you not known of it through me, you would never have heard of it in any other light than as one of Carlo's splendid eccentricities and extravagant entertainments. There is a password which, also, but through me, your Grace's choicest experts would not have been able to surprise. Ah, Monsignore, there is mine under mine; government spies are too often content to believe that when they have explored the topmost one they know all! There, at Antina, will be the Countess Vassalis, and not she alone: Caffradali, Aldino, Villari, Laldeschi, all the Neapolitans who are written in your Livre Rouge will meet. You may strike a great stroke at one blow; by day-dawn Viana and his glittering maskers may fill the Castel Capuano, if you will. Ask for what proofs against them you choose, you can have sufficient to justify the galleys for life against one and all of them; out of their own words shall you convict them, and, once yours, how shall this lawless Empress, this queenly Democrat, this patrician with the Marseillaise on her lips, this liberator with the pride of all the Empires in her heart, ever escape again to mine your thrones with her arts, to sap your creeds with her ironies, to arm your enemies with her riches, to overthrow your policies with her genius, to dare, to mock, to scheme, to revolutionise, to rule—to be, in one word, Idalia? Where will her power be when the same fetters as Poerio's hang on her wrists, where her loveliness when day and night the skies alone look on it from a chink in a dungeon wall, where her triumphs and her victories when the felon's branding-iron eats its hot road into her breast? She will be dead—as dead as in her grave."

The persuasive eloquence with which nature had endowed him left his tongue with a silken stealing sound, like the gliding movement of some serpentine thing, made more ornate in its eloquence by the richness of the Italian words he used. But there was beneath it the hiss of hatred, the ravenous thirst of desired vengeance, the lust that painted to itself her doom, and gloated on its own pictures with a hellish pleasure.

Giulio Villaflor caught that accent, and thought, with his acute trained wisdom:

"He has loved her—he will be true to us, then. There is no hate so sure-footed and so relentless as *that* hate."

"*Figlio mio*," he said, with his mellowest smile, resting his glance so cruel yet so caressing on the man who henceforward would be no longer his master, but his instrument, once having let him glean his secret, "you should have been in our Church; you have an orator's powers. How many souls you would have won!"

"Pardon me, your Eminence! it is more amusing work, more to my taste at least—to lose them."

Monsignore smiled a gentle reproof.

"'Your Eminence!' You give me too high a title, my son."

"Forgive me a mistake the world will soon ratify! I only anticipate the future by a month or two."

Giulio Villaflor was flattered; courted though he was, he was not above the bait to his vanity and his ambition. The Cardinal's hat was the goal of his daring yet wary desires, and in his own mind he foresaw himself soon or late a second Leo X; Pontifex Maximus in all the ancient power of the Papal tiara.

He let his eyes rest for a long moment on those of his companion; they were the deep, soft, full Italian eyes, like the brown, gentle, luminous eyes of the oxen of the Apennines; they could be tender in love as those of Venus Pandemos, they could be spiritual in religion as those of Leonardo's John, but also, they could be impenetrable as those of Talleyrand, they could be piercing in meaning and in discovery as those of Aquaviva, when, instead of the smile of the lover, or the benignity of the priest, he wore the mask of the diplomatist and politician.

"We understand each other, *figlio mio?*" he said, gently, while the violet gem of the episcopal ring glittered like the glance of a basilisk.

"We do."

They understood each other: and thus silently, while the aromatic light shone on the Vinci Passion, and without the melody of the waters beat sweet measure against the swaying orange-boughs, the seal was set to the unholy barter that betrayed a woman, and played the Iscariot to Liberty.

CHAPTER XVI.
"A Temple not made with Hands."

THE day on which Conrad Phaulcon left her was just in the mellow heat of noon, yet not oppressive where the great overhanging rocks with drooping masses of entwined foliage shut out the sun; and where in the privacy of her villa gardens Idalia came, leaving her prosecutor to his half triumphant and half mortified solitude.

Alone, she sank down on the stone bench that overlooked the sea, while the hound Sulla was couched at her feet; alone, a profound weariness and dejection broke down the pride which had never drooped before her foe, while a passionate hatred quivered over the fairness of her face.

"Oh God!" she said, half aloud in the unconscious utterance of her thoughts, "and I once believed in that man as simple women believe in their religion! Fool —fool—fool! And yet I was so young then; how could I know that I worked for myself?—how could I know what depths of vileness were in him?"

The dog before her, lying like a lion at rest, with his muzzle down, lifted his head with a loud bay of wrath, and a snarling growl of menace and defiance: he heard the footsteps of Count Conrad passing downward on the other side of the villa towards the beach, and he hated him with all a hound's unforgiving intensity; once, months before, Phaulcon had been so incautious, in a fit of passion, as to strike the stately Servian monarch, and, but for Idalia, would have been torn in pieces for the indignity. Sulla had never pardoned it.

His mistress laid her hand upon his neck, and her teeth set slightly, while her splendid head was lifted with a haughty action that followed the colour of her thoughts.

"Let him be, Sulla. The man who is *false* is beneath rebuke or revenge!"

And to those who should have known her rightly that proud contempt would have been more than any vengeance she could have given. She sat there many moments—moments that rolled on till they grew more than hours; her eyes watching the boats that passed and repassed below in the Capriote waters, her thoughts far from the scene around her. Her life had been changeful, varied, spent in many countries, and conversant with many things; its memories were as numerous as the sands, but what was written on them was not to be effaced as it could be effaced on the shore. The reverse of Eugénie de Guerin, who was "always hoping to live, and never lived," she had lived only too much, only too vividly. She had had pleasure in it, power in it, triumph in it; but now the perfume and the effervescence of the wine were much evaporated, and there was bitterness in the cup, and a canker in the roses that had crowned its brim. For—— she was not free.

Like the Palmyran queen she felt the fetters underneath the purples, and the jewelled links of gold she wore were symbols of captivity; moreover, conscience had wakened in her, and would not sleep.

She rose at last; she knew many would visit her during the day, and she was, besides, no lover of idle dreams or futile regrets; brilliant as Aspasia, and classically cultured as Héloise, she was not a woman to let her hours drift on in inaction or in fruitless reverie; no days were long for her even now that she rebelled against the tenor and the purpose of her life.

With the hound beside her she left the cliff, and moved slowly, for the heat was at its height, backward towards her house; a step rapidly crushed the cyclomen, the leaves were swept quickly aside, and in her path stood Erceldoune. The meeting was sudden to both. It was impossible that either could for the moment have any memory save that of the words with which they had so lately parted; over the bronze of his face the blood flushed hotly, from the fairness of hers it faded; she paused, and for the moment her worldly grace forsook her. She stood silent while he bowed before her.

"Madame, I had your promise that you would receive me; not, I hope, in vain?"

The words were slight, were ceremonious; she had forbidden him all others; but in his voice were the feverish entreaty, the idolatrous slavery to her, which, repressed in speech, were so intense in his own heart.

"I do not break my promises," she said, gently; "and—and you will not do so either. Are you staying in Capri, that you are here so early?"

His eyes looked into hers with a mute, imploring suffering that touched her more deeply than any words could have done.

"While I have strength to keep my word, I will. I cannot say my strength will endure long—you put it to a hard test. How hard, God only knows!"

She stood silent a moment; then she moved on with a negligent dignity.

"Pardon me—I put it to no test. I but told you the terms on which our friendship can continue. I told you, too, that it were better ended at once. I say so now."

There was far more of melancholy than of coldness in the answer, chill though it might be. One long step brought him to her side as she passed onward, and his voice was low in her ear.

"We said enough of that last night! I will keep my word while I may; till I break it, I claim yours. Make my misery if you must, but let me cheat myself out of it one little hour more."

She turned her head slightly; and he saw that unpitying though her words were, her eyes were humid.

"If I could spare you any pain, I would!—believe me, believe that at least," she said, with an intonation that was almost passionate, almost appealing; she could not have this man, whose life she had rescued from the grave, and over whose agony she had watched in the Carpathian solitudes, think that she could wanton with his wretchedness, or be careless of his sorrow.

"Then—do what else you will with my life, but do not bid me leave you?"

She was silent, and she shook her head with a gesture of dissent; she knew that he prepared himself but added pain, but more enduring suffering, the longer he deceived himself with the thought or the simulation of happiness. Yet, she asked herself, bitterly, why was she bound to send him from her as though she were plague-stricken?—why, since it was his will to linger in her presence, should she be compelled to drive him out of it?

Her honour, her pity, her conscience, her reason said—why delude him with a passing and treacherous hour of hope? Her heart pleaded for him—perhaps pleaded for herself;—her mood changed swiftly, though her character never; a natural nonchalance was combined in her with the dignity and depth of her nature. She was at all times too epicurean not to let life take its course, and heed but little of the morrow.

She gave a half-impatient, half-weary sigh.

"Well! be it so, if you will; for to-day, at the least," she said, with the accent of one who throws thought away, and resigns the reins to chance. "You stay in Capri? Have you breakfasted?"

"I thank you, yes; in a fishing-hut on the beach yonder."

"That must have been but a poor meal. I know what Capriote fare is—some smoked tunny and some dried onions! Come within."

He obeyed her, and forgot all else in the charm of that sweet present hour.

She had repulsed his love; she would have done so again had it been uttered; she had told herself that this man's gallant life must not be cheated into union with hers, this fearless heart must not be broken beneath her foot; though she should have spared no other, she vowed to spare him, over whose perils she had watched while her hand held the living water to his dying lips. In what she now did, therefore, she erred greatly; but it was very hard for her not to err. She was used to reign, and was accustomed to follow her own pleasure, answering to none; she had known the world till she was satiated with it; she was in this moment utterly weary of her associates, weary almost of herself. There was a certain repose, a certain lulling peace, in the chivalrous and ennobling adoration she received from Erceldoune. She knew him to be a high-spirited gentleman, candid to a fault, loyal to rashness; with brave lion's blood in his veins and a noble knightly faith in his love; beyond all cowardice of suspicion, and true unto death to his word. It was as strange to her, as it was sweet, to find such a nature as this; stranger and sweeter than any can know who have not also known life as she knew it—it was like a sweep of free, fresh, sea-scented Apennine air, stirred by the bold west wind, after the heat, the press, the bon-mots, the equivokes, and the gas-glitter of a Florentine Veglione.

It is difficult for any who survey mankind deeply and widely, to retain their belief in the existence of an honest man; but if they meet one, they value him far more than they who affect to imagine honesty as natural amongst men as beards.

The hock, the chocolate, the fish, the fruit, were scarce tasted as he took them that morning: he knew nothing but the shaded repose of the quiet chamber, the dream-like enchantment of the hour, the form before him, where through the green tracery of the climbing vine, the golden sun fell across her brow and at her feet. He was almost silent; his love had a great humility, and made it seem to him hopeless that his hand could ever have title even to wander among the richness of her hair.

To have right to win her lips to close on his, it seemed to him that a man should have done such great and glorious things as should have made his life—

> A tale of high and passionate thoughts,
> To their own music chanted.

The full heat of the noon was just passed, the bells of afternoon vespers were sounding from a little campanile that rose above a jumbled mass of rock and foliage, grey jutting wall, and pale green olive woods; through a break in the foliage the precipitous road was just seen, and a group of weather-browned peasant women, with the silver *spadella* in their hair, going upward to the chapel of S. Maria del Mare. Idalia rose, and followed them with her eyes. In an unformed wish, born of weary impatience, she almost envied them their mule-like round of life, their simple, dogged, childish faith, their nurtured indifference alike to pleasure and to pain.

"That animal life is to be envied, perhaps?" she said, rather to herself than to him. "Their pride is centred in a silver hair-pin; their conscience is committed to a priest; their credulity is contented with tradition; their days are all the same, from the rising of one sun to another; they do not love, they do not hate; they are like the ass that they drive, follow one patient routine, and only take care for their food;—perhaps they are to be envied!"

He rose, too, and came beside her.

"Do not belie yourself! *You* would be the last to say so. You would not lose 'those thoughts that wander through eternity,' to gain in exchange the peace from ignorance of the peasant or the dullard?"

She turned her face to him, with its most beautiful smile on her lips and in her eyes.

"No, I would not: you are right. Better to know the secrets of the gods, even though with pain, than to lead the dull, brute life, though painless. It is only in our dark hours that we would sell our souls for a dreamless ease."

"Dark hours! *You* should not know them. Ah, if you would but trust me with some confidence—if there were but some way in which I could serve you——"

Her eyes met his with gratitude, even while she gave him a gesture of silence. She thought how little could the bold, straight stroke of this man's frank chivalry cut through the innumerable and intricate chains that entangled her own life. The knightly Excalibur could do nothing to sever the filmy but insoluble meshes of secret intrigues.

"It is a Saint's day: I had forgotten it!" she said, to turn his words from herself, while the bell of the campanile still swung through the air. "I am a pagan, you see—I do not fancy that you care much for creeds yourself?"

"Creeds? I wish there were no such word. It has only been a rallying-cry for war—an excuse for the bigot to burn his neighbour!"

"No. Long ago, under the Andes, Nezahualcoytl held the same faith that Socrates had vainly taught in the Agora; and Zengis Khan knew the truth of theism like Plato; yet the world has never generally learnt it! It is the religion of nature—of reason. But the faith is too simple and too sublime for the multitude. The mass of minds needs a religion of mythus, legend, symbolism, and fear. What is impalpable, escapes it; and it must give an outward and visible shape to its belief, as it gives in its art a human form to its deity. Come, since we agree in our creed, I will take you to my temple—a temple not made with hands!"

She smiled on him as she spoke, and a dizzy sweetness filled his life. He did not ask if she had forgotten her words of the past night—he did not ask whether in this lull of dreamy joy and passionate hope there might be but a keener deadliness of disappointment. He was with her; that sufficed. She went with him out into the brightness of the day, down the rocky paths, under shining walls of glossy ilex-leaves and drooping orange clusters of scented blossom. In the fair wild beauty of Capri,—the tranquillity unbroken except by the lapping of the waves far down below and the distant echo of some sea-song, the sunlight that flooded land and water, the shadows sleeping lazily here and there where the lemon and citron boughs were netted into closest luxuriance,—the world seemed formed for love alone.

Since she had bidden his passion die in silence, why did she let him linger here?

He did not ask; he only gave himself to the magic of the present hour, to the sound of her voice as it thrilled in his ear, to the touch of her hair as he lifted from it some low hanging orange branch, to the sorcery of her presence.

The cool sea lay, a serene world of waters, scarcely ruffled by a breeze, and glancing with all the marvellous brilliance of colouring that northern air never can know. The boat waited in a creek, floating there under so dark a shadow from the drooping boughs of lemon and acacia, that it was almost in twilight: a few strokes of the oars, and it swept out of the brown ripples, flinging up their surf against the rocks, into the deep blue of the sunlit bay; below, above, around on every side, colour in all its glory, all its variety, all its harmony and contrast, melting into one paradise in the warmth of the summer day.

"I love the sea more dearly than any land. It is incarnate freedom!" she said, rather to herself than him, as she leant slightly over the boat, filling her hand with the water, till its drops sparkled like the sapphires in her rings. There was a certain aching tone in her words that sent a pang to his heart: it was the envy of freedom. Was she not, then, free?

"That is the charm my own moors have—the

mere sense of liberty they give. Barren though they be, if you were to see them ——"

His voice was unsteady over the last sentence. He thought of the dead glories of his race, of the squandered wealth and the fallen power that once would have been his by right; his to lay at her feet, his to make his fortunes equal with his name.

"You love liberty?" she said, suddenly, almost abruptly, save that all in her was too exquisitely harmonised, too full of languor and repose ever to become abrupt. "Tell me, would you not think *any* sin justified to obtain it?"

"Justified?"

"Yes, justified!" she said, impatiently, while her eyes flashed on him under their drooped lids. "What! do you know the world so well, and yet do not know that there have been crimes before now glorious as the morning, and virtues base as the selfish chillness that they sprang from? What was Corday's crime—what was Robespierre's virtue? Answer me. Would you think it justified, or not?"

A flush rose over his face; he thought, he felt, that it was of her own liberty she spoke.

"Do not ask me!" he said, hurriedly. "You would make me a sophist in *your* cause. Evil is never justified, though done that good may come; but to serve you, to succour you, I fear that I should scorn no sin, nor turn from any!"

The words were almost wild, but they were terribly true. Though perhaps the less likely thus to fall because he knew his own weakness, he felt that the inflexible justice, the honesty of purpose, the unerring loyalty to knightly creeds, which were so ingrained in him that they were scarce so much principle as instinct, might reel, and break, and be forgotten if once this woman whispered:—

"Sin—and sin for me!"

He thought he could deny her nothing—not even his sole heritage of honour—if she could bend to woo it from him. A look of pain passed for one moment over her face. She thought of him as he had lain in his extremity, while her hand had swept back the dark luxuriance of his hair, and his eyes had looked upward into hers without sense or sight. Was it possible that she had saved him then only to deal him worse hereafter? She shook the sea-drops from her hand with a certain imperious, impatient movement, and replied to him with the haughty negligence of her occasional manner.

"I asked you an impersonal question—no more; and if you cannot frame a sophism contentedly, you are terribly behind your age. We have rhetoric that proves fratricide only a *droit d'aînesse*, and logic that demonstrates a lie the natural right of man!"

He answered her nothing. She saw a look come on his face mortified, wounded, incredulous. There was something in her words, and in the accent of their utterance, that seemed to chill him to the bone, and freeze his very heart. The stately simplicity of his own character could not follow the manifold phases of hers. Moreover, he had spoken in the fervour of passion: she had answered him with what, if it were not half scorn, half cruelty, trenched close on both.

A certain pitying light glowed in her eyes as they read this, the languid and ironic smile passed from her lips, she sighed slightly, though it was half with a laugh that she spoke:

"Caro es, non Angelus."

Do you not remember the old Latin line? Be sure that you may say it to any human life you meet; above all, to a woman's! There is no angel amongst us; some faint rays of purer light here and there; that is the uttermost, and that so often darkened! I will give you the surest guard against the calamity of disappointment. Learn to say, and realise, of all you fancy fairest or noblest, this only—'*Non Angelus.*'"

He looked at her wistfully still; the temper of the man had too much directness, too much singleness, to be able to divine the veiled meanings of her varying words, the seductive changes of her altered tones: he only knew that he felt for her what he had felt for no other woman.

"Non Angelus?" he repeated. "Well!—might I not also be answered with its companion line, 'Homo es, non es Deus?' I am no sophist; you have reproached me with it. Sophism is to me the shameful refuge of cowards who dare not own themselves criminals; but—but—even while I condemned what I loved, my love would not change; though she erred, *I* would not forsake her. 'Non Angelus?' What knell to love is there there? It is but to admit a common bond of weakness and mortality."

His voice was low and unsteady as he spoke, but it had a great sweetness in it; the love he was forbidden to declare for her he uttered to her in them.

She stooped and leant her hand over the side again, toying with the coolness of the water. His words had touched her keenly, and their loyalty sank deep into her heart. She shook her head with a slight smile—a smile of great sadness, of great compassion.

"You will be still in error! While you say the 'Non Angelus,' in *your* meaning, you will still expect more divinity than you will ever find on earth. It is, not that we are not angels—that only idiots dream—it is that we are—"

"What?"

"Worse than the worst of men too often! Hush! we will talk no more. We shall soon be near my cathedral."

She leant back in silence, while the vessel swept with a free, bird-like motion through the water, the boat-song of the Capriote rowers rising and falling with the even beat of their sculls, while behind them they left the rock of Capri, orange-crowned in the sunlight, with the soft grey hue of the olives melting down into the many-coloured sea.

A low and darkling arch fronted them—the porch of the temple,—where the broad bay lay coolest and darkest, and the waters deepened into deeper blue. They bowed their heads; the boat shot down into the gloom, passing under the narrow passage-way, close and contracted as a cell; then out of its darkness the skiff glided, without sound, into the silent and azure vault of the cathedral to which she brought him.

It was the Grotto Azzuro.

The sea lay calm as a lake beneath, the blue and misty light poured through the silence, the Gothic aisles of rock rose arch upon arch in awful beauty; there was no echo but of the melody of the waves chanting ever their own eternal hymn in a temple not built of men. It was beautiful, terrible, divine in its majesty, awful in its serenity, appalling yet godlike in its calm; while through the stillness swept the ebb and flow of the sea, and all the sunless shadow was steeped in that deep, ethereal unearthlike, azure mist which has no likeness in all the wide width of the world. The boat rested there, alone; and high above the arched rocks rose, closing in on every side, like the roof of a twilight chancel, lost in vague and limitless immensity; while through the calm there echoed only one grand and mournful Kyrie Eleison—chanted by the choir of waves. Perfect stillness,—perfect peace, —filled only with that low and murmuring voice of many waters; a beauty not of land, not of sea, sublime and spiritual as that marvellous and azure light that seemed to still and change all hue, all pulse of life itself; a sepulchre and yet a paradise; where the world was dead, but the spirit of God moved on the waters.

Passion was stilled here; love was silenced; the chastened solemnity, the purity of its mysterious divinity, had no affinity with the fevered dreams and sensuous sweetness of mortal desires. The warm poetic voluptuous light and colour of the land that they had left were the associates of passion; here it was hushed, and cast back in mute and nameless pain on its own knowledge of its own mortality; here there were rather felt "the pain of finite hearts that yearn" for things dreamt of and never found; the vagueness of far-reaching futile Promethean thirst; the impulse, and the despair, of immortality.

The boat paused in the midst of the still, violet, lake-like water. Where he lay at her feet, he looked upward to her through the ethereal light that floated round them, and seemed to sever them from earth.

"Would to God I could die now!"

The words broke unconsciously from him rather in the instinct of the moment than in conscious utterance. Her eyes met his, in them that dreamy and beautiful light that seemed to float in unshed tears. She laid her hand one moment on his forehead with a touch so soft that it was a caress.

"Hush!—for what is worth life in us there will be no death!"

And the boat swept, slowly and noiselessly, through the crystal clearness of the waters, through the cold and solemn loveliness, through the twilight of the blue sea-mists, down into the narrow darkened archway of the farther distance, and out once more into the golden splendour of the living day—even as a human life, if men's dreams be true, may pass through the twilight shadows of earth down into the darkness of the valley of death, thence only to soar onward into the glory of other worlds, the radiance of other days.

She stooped to him slightly as the vessel swept away into the breadth and brightness of the bay.

"Is not my temple nobler than those that are built by men?"

He looked upward at her with a look in his eyes that had never been there before.

"You have taught me to-day what I never learned in all the years of my life!"

And the boat passed softly, silently, out of the sea-built temples that the waves had worn, out of the stillness and solemnity of that aërial light, onward through the heavy perfumes wafted from the shore, onward to where the Syren Isles laughed in their smiling loveliness upon the waters, half of earth and half of heaven.

CHAPTER XVII.

"Cravest thou Arcady? Hold is thy Craving. I shall not content it."

The day had sunk away into evening before the boat returned; the splendour of the Capri moonlight was on sea and land, on the grey terraces of olives, with their silvery plumes of foliage, and on the green vines, clustering in the early summer over the steep stairs of rock and the stones of high monastic walls.

As they passed up the winding ascent, an old peasant, sitting watching for the boat under the orange-boughs, a nut-brown, withered Capriote woman, of full seventy years, started from the shadow in Idalia's path, and fell on her knees before her, pouring out on her gratitude and benedictions. Idalia stooped and raised her:

"Do not kneel to me, old friend. You owe me nothing."

"I owe you my children's life, my children's souls!" cried the Italian, in the patois of the bay, lifting her brown stern face all bathed in tears. "To whom should I kneel, if not to you? Day and night I prayed to S. Theresa to save them, and she never heard my words; *you* heard them. The saints in glory never had more fairness than your face, 'llustrissima;—they never had the pity of your heart, the charity of your hand. They let us pray on, pray on, and never speak; you heard and saved us."

The one she blessed raised her once more, with a gentle veneration for age in the action.

"You have thanked me too much, *madre mia;* far too much. The little any one of us can do to relieve sorrow is but such slight payment of so great a human debt. When Fanciulla is old enough to marry, tell her I will give her her silver wreath and her dower. No! no more thanks—you shame me! You, who have led so long a life of goodness, to bless *me!*"

She stooped lower still towards the old peasant, to drop some gold into her kerchief unperceived, and passed on, while the praises and prayers of the Capriote were poured out, with tears staining weather-beaten, age-worn cheeks that in youth had never known so sweet a rain of joy and peace.

"Ah!" murmured Erceldoune to her, "you cannot ask me *now* to believe you, when you say 'Non Angelus!'"

She turned her eyes on him with a sudden weary wistfulness, a sudden ironic scorn intricately commingled:

"I *do* say it. Repeat it till you believe it; it is a terrible truth. Here and there we do a little good;— save, as I saved to that poor Capriote, the life of starving infants, a legacy of grandchildren that her dead son left to drag her into the grave; children as bright as the morning, dying for want of the bread we throw away as we eat guinea peaches and two thousand-franc pine-apples!—what is the worth of it? It is a grain against a mountain—of evil!"

He looked at her with appealing pain; he felt vaguely that she, who to him was stainless as the morning, had the darkness of some remorse upon her, and yet he could neither follow the veiled intricacies of her nature, nor divest her of that divinity with which to-day yet more than ever he had clothed her. She glanced up at him and laughed.

"Do not look so grave! I never murdered any one in poisoned wines, or medicated roses; it is a good deal to say in these days of artistic slaughter! Believe me —a woman. If you rightly understand all those words say, you will never attribute me too much divinity, or ask me to oblige you with consistency. Mephistopheles always takes a woman's guise now; he has found he can change his masks so much more quickly! Will you dine with me? Dress? Oh! I will pardon your costume —it is velvet, picturesque, rather Spanish."

She motioned him to take his way into the deserted library, and went from him down the corridors of the Villa Santilla, that they had reached whilst she spoke.

Had she any love for him? He had no belief that she could have. And yet—if there were none in her heart, was it not rankest cruelty to toy with him thus? No—he could not reproach her that it was; she had bidden him over and over again leave her, she had refused to hear words of love from him, she had only acceded to his remaining near her at his own persisting prayer; there was no blame here. He had no thought that she could care in any way for his fate; the caprice of her manner, the mockery of her satire, the profound pathos that had tinged her words, the strenuous force with which she had bidden him think evil of her— these were not the ways of women to one they loved; they were the inconstancies of a heart ill at ease, of a spirit without rest and not without regret, but they were not the ways of a woman who loved. And yet an agony of passion was on him; he only felt, lived, thought, breathed, for her; and the purity of the sea-temple in which he had looked upon her face in the past day shed on her its own sanctity, its own exaltation. Nothing loftier, purer, more superb, ever rose in a poet's vision of idealised love than he had incarnated in his worship of her—worship whose grandest element was faith sublime in its very blindness.

At her villa that night there were a score of guests; all men, and all unknown to him; amongst them the Italian, Carlo of Viana, whose subjugation to her sway had been so proud a triumph. Men of the world though they might be, there was not one of them, not even the brave, bright, cordial southern Prince, who could wholly conceal the surprise and the dislike, almost the offence, with which they saw a stranger; their glances ranged over him curiously in a jealous challenge, and he felt as little amity to them.

"Count Phaulcon is not here?" asked the Prince of Viana of her.

"No. I regret to have to make his apologies; he is unhappily prevented the honour of meeting your Highness," she answered him, as they passed into the dining-chamber.

"And this foreigner; has he your pass, madame?" asked Viana, softly bending his head.

"He is not one of *us*, but he is my friend."

"Your friend, madame!" said Viana, with a certain smile that Erceldoune caught, and for which, though he could hear no words accompanying it, he could have tossed the Tuscan prince into the sea sounding below the cliffs. "A fair title, truly: but one with which none, I think, ever rest content!"

Viana said no more on the subject, but Erceldoune saw that, as in Turkey, so also in this larger gathering, his presence was unwelcome, and imposed a restraint on her guests, though not apparently on her. He was a curb put on them, and they bore it with chafing impatience, deepened in many of them by a jealous, surprised intolerance of this fóreigner, with whom their hostess had entered the salons.

He himself sat in almost unbroken silence, eating little, drinking unconsciously much more than his wont. His thoughts whirled; he felt a fierce, reasonless hatred for all the men by whom he was surrounded. He saw her, through the haze of light and perfume and wine-odours and incense; he felt giddy, maddened, reckless; the fiercest jealousy was at riot in him, and the spiritual beauty of the earlier day was gone for the while from him, as it was gone from her.

He saw her now as she was in all the varied scenes of her dazzling and careless world. She took little heed of him, rarely addressed him, rarely looked at him; her silver wit, barbed and ironic, scathed all it touched; her delicate laughter rang its mocking chime at things human and divine; the diamonds on the rose hues and black laces of her costly dress glittered like the dews on a pomegranate. Her resistless coquetries enslaved whomever she would, and cast their golden net now on one and now on another; the heartlessness of a heartless code, the caprices of a world-wise imperious woman, used to be adored, and to tread the adoration at fancy beneath her foot, the recklessness of one accustomed to defy the world, and to stake great stakes on fortune, ruling her as utterly as a few hours before in the Grotto Azzuro high thoughts and noble regrets had reigned in her.

Which was truly herself of those characters so dissimilar? It would have been hard to tell. He would best have comprehended her who had judged—both. But to the man who loved her, let her be what she should, let her treat him as she would, the Protean changes in her tortured him as with so many masks that shrouded her beauty from him; the frank singleness of his nature was without key to the intricate complexity of hers. Had he seen her first and solely as she was to-night,—lying back in her chair, toying with her exotics glowing with rose and purple, touching the golden Lebanon wine or the luscious Lachryma, letting her eyes dwell with their lustrous languor now on one, now on another, and holding all those about her with a silver chain, surer than steel in its hold on them, ductile to her hand as silk,—he would have dreaded her power, he would have doubted her mercy, he would perhaps never have loved her.

Erceldoune listened to the words around him, but insensibly and uncertainly; his thoughts were on her alone; but when they reached his senses he heard the most advanced opinions of Europe, with the politics of the extreme Left, form the staple of all deeper discussion, and the basis of a thousand intricate intrigues and abortive projects that were circulated, often to be passed current with the seal of Idalia's approbation, much more often to be broken in two by some hint of later intelligence than theirs, or some satirically suggested comment languidly let fall by her on their excited warmth, like the fall of an icy spray. And yet there were moments when she was not thus, when she was more seductive in her eloquent expositions, her sudden and then impassioned earnestness, than in her nonchalance; moments when she spoke low, swiftly, brilliantly, with a picturesque oratory, persuasive, vivid, irresistible, till her guests' bold eyes glowed with admiration as they listened, and they were ready to lend themselves to her hands, to be moulded like wax at her will, without a will of their own. Then, as often, when she had roused them or wooed them to the height of the enthusiasm, the rashness, or the sacrifice she had sought to win from them, she dropped the topic as suddenly, with a languid indifference or a sarcastic jest, sinking back among her cushions, playing half wearily with the scarlet blossoms of her bouquet or the velvet ears of the hound, with hardly a sign that she remembered the presence of her numerous comrades.

Varied and glittering though the conversation that went on round him was, infectious and free as its gaiety of tone was also, marked as might seem her confidence in him to introduce him there, and intoxicating to every sense as the entertainment to which she had brought him might be, Erceldoune was wretched in it; he could comprehend nothing; he was jealous of every man at her table; everything he heard related to a party, but to which he referred, however indefinitely, his seizure in Moldavia. She scarcely looked at, rarely addressed him; in nothing, save her personal loveliness, could he recognise the woman with whom he had floated through the azure air of her sea-temple before the sun had set.

It was late when they rose from the table; cards were begun, while the windows stood open to the midnight, where the southern moon flooded the Mediterranean. Idalia threw herself into the hazard with the eagerness of a gamester; she played with the utmost recklessness, a hectic excitement shone in her eyes, the

insouciant defiance of her wit rose with the risks of
chance; she staked heavy sums, lost them, and only
played the more eagerly still. Impair her charm even
this insatiate passion could not do, distasteful though it
be in women, and even abhorrent in women who are
in their youth; as seductive she was, but there were
danger, levity, heartlessness in the charm. She was
now at her worst.

Once she glanced at the solitary form of Erceldoune
standing out against the flood of moonlight; his face
was pale and very grave, while his eyes had a pathetic
wonder, rebuke, and pain in them;—she never looked
at him again. The hours went on, and the play with
them; only broken by intervals when hookahs and cool
drinks were brought round, and the homage offered to
hazard was offered to its beautiful empress. She lost
very considerably for a while, but the more she lost the
more extravagantly she staked upon the cards; and
fortune changed, pouring in on her its successes at
length as lavishly as it had previously squandered her
gold. So the short sweet night passed away, over the
scattered hamlets that crowned the piles of rocks or
nestled in sea-grey olive-woods;—passed away in the
whirl of gambling, and the bitterness of jealous heart-
burning, and the stir of restless passions. Without,
where the waters lapped the shore so softly, and the
islands hung in the starlit air like sea-birds' nests brood-
ing above the waves, the aged, dying peacefully, dreamt
of immortality, and children slept with smiles upon
their lips under the low brown eaves of cabin roofs,
and the eyes of poets, wakeful and laden with voluptuous thoughts, dwelt, never weary, on the silent sailing clouds, warm with the flush of earliest dawn; but

here, within, there was but the fever of unworthy things.

Erceldoune, where he stood apart, glanced once or twice at that fair tranquil neglected night with an impatient sigh, as though to take relief from its balmy freshness and cool serenity amidst the glittering martyrdom of the scene before him and the tumult of passion at work in him.

In the intensity of his pain he could have believed himself like the men in the old legends whom a sorceress bewitched; it was anguish alike to stay or to go; every moment he spent there was suffering as intense as when he had lain prostrate with the vultures wheeling above his eyes in the sickly light of the sun, yet he could not tear himself from its terrible fascination any more than he could then have torn himself from the power of the carrion birds. He believed in her; yes, not less utterly than when a few hours before he had heard her lofty and spiritualised thoughts unfold all diviner things, and lead him through the dim and glorious mysteries of a poet's speculations of eternal worlds. But he felt like a man in delirium tremens, who struggles with a thousand hideous and revolting shapes, that rise again as fast as he overthrows them. The atmosphere about her, the glances that dwelt on her, the profane mocking wit that woke her laughter, the eyes that met her own in such bold language, the gaming-passion that, while it possessed at least enslaved her, all these were so much desecration and profanation to his idol, so much blasphemy against the woman who had been with him in the pure stillness of the Grotto Azzuro.

The sun above the eastward circle of the bay rose,

breaking over the sea, while the stars were still seen through its golden haze, in which they would, with another moment, die. Idalia looked at the sun, then left the gaming-table.

"There is the day rebuking us. Good-night!"

As she spoke she paused one moment, the full fresh light of the broken morning falling upon her, while around was still the wax-glare of the chandeliers; the pure light lay before her, the impure glitter was behind.

She paused one moment, looking seaward, then turned negligently to her guests and dismissed them, with much carelessness, little ceremonial.

Viana pursued her with eager whispered words; she put him aside with a coquette's amusement and a graceful gesture of denial, and passed out, while the Nubian appeared and followed her.

The Prince, with stormy petulant anger on his face, left the room with his equerry. The others went out one by one.

Erceldoune remained silent and motionless, he neither saw nor heard what passed before him; he had bowed his farewell instinctively, but all that he knew were the smiles he had seen cast on others, and the bold look with which Viana had followed her, and for which he could have struck him down as men of his race struck their foes when a back-handed sweep of a heavy iron gauntlet dashed down all rivalry, and washed out all insult. Each of her guests, as they passed out, cast a look of suppressed and envious dislike at him where he stood, as though he had a right to remain thus behind them. He noticed nothing, was conscious of nothing; an intolerable agony, a burning, boundless jealousy alone were on him. He stood there like a man stunned, looking blankly out at the sunlit sweep of waters. Evil passions were not natural to him; but the life he had led had left the free untameable strength of the old Border Chiefs unaltered in him.

He stood there with no remembrance of how little right he had to remain, scarcely any remembrance even of where he was. All at once he started and turned. As a dog feels, long before human eyes can see or human ears can hear it, the approaching presence that he loves, so he felt hers before she was near him; through the inner chambers, dark in twilight, where the lights were extinguished and the dawn could ill penetrate, Idalia returned. Her step was weary, and her face, as the illumination from the chandelier, still burning in the window where he stood, fell on it, was pale, even to the lips on which, as some poet has it, "a sigh seemed set"—unuttered.

"You have remained after the rest!—how is that? It is as well, though, as it is. I wish to speak to you —alone."

The words themselves might have fed many a wild hope, many a vain thought, in any man less single-hearted and less incapable of misconstruing her meaning than he was. With him all the light died out from his face as he heard: he knew that if she would have listened to his passion she would not have returned to him now—she would not have addressed him thus.

He bowed gravely, and stood waiting for her pleasure. The forbearance was not lost on her. Idalia, more than any other woman, could appreciate this deference which gave her untainted comprehension, this delicacy which took no advantage of her return to him in solitude. She moved on towards one of the windows, and stood there, between the grey light of the rising day and the radiance of her own card-room.

"You have offered me many pledges of your service," she said, gravely, "nor do I doubt their sincerity. I am now about to test it; not on any ground that, as you think, my past slight aid to you gives me any claim upon your life—I have none whatever—but rather simply because I trust you as a gallant gentleman, as a chivalrous nature, as a true-hearted friend."

He bent his head in silence; he offered her no protestation of his faith: he knew that none was needed.

"I am about to ask you much," she resumed. "To ask you to undertake a service of some danger, of immediate action, and of imperative secrecy; it may involve you in some peril, and it can bring you no reward. Knowing this, are you prepared to listen to it?"

His face grew a shade paler beneath its warm seabronze. He divined well what her meaning was in those few words, "it can bring you no reward." But he answered without a second's hesitation.

"Do with me what you will," he said, simply; "I am ready."

There were no asseverations, no eager vows, no ornate eloquence; but she knew better than they could tell her that he was hers, to send out to life or to death at her choice.

She put out her hand to him with royal grace to thank him as sovereigns thank their subjects. She let his lips linger on it mutely, then, with no more emotion than queens show at that act of homage, she sank into a couch, and bent slightly forward.

"Listen! I want no political controversy, but it seems to me unutterably strange that you, with your bold high spirit, your passion for liberty, your grand contempt for conventionalities and station, should have no sympathy with a party whose cause is essentially that of freedom."

He looked at her wearily. What were creeds and causes to him now?

"I am no politician," he said, briefly. "I have never mingled in those matters. I am neither a student nor a statesman. I hate tyranny. I would stamp it out wherever I saw it; but the codes of my race were always conservative. I may unconsciously have imbibed them."

She smiled with ironic disdain. He had touched the qualities in her with which she could rule men like children, and could have swayed a kingdom with the sceptre of Russian Catherine or of Maria Theresa.

"'Conservative'! To reverence the divinity of rust and of corruption—to rivet afresh the chains of tradition and of superstition—to bind the free limbs of living men in the fetters of the past—to turn blind eyes from the light, and deny to thirsty lips the waters of truth—to say to the crowned fool, 'You are God's elect,' and to the poor, 'You are beasts of burden, only not, like other beasts, worthy shelter or fodder'—to cling to falsehood, and to loathe reason;—this is what it is to be 'Conservative'! Do you, who love freedom like any son of the desert, subscribe to such a creed as that?"

Now he saw her as those saw her who were subdued to her will, till no sense was left them save to think as she thought, and to do as she bade. The magic of the voice, the charm of the eloquence, the spell of the fearless truths, uttered with an imperial command, wrought on him as they had always done on others—as they could not fail to do on any man with a heart to thrill and a soul to be moved.

"I will believe what you believe!" he cried, passionately. "*You* are my creed; I have forgotten all others."

The brilliant fire which had been upon her face as she spoke, faded.

"Too many have made me their creed;—do you take some surer light to guide you. I do not seek a convert in you. You are happier, perhaps, if you can live thinking of none of these things. What I seek of you now is your service, not your adhesion. I want little else except your high courage; and I know that will never fail either you or others."

"Try it as you will."

There was a curious conflict of feelings in him as he heard her. He was moved to strong pleasure by the mere thought that she placed confidence, of whatever sort, in him, and he knew by her words that she held his honour, his faith, and his courage in full esteem; yet as strong a pain smote him heavily. He felt that these great purposes of her life, vaguely as he could imagine them, were dearer to Idalia than any individual love could become, and he felt also that in her manner to him which seemed to place him farther off from her than he had ever been.

She bowed her head in thanks to him.

"What I need is told in few phrases," she resumed. "The Conservative faction, that you favour, is in the full exercise of its iniquity in Naples—for a little

while longer; a very little. There are to-night in my
house—concealed here, I do not shirk the word—
two of its greatest victims, an old man and a young,
father and son. The elder is as noble a patriot and
scholar as Boethius, with no other crime than his;—
he wishes the freedom of his Italy. King Francis plays
the part of Theodoric. Once arrested, the fate of Boethius will be his. Less severity, perhaps, but the gal-
lays, at best, awaits his only son, fresh from the cam-
paigns of Sicily. By intelligence I have of the government's intentions, I know they will not be safe here
three hours longer. I left my own yacht at Trieste;
besides, it could not approach Naples without being
searched, or probably brought-to by a broadside. Yours
is here; will you save these men, take them secretly on
board, and land them on the coast of Southern France?
I give you my word that they have no other sin than
one that is the darkest, perhaps, in the world's sight
—to love truth and liberty too dangerously well;—
how much they have suffered for these you will know
when I tell you that they are Paolo and Cesario Fie-
sole."

An eager light flashed into his eyes, a noble indig-
nation flushed his face; he knew the names well—the
names of men who, for the choicest virtues of the patriot's and thinker's and soldier's characters, had endured the worst persecutions of the Neapolitan Bourbons. Whatever he thought of creeds and causes, he
loathed tyranny and oppression with all his heart and
soul.

"Save them? Yes, if I lose my own life to do it."

She looked at him with a smile; how often she had

seen that lion spirit, that eagle daring, lighten in temperaments the most diverse at her bidding!

"Ah! I thought your sympathies must always rise with liberty, and your hatred with oppression, or you would have belied your whole nature. I would make you 'with us' in an hour's reasoning."

His eyes met hers with something pathetic in their wistful gaze—as though they besought her not to trifle with him.

"You never need to reason with *me*. You have only to say, 'I will it.'"

An absolute obedience this, an utter unquestioning submission, prostrate as any that ever laid Marc Antony at Cleopatra's mercy, or Héloise at Abélard's; yet he did not lose his dignity in it; it was lofty even while it was subject. It touched her, yet it pained her; it brought home to her the intensity and truth of this man's devotion; she would not, or could not, return it or repay it; she had no right, she bethought her, with a pang, to use it as she had used it with so many, to the furtherance of her own aims, however generous or just those aims might in this instance be. Moreover, she had come to say other and more bitter things to him than this.

She was silent a moment, looking at him where his gallant height rose against the clear subdued light of the breaking day; her future task was more painful than she, consummate mistress of every toil and art, and used to control every mood and every passion of men, had ever known one yet to be.

"Weigh the peril well," she said, after a pause, with something of restraint upon her. "It must be great—I mean, if you are discovered. Discovery may be guarded against, but it cannot be positively averted at all channels. If you will risk the danger of detection, your yacht can weigh anchor at once. She is, of course, in readiness? The Ficsoli, father and son, disguised as Capriote fishermen, can row you to the vessel amongst others. They are ready to take the alarm at any instant, and sleep dressed in their disguises. They will probably pass in safety; the Marinari here are dull and unsuspicious, nor would they harm what I shelter for a thousand ducats each. But, should detection occur, remember, the Bourbon government will not spare you even for your country's sake. You will have rendered yourself liable to the law for assisting the escape of condemned 'conspirators' and 'insurgents,' as the Court terms them, and you will share the fate they suffer."

The words were almost cold, but uttered with a visible effort; in the instant, even though the urgency of peril for those she sought to save, and the motive for which she bade him expose himself to this risk at her command, excused it to her, she loathed herself for sending him out to chance the slightest danger in fealty to a love that would never bring him anything except its pain. Indeed, his life was dearer to her than she, disdainful of all such weakness, yet would know.

He raised himself erect.

"I have given you my word; I am not used to weigh the hazards of any dangers that may accrue to me through keeping it."

She answered him nothing; the implicit obedience this man was ready to render her, even to the rendering up of his life or liberty at her word, moved her the more deeply beside the bold honour and the fearless independence of his carriage towards men, such as now flashed out even to her in his reply. Once again unseen by him as she leaned her brow upon her hand, there came upon her face the warmth, and in her eyes the look, with which she had gazed upon him in the previous night. It passed; she rose and stood again in the shadow of the myrtle-covered casement, looking from him out towards the sea.

"When will you be ready, then?"

"I am so now. Your friends can row me on board when you will, and the yacht can weigh anchor with them at once."

"And you take no more thought than that of perilling your life for strangers?"

"I have never taken much thought for my life that I can recollect. Besides, what need is there of thought? You wish it."

He spoke only in the singleness of his fidelity, in the earnestness of his devotion to her; but the most refined subtilty of art and purpose could not have taught him a better means to win his way towards the tenderness of Idalia's nature, and an infinite tenderness there was, let her lovers and her foes say what they would.

Her cheek lost the warmth it had regained, her face had the same sadness on it which it had worn as she had entered the chamber, the intense melancholy which now and then fell on her at rare intervals gathered in her eyes. She pitied him, she honoured him; she would willingly, at all cost to herself, have effaced every thought which bound him to her, and saved him from every pang that came to him through her; but she was too proud and too world-worn to recognise that

there might be a feeling even beyond this in her heart
for him. Even had she recognised it, it would not have
changed her purpose—the purpose which had made
her let him see her as he had done through the past
evening—the purpose to toy with him no more, but
to put from him, now and for ever, the vainness of
hopes which could but fatally beguile, only to as
fatally betray, him.

She could do this as no other woman could have
done; she had dealt with men in all the force of their
enmities, all the height of their follies, in their most
dangerous hours as in their most various moods; through
paths no other of her sex could have approached, Idalia
passed unhesitating and with impunity, and one of the
secrets of her great power lay in her perfect and unerring knowledge of human nature. With the first
hour in which she had seen the man who now stood
with her, she had known his character as profoundly
as she knew it now. She turned to him, and spoke
softly, yet with a certain grave and haughty grace.

"I do not pretend to misunderstand you; to do so
would be but to imitate the mock humility of foolish
women. You would do this thing for my sake; if
done at all, it must be done for the pure sake of justice
and compassion, not for mine. You gave me your
promise that no other words like these should pass between us, and I told you if it were broken we could
meet no longer."

He looked at her bewildered; she seemed to him to
toy with him most recklessly, it was a deadly trial to
his faith not to believe most mercilessly also.

"That promise I must break, then. It is the only

one broken in my life. My God! why do you play with me so? You *know* what my love is!"

His voice sank to a breathless fervour; he stooped forward, his lips trembling, his eyes seeking hers with an anguish of entreaty. That look almost broke down her resolve; it was so easy to soothe this man's loyal heart with a smile, with a glance; it was so hard to put an end for ever to that imploring prayer. Hard to her at least, now, when for the first time some portion of the heavy blow she had so often dealt fell on her, some scorch of the fiery pain she had so often caused touched herself, if it were but by sympathy and pity. Yet she was unmoved from her resolve; she was unflinching in a course once chosen, and she was resolute to fool him on no more with empty hope, to let him blind himself no longer. She wished to save him, as far as she could still effect this, from herself, and to do so she sacrificed his faith in her with a ruthless and unsparing hand.

"I do know it," she answered him; and her voice had no tremor in it, her face no warmth, her eyes dwelt on him with a melancholy in which no softer or weaker consciousness mingled. "And because I know it, and know its strength and its nobility, I will not dupe it or dupe you. What avail to lead you on after a mirage, to let you cheat yourself with fond delusions? Better you should know the truth at once—that what you feel for me can only bring you pain; strive against it for your manhood's sake."

He staggered slightly, and bent his head, like a man who receives a sudden sickening blow; despite the revulsion of the last few hours, it fell on him with

the greater shock after the peace and beauty of the day
they had passed together on the sea.

She looked at him, and a shadow of his own suffering fell on her; she could not strike him thus without herself being wounded—without a pang in her own heart. Yet what she had determined to do as she saw him standing aloof that night with the rack of wondering grief, of incredulous reproach upon his face, she carried out now, cost her in its loss—even to her fair fame—whatever it should.

She turned to him with a sudden impulsiveness most rare with her, and in her eyes something of the defiance with which she had fronted Conrad Phaulcon mingled with an infinitely softer and more mournful thing.

"Listen! As you have seen me to-night, *I am*. That higher, holier light you view me through is in your own eyes, not in me. Ask those whom you saw with me; they will tell you I am without mercy—believe them. They will tell you I have ruined many lives, blessed none—believe them. They will tell you you had better have died in the Carpathian woods than have fallen beneath my influence—believe them. Take the worst that you can learn, and credit it to its uttermost. Tell yourself till you score its truth into your heart, that I have never been, that I shall never be, such as you imagine me. Your love can be nothing to me; but I would save it from its worst bitterness by changing it into hate. I would not even forbid *you* to change it into scorn."

Her eyes were prouder than they had ever been as she thus bade the man, who had centred in her his purest and most exalted faith, give to her the shame of his disdain. As she spoke, with her resistless beauty touched to a yet nobler dignity as she uttered this attainder against her own life, he must have loved her less, or have believed evil swifter than the one who heard her now, who could have followed out her bidding, and stamped the warning down into his soul, till all love of her was dead.

He looked at her in silence, and in the heart-stricken pathos of that look she saw how utterly she laid life desolate for him—she felt the recoil of the living death she dealt, as now and then the hunter feels it when he meets the upward dying gaze of the stag his shot has pierced.

In that instant, while his faith was beaten down for the first moment under the scourges of her words, and the chivalrous idolatry he bore her was bent and blinded under the dead weight of her own self-accusation, the baser alloy of passion alone was on him—he was only conscious of that madness in which men are ready, as to yield themselves to an eternity of shame and torture,

"So that this woman may be mine!"

She saw that in him; she knew its force, its meaning; she knew that in this instant of his anguish her loveliness was all he felt or sought.

"No matter what you are," he muttered, breathlessly, "no matter what you bring me—I love you, O God! as no man ever, I think, loved before. Have you no pity on *that?* Be what you will, if—if—"

His voice sank, leaving the words unfinished; he felt powerless to plead with her; he felt hopeless to touch, or sway, or implore her; and also, beyond all, he could not even, on the acceptance of her own testimony, dethrone her from his stainless faith, any more than a man can at a word tear out from him as worthless a religion that he has cherished as divine through a long lifetime.

The darkest passions had no terror for her; she had known them over and over again at their worst, and had ruled them and ruled by them. But deepest pity was in her heart for him; she sought to save him, even at all sacrifice to herself, and she saw that it was too late; she knew, as his eyes burned down into hers, that, though they should part now and for ever, this longing she had wakened would consume him to his grave.

A woman weaker and more pliant would have yielded to that impulse, and have given him tenderness: to the pride and to the truth of Idalia's nature to have stooped so far had not been possible.

"Love is no word for me," she said, with calmness, underneath which a vibration of deeper feeling ran. "I am weary of it; and I have none to give. I have played with it, bribed with it, ruled by it, bought by it, worked on it, and worked through it—evilly. I cannot do that with you. I must give you suffering, I will not also give you danger. Take your promise back; I absolve you from it."

Her eyes were turned towards the sea, and not to him, as she spoke; she could not watch the misery she dealt. She knew as though she saw it the look that came upon his face — darker and deadlier than the physical anguish that had been upon it when she had found him dying in the Carpathian pass. She had stricken him strengthless; she had refused his love;

she had refused even his belief in her, even his homage to her; she had condemned herself for the evil that she wrought, and she stood aloof from him, imperial, world-weary, rich in the world's wealth, without a rival in the sovereignty of her beauty and her will. Rich himself in those accidents of power and possession which she owned, he might have pleaded still, on the ground of his wretchedness, against her fiat; but in the pride of his beggared fortunes his lips were sealed to silence; he could not force his love, having no treasure upon earth save that to give, upon the empress of those brilliant revels on which the dawn had lately broken, upon the mistress of those high ambitions which seemed alone to reach her heart; upon a woman so proud, so peerless, so throned in every luxury and every splendour as this woman was. She was not haughtier in her magnificent command than he in his ruined poverty; and in that moment he had not force, nor memory, nor consciousness left to him. He only suffered dumbly and blindly, like a dog struck cruelly by the hand he loves, the hand he would have died in striving to obey.

She looked at him once—only once—and a quick sigh ran through her. Had she saved him from the fangs of the carrion beasts and the talons of the mountain birds, merely to deal him this? Better, she thought, have left him to his fate, to perish in a nameless grave, under the eternal shelter of the watching pines! Yet she did not yield. Without a glance or sign she moved slowly away across the chamber;—their interview was over, its work was done.

His step arrested her: he moved forward with a faint slow effort, like one who staggers from the weakness of long illness.

"Send those you spoke of to me; I do not take my promise back."

She turned her eyes full on him with a sudden light of wonder, of admiration, of amaze.

"You would do that—*now?*"

"I have said—I will."

She looked at him one lingering moment longer; all that was great, and high, and fearless in her nature answering the royalty in his; then she bent her head silently.

"I thank you. Be it so."

And with those words only, she left him.

CHAPTER XVIII.
"The Light in the Dust lies Dead."

IN a distant apartment of the villa a youth lay sleeping, his richly-tinted face with the black curls falling back from the bold brow, like one of the beautiful boys who loved, and laughed, and danced, and sung in one long carnival, from sunset to sunrise, in the glad Venice of Goldoni. He slept soundly, as only youth sleeps, dressed in a Capriote fishing suit; and on his chest, as the striped shirt fell back from it, there were the scars of deep wounds just healed—no more —over the strong fearless beatings of his young heart. A little distance from him sat his father, an old man, with the grand head of a noble of Tintoretto's or Bassano's canvas—the head of the great mediæval signori who filled the porphyry palaces, and swept through the Piazza San Marco, in the red gold of glowing summer evenings, when the year of revel was held in Venice for the Foscari's accession, and the City of the Waters was in her glorious reign. The elder man was not sleeping; his eyes were on his son. He had lost three such as that sleeping boy for Italy—three trampled down under the tread of Austrian armies or of Pontifical mercenaries; the one left was the last of his name. But he would have sent out a hundred more, had he had them, to bring back the dead grandeur to Rome, to see the ancient liberties revive, and the banner of the free republic float in spring-tide air above the fresh lagoons and over the green-wreathed arches of his beloved Venezia.

They had suffered much, both of them, for liberty; but they were both willing to suffer more—the boy in the dawn of his manhood, and the elder in the weariness of his age. There was no sound in the chamber; food and wine stood near; the shutters were closed; through a small oval aperture the glowing sun in the hour of its sunrise alone penetrated, flooding the floor with seven-coloured light. From the dawn without there came a faint delicious odour of carnations, of late violets, of innumerable leaves. The door opened noiselessly; through it came Idalia. The old man started and rose, took her hand and pressed it to his lips, then stood in silence. She glanced at the sleeping youth, lying there in so profound a rest with a smile on his arched full lips.

"Poor boy!" she said, softly; "it is a cruelty to waken him. Dreams are the mercies of life. Yet there is no time to be lost. You may be saved still."

"What! your friend will serve us so well as that?" asked the Italian, wonderingly. "But it is not strange; the English are a bold people, they never refuse to resist oppression."

Over Idalia's face swept an unspoken contempt.

"The individual English, no!—but the nation would let any freedom be strangled like a hanged dog, rather than risk its trade or lose a farthing."

"But it is a great risk for him. We have no right to expose him to it."

"No; we have no right," she answered, almost bitterly. "Not a shadow of right!—still he accepts it: he does not heed peril. What brave man does?"

"For you."

The words were softly added; the old Venetian looked at her with a mournful fixity, an unuttered interrogation. She turned slightly from his gaze; she knew what was in his thoughts; she knew that he reminded her of the many who had gone out to peril, and fallen beneath it, for her sake.

"We can waste no time, caro amico," she said, rapidly, in his own liquid, caressing Venetian tongue. "The earlier you leave, the less likelihood of detection. He will wait for you on the shore; you will row him to his vessel amongst others; nothing can be simpler. You will be safe with him."

Something that was almost the weakness of tears rose in her eyes as she spoke; she thought how entirely her trust would be preserved, how surely, at risk of very life, he, whom she recompensed with cold words and bitter neglect, would redeem his promise.

Over the browned, stern, noble face of Filippo Fiesoli the warmth of his lost youth stole; a look came into his glance that only was not love because chastened by so utter a hopelessness, and purified from all touch of passion.

"Ah!" he murmured, in his snow-white beard,

"I can give you nothing, save an exile's gratitude and the blessing of an old man near his grave. You noblest among women!—what you have risked for us!"

Idalia's eyes softened with a mellow wistful tenderness, with an unspeakable regret.

"Ah, Fiesoli! if all patriots were pure, all liberators true as you are, my best friend, I would count every loss my highest, holiest gain! But there is so much dross amidst the little gold, there are such coward villanies masked under freedom's name. *I*, too, 'noblest amongst women!'—O God, sometimes I think myself the vilest."

He sighed; he knew her meaning; the grand pure heart of the old patriot would not take on itself the falsehood of flattering disguise.

"You are noblest in much," he said, softly; "something too pitiless, something too alluring, it may be, to the many who love you; but your errors are the errors of others, your nobility is your own."

She shook her head.

"Gentle sophisms and full of charity, but not true. My errors are my own, woven close in my nature and my mind; such nobility as you speak of—if I can claim it—comes rather from the recklessness of courage, the passion for liberty, the hatred of tyranny, than anything better in me. But I am not here to speak of myself; there is not an instant to be lost; wake Cesario, poor child, and then leave me. We are too used to life and partings to feel this sudden or strange; but, my dear friend, my honoured friend, peace be with you, if we never meet again."

She held out both her hands to him with a look on her face that her lovers had never seen there, so gentle,

so softened, so full of reverent sweetness. Filippo
Fiesoli stooped over them in silence, pressing them in
his own; he was an old man, very near his last years,
as he had said, but perhaps in all the homage that had
been lavished on her she had never had one heart more
nobly and more purely hers than was that of the great
age-worn patriot's. His voice was unsteady as his farewell was spoken.

"Death will take me, most likely, before I can ever
look upon your face again; but my dying breath will
be a prayer for you."

There was an infinite dignity, a sublime pathos, that
were beyond all pity in the benediction; age had set its
barrier of ice betwixt them, and the grave alone waited
for him, but the love wherewith he loved her was very
rare on earth.

Without another word he turned from her, and
awoke his son. The young soldier sprang up alert and
ready on the instant: he had often wakened thus with
the Sicilian legions. As he saw Idalia, his beautiful
Titian face flushed, his eyelids fell shyly as a girl's,
he sank before her on one knee with the old grace of
Venice, and touched the hem of her dress with his lips.
She smiled at him, an indulgent, gentle smile, such as
she would have given a caressing animal.

"There is no time to spare in courtesies, Cesario.
The moment is come. You are ready?"

The boy's lips trembled.

"A soldier is always ready, but—if you would
rather let me die near you, than send me out to
exile!"

She passed her hand lightly, half-rebukingly, over
the silk of his dark curls.

"Foolish child! you talk idly. To stay here were to be locked in the dungeons of the Capuano. Go with your father, Cesario mio; your first duty is to him, your second to Italy and to liberty."

The youth's eyes gleamed with the fire of the south and the fire of the soldier—the fire that her words could light as flame lights the resinous pinewood.

"My *first* is—to you."

She smiled on him; she knew the romantic adoration that he bore her would harm him little, might lead him far on noble roads.

"Scarcely!—but if you think so, then obey me, Cesario. Give your thought, beyond all, first to your father; give the life that remains through all trial and all temptation to Italy and to freedom."

The boy's earnest, impassioned gaze looked upward at her through a mist of tears.

"I will!" he murmured, fervently—"I will."

She drew her hand from him with a slight gesture of pain; she had seen that gaze from so many eyes, she had heard that vow taken by so many voices. Eyes that were sightless; voices now for ever stilled.

"Farewell," she said, gently, to both. "I will send my Albanian to you—he can be trusted; and you must go down alone to the shore. Give this to my friend, and he will know you. He will be in waiting."

She took from her hand one of her rings, a lapis-lazuli stone of ancient workmanship, and held it out to the elder Fiesoli; then, without longer pause, she passed from their presence. The boy Cesario flung himself down on the couch she had just risen from, and with his head bowed on his arms sobbed like a woman, he was a bold and gallant soldier, but he was but a youth; his father stood motionless, the morning sunlight, as it strayed through the oval in the casement, falling with a golden hue upon his grand bronzed brow and the white sweep of his patriarch's beard. Differently they both loved her, equally they alike knew their love hopeless.

Idalia passed on to her own apartments. These were not the first lives she had saved by many; at personal cost, personal peril; saved with courage, and daring, and fertile expedient; but they were as nothing to her in this moment beside the many more that through her had been lost. She had not yet slept or rested for a moment, but she felt no sense of fatigue, no willingness to sleep. Alone, the proud sapphire-crowned head of the coquette, the *lionne*, the sorceress, the brow that would have borne so royally the Byzantine diadem of her ancestral Comneni, drooped wearily, yet not from physical weariness; the flush upon her cheeks had faded, and her form, with its trailing rich-hued skirts, and jewels flashing in an eastern splendour, was in strange contrast with the melancholy of her attitude and of her thoughts as she stood there in solitude at last, with the dawning light of the young day shut out by draperies of falling silk, and a single Etruscan lamp only burning near.

"Now he has seen me as I am," she thought—"as I am!" A smile crossed her lips, but it was a smile more sad than tears;—there was in it so much hatred of herself. "It was but just to him. No cruelty from me would kill his love, but his own scorn may. *They* love me for my beauty, because I charm their sight and their senses, because they are fools, and I know how to make them madmen! So that a woman were lovely, they would care not how vile she might be! But he — he has the old knightly faith, the old gallant honour; he gives his heart with his passion; he must revere what he adores. He has seen me as I am to-night; the pain was deadly to him; yet, if it rend me out of his memory, he may live to be grateful for it."

The warmth of the chamber seemed stifling to her, the perfumed oil of the lamp oppressive; the room itself, with its hangings, its cabinets, its decorations, its countless bagatelles of art and wealth, of extravagance and of effeminacy, struck on her loathsomely.

"Ah! how like my life!" she thought, with an impetuous scorn. "The pure day is shut out, and all that is heated, unreal, luxurious, meretricious, worthless, is chosen instead! A diamond-studded, gas-lit, dangerous lie, instead of the sunlight of truth!"

She pushed the heavy folds of a curtain back, and opened the casement beyond it; as the villa overhung the sea, so the window jutting out overhung the rock, and gave to view in one grand sweep the whole bow of the bay, with the white mists of earliest day resting still midway between earth and heaven. Sound there was none, save close at hand the low music of a monaco's wing, and from afar the swinging cadence of a chiming angelus.

She stood silent, looking long outward through the fragrant coils of orange-blossom and of climbing ivy that hung in their green shadow before the oval of the window, towards the waking world that smiled below.

To her, whose heart had never beaten for one of those which had throbbed for her, there came at last some recoil of the suffering which she had so often dealt, some touch of that futile pain which for her and through her had been so often borne. She saw still, in memory, the wondering and grieved reproach of the eyes which had haunted her throughout all the past hours.

"Do I love!—*I!*" she thought, while a laugh half haughty, half ironic, and yet more mournful than either, came on her lips. And she turned back again from the brightness of the day with a gesture of her old imperious disdain. She was too proud, too sceptical, too used to command, too unused to weakness, not to be loth to admit such yielding folly in her, not to be contemptuous of her own softer thoughts and tenderer impulses. Love!—to her it was a fool's paradise, a gay and glittering masquerade, a sceptre with which to sway a court of madmen, a weapon with which to reap the harvests of gold and power, a passion that men got drunk with as with raki, and through which, as they pampered or inflamed it, women could indirectly rule the world. Her contempt for it had been as great as the sovereignty with which she had used it.

It was bitter to her to think that she could have so much weakness in her—so much living still beneath all that she had seen, known, done, to slay it by the roots. Something of the warmth of passion, something of its tenderness, were on her; and she flung them away, she would not have them. The unquestioning fealty which was ready to do her will at all and any cost, the devotion to her which, without any recompense, any hope, any self-interest, accepted the peril from which she had offered to free him, and with a simple grandeur claimed the right to be true to his word: these moved her as nothing else could have done. Tempests had swept over her, leaving her utterly unswayed by them; the rarity which touched her as something strange and unfamiliar was the unselfishness of the love he bore her. Many had loved her as well; none so generously.

She could see the shore far below—down through a wreathing, shimmering interspace of green leaves. She had rescued men at far keener, closer danger than there was in this. She had gone to Russian masked-balls, ignorant whether at any moment the hand of an Imperial officer might not be laid on her domino, and her fettered limbs be borne away without warning, through the frozen night, over leagues on leagues and steppes on steppes of snow, to the Siberian doom which awaits the defenders of Poland. She had swept at a wild gallop through the purple gloom of the midnight Campagna with her courage only rising the higher, her eyes only gleaming the darker. She had glided in her gondola through balmy spring sunsets, when all Venice was wreathed and perfumed with flowers in some Austrian *festa*, and had laughed, and coquetted, and stirred her fan, and listened languidly to the music, while hidden beneath her awning was one whom the casemates of the Quadrilateral would enclose only to let him issue to his death, unless her skill could save him. She had passed through many hours of supreme peril, personal and for others, and the disquietude had not been on her that was on her now.

She leaned there against the casement watching the beach beneath, where it stretched out along the glittering sea. It was still only the daybreak, but the fisher-folk were astir, in different groups, spreading out their nets in the warmth of the rising sun, or putting out in their boats from the shore. There was glowing colour, picturesque movement, life, healthful, active, innocent, along the grey line of the sand; she sighed half impatiently as she watched it. Was it good to have no thought, save of a few fish?—no fear, save of the black swoop of the mistral?—no care in life, save for those striped sails, and those brown keels, and those sun-browned, half-naked children tumbling in the surf?

No; she did not so belie herself as to cheat her thoughts into the lie; she would not have relinquished the power, the genius, the vitality, the knowledge of her life, for a thousand years of the supreme passionless calm that looks out from the eyes of Egyptian statues, far less for the dull brute routine of peasant ignorance and common joys.

On the sands Erceldoune waited, leaning against a ledge of rock, with his eyes fixed absently on the waters. Even at the distance he was from her she could see the profound weariness that had altered his bold and soldier-like bearing, the hopeless melancholy that darkened his face as the light of the dawn fell upon it. She was not a woman to wish things done undone, or to know the vacillations of regret; yet, in the moment, she almost wished the words unspoken which had been uttered by her in a sudden impulse and resolve to let him blind himself no longer.

"It is useless to try and save him now," she thought; "*he* will never forget."

There was something which touched her infinitely

in that guard he kept there; patient as the Pompeian soldier standing at his post, while the dark cloud of the ashes and the liquid torrent of lava-flame poured down, certain as he that no reward could come to him for his unrecompensed obedience, save perhaps one—death.

The Venetians left her garden. She saw them approach, and address him; she saw him start as the elder man handed him the ring, and, as he took it, give one upward glance at the eyrie of the villa where she leaned. Then he signed to him the sailor whom he had first spoken with on the night of his arrival at Capri.

There was an instant's terrible suspense as the Capriote stood curiously eyeing these two unknown sailors, whose presence on his shore he felt to be odd and unwelcome, since living was poor in the Picola Marina, and strangers likely to take a share of it were commonly roughly handled: then he gave good-humoured assent to whatever had been asked of him and launched his boat into the breakers with the single force of his broad breast and brawny arms. He motioned the unknown fishermen to take the oars, with somewhat of a sullen grace, as though their advent still annoyed him; he took the helm himself; Erceldoune flung his limbs down across the benches; the little skiff put out to sea. Thus far the work was done.

As the boat left the shore he turned, rose slightly, and looked back at Capri: that mute farewell, that speechless witness of how his promise had been redeemed, smote her keenly.

She watched the movement of the boat through the waves, with the daybreak light upon the stripes of its orange awning—watched it as it receded farther and farther, the tall figure of the Capriote standing at the stern, in his loose white shirt and his brown brigand-like Italian beauty—watched it till it swept out unarrested, unobserved, to where the yacht rocked at anchor.

The boat reached the vessel's side; a while longer, and the anchor weighed in the quiet of the dawn, whilst the only things that stirred on the whole width of the bay were a few scattered fishing-craft. She, leaning there against the grey of the stone, looking out through the wreaths of the leaves, never left her watch, never relaxed her gaze. She knew the tigers who slept yonder where Naples lay; she knew the cannon that would boom out through the sunny air if the errand of the *Etoile* were dreamed of; she knew the dungeons that yawned in the Vicaria for those who fled. She could not tell how much, how little, of the escape that she had organised was known to the Bourbon court; she could not tell that the government of Francis might not be only seeming to slumber, that it might crouch like a jungle-beast the surer to seize. She could not tell, even though to no living being had a word been whispered of her intent; she could not tell, for walls have ears where tyranny rules and priestcraft listens.

Any moment while the anchor was slowly wound upward, and the rigging of the yacht covered with eager sailors, the alarm-gun might boom from Naples, and the pursuit run down the schooner, boarding and swamping her in the midst of the smiling seas of the tranquil dawn.

At last she moved; her white canvas filled with a fair wind, her helm was turned straight westward, her ensign of St. George fluttered in the favouring breeze. With an easy gliding motion, like a swan's, she passed through the sun-lit waters, unnoticed, unpursued. Against her rails one figure leaned motionless; his eyes were turned towards the rock, hanging so far above, where the villa was suspended like a falcon's nest; turned there always whilst the yacht passed onward, out beyond Capri, beyond Ischia, beyond the range of Neapolitan guns and the pursuit of Neapolitan ships, outward to round the snow-peaks of the eyrie of the Buonaparte eaglets, and to steer on towards the southern coast of France, in safety.

As it receded, slowly, surely, till its sails looked no larger than the sea-gulls that flew past her, and the busy day of the young summer awoke all round the semicircle of the bay, then, only then, Idalia moved and left the ivy-sheltered casement. From the glittering stretch of the azure seas, as from the thoughts newly arisen in her, she turned, with a pang of pain, with a throe of regret, the bitterness of pride repelling weakness, the bitterness of pride warring with remorse.

CHAPTER XIX.

"More great in Martyrdom than throned as Cæsar's Mate."

At the Prince of Viana's villa in the interior there was a masquerade; brilliant, gorgeous, like the splendid *feste* of mediæval Italy, of Venice in its Dandolo glory, when the galleys swept home with the rich Byzantine spoils; of Florence while Isabel Orsini was in her loveliness, and the Capello beamed her sunny fatal smile, and even grave Macchiavel sauntered well amused through the festive Gardens of Delight, when the Embassies of the Ten came in their purple pomp, or the City of Flowers laughed through endless mirth and music. The fête was very magnificent at the palace at Antina, given by lavish princely hands that scattered their gold right and left, and vied with the Grammont and the Doria brilliance away yonder in old Rome. That at it other masks were worn than those black Venetian ones of pleasure, that beneath the swell of the music words of menace and danger were exchanged, that the domino was only donned that the sword might be surely drawn hereafter, that under the dewy orange-boughs, and beside the starlit waters and on the marble stairs, and under the light exchange of frivolous wit, intrigues were woven and dark plans made perfect,—these no more disturbed the gaiety and the glory of the Antina masquerade than such had disturbed the laughing tide of festivities in Venice, or the garden fêtes of the Tuscans in the Cinque Cento. Rather they suited and enhanced it; it was in Italy, and they made it but the more Italian. It was the dagger of Sforza glancing beneath the Arlecchino spangles and colours of Goldoni. Whoso cannot understand this mingling —the laugh and the arlequinade as really joyous as the steel and the stroke are surely subtle—can never understand the Italy of the Past: perhaps not the Italy of the Present.

Around one the maskers gathered with pressing homage, around one the groups were more eager, more sedulous, more vivacious in their wit, more earnest in their under-current of political discussion than round any other; for on the elegance of the scarlet domino was the well-known badge of the Silver Ivy, that rallying symbol which brought to her all the lovers and the vassals of Idalia. She reigned there, as she had reigned wherever her foot fell, since the day eight years before, when she had left the leafy shadows and the yellow corn-lands of Sparta to come out to this world of mystery, intrigue, romance, danger, and pleasure, which she had made so wholly her own.

It has been said, "Every woman is at heart a Bohemian." Idalia was one to the core, all proud and patrician though she was. The excitement and the peril of her life, with its vivid colour and its changing chances, she would not have exchanged for the eternal monotony of the most perfect calm; not even when she most utterly loathed, most utterly rebelled against the bondage which had entered in with the life she pursued. She was weary with herself often for the evil that she had done, she hated with an intense hatred the chains that had wound themselves round her freedom-loving, liberty-craving nature; but all the same, once plunged into the whirlpool of the dangers she directed, of the excitations she enjoyed, Idalia would not have laid them down and left them—left her sceptre and her peril—without a pang bitter as that which tears life out, without a lingering and unbearable regret. It is false philosophy to say that those who have been once launched on a career which bears them now in the sunlight, now in the storm-shadow, now high on laughing waves of pleasure, now low sunk down under black bitter waters, varying ever, yet ever full of a tempestuous delight, of a headlong risk, of an abundant luxuriant glow and intensity of life, will ever willingly return to the dull flow of tideless and unchequered streams. They may in moments of exhaustion fancy that they would willingly take the patience and the monotony of serene unnoted lives—human nature will ever at times, be it in king or peasant, turn from what it has to sigh for what it has not;—but it is only a fancy, and a passing one; they would never for a second make it a reality.

Thus it was with Idalia now; remorse haunted her, captivity in a sense galled her with terrible fetters, often she hated herself and hated those around her; yet once in the vortex of the intrigues and the ambitions which had so long possessed her, she forgot all else. Thus she forgot all save them here at the Antina masquerade. It was not that she was changed, it was not that her other impulses were not vitally and deeply true; it was simply that the dominant side of her character now came into play, and the love of power that was in her usurped its ancient sway.

Moreover here, though she scorned and abhorred many of the companions and tools that the cause necessitated and employed, the cause itself was a pure and lofty one; one for which her will could never slacken, her love never grow cold;—it was the freedom and the indivisibility of Italy.

This was in the hearts, often on the lips, of all those to-night at Antina; amidst the music, the laughter, the wit, the balmy air breathed over a million flowers, the melodies of nightingales' tender throats, the flash of fire-flies among the groves of myrtle; and in the endless reception-chambers, with their jasper and their onyx, their malachite and their porphyry, stretching onward till the eye was lost in the colonnades of pillars, in the flood of light, in the sea of colour. It was a scene from the Italy of the Renaissance, from the Italy of the Cinque Cento, from the Italy of Goldoni, of

Boccaccio, of Tullia d'Arragona, of Bembo, of Borgia;
—but beneath it ran a vein of thought, a stream of
revolution, a throb of daring that gave it also a memory
of Dantesque grandeur, of Gracchan aspirations, of
Julian force: "One Italy for the Italians!" vibrated
through it; an echo, though a faint and distant one,
of the ancient challenge, "The whole earth for the
Romans."

Suddenly through the glittering gaiety of the masquerade, the magnificence of the princely banquet, the mirth of the Neapolitan revelries, an icy whisper ran; it was vague, unformed, it died half spoken upon every lip, yet it blanched the boldest blood; it was but one sickening, shameful, accursed word—"*betrayed.*"

The music ceased, the laughs hushed, there was a strange instantaneous pause in all the vivacious life, filling the palace and the gardens with its colour and its mirth; there was such a lull as comes over sea and land before the breaking of the storm. Men looked in each other's faces with a terrible dread responsive in each other's eyes; glance met glance in a mute inquiry; friend gazed at friend in a wild search for truth, a bitter breathless thought of unmeasured suspicion; there was a chill, black, deadly horror over all—none knew whom to trust. On the stillness that had succeeded the music, the laughter, and the festivity, sounded dully the iron tread of heavily armed men; where the golden fireflies glistened among the leaves, glistened instead the shine of steel; on the terraces and far down the gardens gleamed the blades of bayonets, the barrels of musketry; the earth seemed in a moment to grow alive with swarming men, and bristling with levelled weapons; gendarmes filled the piazza and the courts; the soldiers of Francis were upon them. There was an instant's silence so intense that the murmur of the bubbling fountains alone reigned in it; then with a shock like thunder, the bold blood of the sons of liberty, growing desperate, threw them in headlong violence unarmed upon their foes. Little avail;—the solid line of steel was drawn around, with not an inch unfilled; they were hemmed in and caught in the toils.

Carlo of Viana, with his careless eyes alight like a lion's in its wrath, tore down from where it hung a keen Damascus sword, placed amidst a stand of curiously wrought and antique arms, and strode over the mosaic pavement to one of his guests, whose azure domino was broidered and fastened with wreaths of silver ivy.

His voice shook as he stooped to her ear.

"Madame—Idalia—this is more for you than us. Follow me at once; there is a secret passage that no living creature knows besides myself; I can save you —I *will* save you!"

"I thank you deeply. But—I shall not fly from them!"

"My God! Not fly? Do you not know that if you are taken——"

Her lips might be a shade whiter, but her voice had no hesitation as she answered him:

"My fate will not be worse than others'; whatever is theirs, I share."

Carlo of Viana drew the broad blade with a ringing echo from the sheath:

"Mother of Christ, then, we will defend you while life is in us!"

At that very moment the storm broke, the tumult began; the gay maskers fled in from the terraces and gardens like sheep driven wild by a wolf-dog; the banqueters seized the antique weapons, the weighty candelabra, the bronzes, the toy daggers—all and anything that would crash through like iron or be hurled like stones; the double lines of steel drew closer, and filled in every aperture, blocked every door of egress; an officer advanced to the centre of the great arch that spanned the entrance of the first reception-room, and addressed the Prince himself:

"Eccellenza, in the King's name, I demand your unqualified submission, and your surrender to me of all suspected persons—notably, first, of the notorious revolutionist known by the title of the Countess Vassalis."

For all answer, with a mighty oath that rang through all his banqueting-chambers, Viana lifted his arm, and whirled in a flashing arc above his head the bright blade of the Persian steel;—Idalia bent forward with a swift gesture, which caught his wrist, and arrested the sabre in its downward course; then, turning to the King's officer, she removed her Venetian mask, and looked at him calmly.

"If it will spare the shedding of innocent blood, you know me now."

For one moment there was a dead silence—the hush of speechless surprise, of speechless admiration; the emotion of a passionate love, of a passionate pride, in and for her filled the hearts of her own people with an agony of homage and of grief; the soldiers of the Bourbons were arrested for the instant, paralysed and confounded as they looked on her, fronting them with a proud serenity, a dauntless, tranquil contempt, with the light on her diamond-bound hair. Then, as the officer

of the Palace troops advanced to arrest her, his soldiers
drawn closer and firmer round the banqueting-hall;
the shouts of "Viva l'Italia!" "Viva la libertà!" shook
the walls with the roll of thunder; a hundred who
would have died at her feet to save a dog of hers from
injury threw themselves round her as in a guard of
honour; driven to bay, the lovers of freedom, the haters
of tyranny, were ready to perish, shot down like hunted
beasts, rather than ever yield. Carlo of Viana flung
himself in the van, his sabre flashing above his head;
the gay and splendid dresses of the maskers, glittering
in the light, seemed to heave and toss like a sea of
colour; they circled her like gardes du corps; their
improvised weapons, torn from the tables, from the
cabinets, from the walls, whirled in the radiance that
burned from innumerable lamps. Idalia's eyes gleamed
with such fire as might have been in the eyes of Artemisia when she bore her prow down on the Calyndian;
of Antonina when she pierced the armies of the Goths,
holding watch and ward to sack Imperial Rome; of
Boadicea when she led the Iceni on to the fasces and the
standards of the conquering legions. She would have
given herself to save them; but since they, with or
without her, must be doomed, her whole soul rose
responsive to the challenge of danger, to the defiance
of submission.

Her glance beamed on them with a superb light;
sign of fear, thought of terror, there were none on her;
she stood unmoved, the centre of that tossing ocean of
colour, of steel, of floating dominoes, of levelled pistols,
and glanced at Viana with a glance that thrilled him
like flame and made him drunk like wine.

"Right! If they must take us, let us be dead first!"

As touchwood to the flash of fire, their blood and their wills answered her bidding; with a single sweep of his arm Viana felled down the commander who faced him, in a stroke that cleft straight through bone and brain; it was the signal of a life-and-death resistance. With a yell of fury, the soldiers closed in; a single voice from one unseen rose clear above the din.

"Reserve your fire; cut those carrion down like straw, and capture her alive!"

The voice was the voice of supreme command; officers and troops alike obeyed it; it was the mellow clarion tone of Giulio Villaflor, if the Priest of Peace could be the chief of such an errand. With bayonets fixed, in ranks three deep, pressing steadily through the courts and chambers, the soldiers of Francis came on to the band of the maskers. Not a man wavered as the pointed file of steel pressed towards them: their masks flung aside, lest in that moment of supreme danger any should deem them guilty of the wish to hide beneath disguise, their right arms lifted, their brave faces set, the Revolutionists waited the approach of the Royalists—waited till there was scarce a foot's breadth between their circle and the naked blades levelled against them. Then, with a marvellous unison, as she raised her hand, they launched themselves forward, Viana in their van, and the weapons with which the haste of extremity had armed them fell with furious strength and lightning speed crash down on the ranks of the soldiers. Strange weapons—the embossed barrels of old Florentine arquebuses, the butt-ends of toy ivory pistols, the bronzed weight of lifted statuettes, the gold-handled knives of the banquet-tables, the massive metal of Cellini vases, the arabesqued steel of mediæval rapiers,—anything, everything that could have been torn down in the moment, from the art-treasures round, were hurled—as stones are hurled from a barricade,—down on the advancing troops of the king with mighty force, with tremendous issue. The Bourbon legionaries reeled and wavered under that pitiless storm, that fell like thunder-bolts upon them; more than one swayed back stone dead as the bronze or gold missile of some statuary or amphora felled him to the ground. Forbidden to fire, they hesitated dismayed before that terrible band of revellers turned to warriors, of maskers changed to foemen, of idle laughing wits and dancers grown desperate as men who fought for more than life. The Royalists recoiled; they were chiefly the dross of various nations; they could not front the blazing glance, the tiger-swoop, the proud, passion-heated scorn, the fearless menace of Italian nobles and Italian patriots. From the gloom of the night without, the same clarion voice rolled, clear as a bell's, merciless as a Nero's.

"Cowards! perdition seize you. Advance and fire on them."

It was a strange battle-field;—the beautiful ball-room and banqueting-halls of Antina! It was a strange battle-scene!—the circle of the dominoes like a ring of many colours were belted round the form of Idalia like guards around their menaced queen; the dead men were lying with their blood slowly welling out over the rich mosaics and the velvet carpets; the soldiers of the Throne had halted in a broken line; the light that had been lit for the gaieties of the masquerade was shining on carnage and on combat; the splendours of the palace were stretching out and away beyond aisle on aisle of porphyry columns, through circle on circle of rose-wreathed arches, while without, through the marble pillars of the piazza, were the silver silence of the night and the shadows of innumerable forms gathering closer and closer to seal all hope from those who fought for liberty.

Idalia stood tranquil; and as they saw the serene disdain, the unwavering courage, the mercenaries of the king paused involuntarily. They *dared* not fire on her.

The voice from the gardens rang imperiously through the stillness.

"Dastards! you shall be shot down with them. Fire!"

The last word was not for the halting and paralysed soldiers of the front; it reached farther, to where, unseen, the picked men of Francis's Guard had marched noiselessly through the opposite doors of the banqueting-room, and circled the band of patriots in the rear with an impassable barrier—meshing them in one net beyond escape. They had not heard, they had not seen, they knew nothing of the ambuscade behind them, where they stood gathered around Idalia, facing their foes and holding them back by the menace of their eyes, as men hold back wild beasts, in gallant and dauntless chivalry, willing each one of them to lay down his life that night rather than yield her up in passive cowardice to her foes. They never saw, they never heard—behind them stole the murderous tread, filling up the rear of the lofty hall with rank on rank of soldiers. Then suddenly, as the word to fire rang in its merciless command from the outer court, the line of rifles belched forth its flame; the sullen roar of the shots echoed through the chamber, raking the glittering colours of the masquerade robes as the driving hail rakes the wheat and the flowers of a full corn-field. Shot down from the rear in that craven murder, they fell, the balls in their brains or their shoulders—a fourth of them levelled low; yet not a moan, not a cry escaped one of them, not a prayer broke from the lips wet with their life-blood, not a sigh escaped those whose nerves were rent, whose bones were shattered, whose lungs were pierced by that dastardly masked attack. Not a cry, not a supplication, broke even from Idalia, as the crash of the firing rolled over the devoted band that guarded her. Not for the first time did she look on bloodshed, nor for the first time meet the likeness of her death; but as they fell downward at her feet, stricken like felled trees, a mortal anguish came into her fearless eyes; she stretched her arms out less with entreaty than command.

"Spare them! To save *them*, I will surrender."

"By Christ, not for ten thousand lives!" cried Carlo of Viana, where he stood out of the deadly press, his reeking sword held aloft before her. "Surrender you! They shall only take you when we all lie dead around you!"

She grasped his arm and looked up in his face: there was no more of fear, no more of shrinking, than there were on his own; only in her eyes a superb heroism, on her lips a passionate entreaty.

"Serve me better still, my noble friend! Turn your sword *here*."

The tumult was at its height; emboldened by the fate of those shot down from the rear, the Royalists of the front pressed in. Wedged between two barriers, the patriots fought with mad despair. Where Vinna stood, pausing one instant as she turned and made her prayer to him, he knew that death were sweeter far to her than the fate that would await her from her foes; he knew that she had in her the courage of Lucretia, the force of the wife of Pœtus; but to slay with his own hand that perfect loveliness, to destroy with his own steel the pulse of that splendid and gracious life! —he drooped his head with a shudder, "*I cannot!*"

Scarcely had the words left his lips when the blade of a bayonet pierced his lungs; he fell like a mighty cedar lightning-stricken, not dead, but dying fast. The roar of the combat, the ring of the shots, the tumult of the conflict, as the betrayed were pressed between the wedge of the Royalist van and rear, were filling his palace-chambers with their riot; he knew no more of sight, or sound, or life. He only looked up with blind eyes, that, through their mists, vainly and solely sought for one; his lips parted with a murmur, "Idalia!— Italy!" Then, with those names his latest utterance, a shiver shook him as the red blood streamed through all the laces and the silks, the violet and the silver and the jewels of his dress, and, with one other deep-drawn, lingering sigh—he died.

She sank beside him on her knees, and her own danger and the conflict of the night that raged in its fiery struggle, its mortal misery, around, died from her memory, and grew dull upon her sense. She only remembered the man who lay here at her feet—dead; dead through the love he bore her; dead through the creeds she had breathed in him; dead·for her and by her, as though her hand had slain him.

The fearless grandeur faded from her face, that

had been there throughout all chance of her own death; it grew white, and cold, and fixed; a tearless grief, a burning remorse, were in her eyes, which only saw that crimson stream of flowing blood staining the tessellated floor, and that brave, bold, serene face turned upward to the light of million lamps studding like stars the vault of the dome above.

"Let them take me," she thought, "it is just. What am I better than a murderess?"

From the gloom of the outer court rang once more the voice of command.

"Seize *her!* You can choke the dogs of rebels at your leisure."

She never heard the pitiless clarion of those clear tones; she never felt the hiss of the balls past her; she never saw the ghastly conflict that filled the palace festive chambers with its clamour and its carnage, as men armed strong with the weight of tyranny and law pressed down on men who fought for liberty, for conscience, for their land, and for their lives. She thought only of the dead who lay around her.

Two officers of the guard, obedient, stooped and laid their grasp upon her; the action roused her from the unconscious stupor with which she knelt beside the lifeless limbs; she shook them off and rose facing them, still with that look of terrible remorse in her tearless eyes, though on her face were a scorn and a daring which held those whom she threw off at bay as surely as the most desperate resistance of shot or steel.

She glanced down the hall, under the dome of the light-studded ceiling that stretched over so vast an area, that had been a few brief moments before filled with music and mirth and the murmur of laughing voices. She took no heed of those who had sought to seize her, but her eyes gazed with an infinite yearning out on her defenders holding that unequal life-and-death struggle between the closing bayonets, and her voice échoed, clear and eloquent, yet with a misery that thrilled the hearts even of her enemies.

"My friends—my friends!—lose no more for me. Death is liberty, but it cannot be mine; give me no other murdered lives to lie heavy on my own. Save yourselves by surrender, by flight, how you can, and think no more of me. The future will yet avenge us all."

The voice of the chief in command rang down again from the dusky shadows of the piazza.

"Soldiers! seize and silence her. She speaks sedition."

The officers, gentler than he who hounded them on to their work, stooped, hesitating, to her.

"You surrender?"

She looked at them with a look that for the moment flashed back all the proud contemptuous light upon her face, and lit in her deep eyes the glow of the old heroism.

"If the carnage cease."

The voice from the outer courts answered her, imperious and unyielding—

"We make no terms with revolutionists and rebels."

"I make no peace with tyrants and assassins."

Her return-defiance challenged her unseen foe with a calm grandeur; she stood above the fallen dead as some prophetess of Israel, some goddess in the Homeric age, might have stood above the slain, and called down vengeance.

From the darkness of the piazza a hot and heavy oath broke through the clamour.

"Yield! or we will deal with you as we deal with men."

A smile of utter unspeakable scorn passed over her lips—scorn for the cowardice that could threaten her thus—scorn for the craven temper that could deem death so victorious a menace.

She looked down tranquilly on the gleaming barrels of the rifles, and as her lover, in the far Carpathian pass, had given the word for his own death-shot, so she gave hers now. Her eyes rested steadily on the Royalists.

"Fire!"

The soldiers of the King gazed at her, then dropped the muzzles of their muskets slowly downward and downward; they hung their heads, and their eyes fell, while from one to another ran a sullen rebellious murmur,

"*Non possiamo!*"

There was an instant's intense stillness once more; the tumult ceased, the clamour died away, the uplifted steel sank, the iron grip relaxed; aggressors and defenders, revolutionists and royalists, alike were mute and awed before the courage of one woman. Then, with the fury of a mighty oath, a fresh command was hissed in its ferocity from the garden gloom, where the chiefs looked on into the courts and chambers.

"Make her captive, dead or living!"

There were ruffians in that Royal Guard, brigands of the Abruzzi, mountaineers of Calabria, who had imbrued their hands in innocent blood, and knew no check upon their crimes, though they would mutter Aves for their black and poisonous souls like any nun before her crucifix. These heard but to obey. They launched themselves upon her; they flung themselves through the press to seize her; their swords flashed naked above her head; their ravenous eyes fed gloatingly upon her jewels and her beauty; their brutal hands stretched ruthlessly to grasp and crush the gold of the shining hair, the mould of the delicate limbs, the fairness of the transparent skin; their gripe was on her shoulder, their breath was on her bosom. With the horror, and the grace, of outraged dignity, Idalia shook their hold from her, and drew herself from the loathsome insult of their villanous contact; her eyes shone with the lustre of a passionate scorn, her voice mellow, imperious, unshaken, rang outward to the terrace where her tyrants herded.

"I surrender!—not to escape death; but to escape the pollution of your touch."

END OF VOL. I.

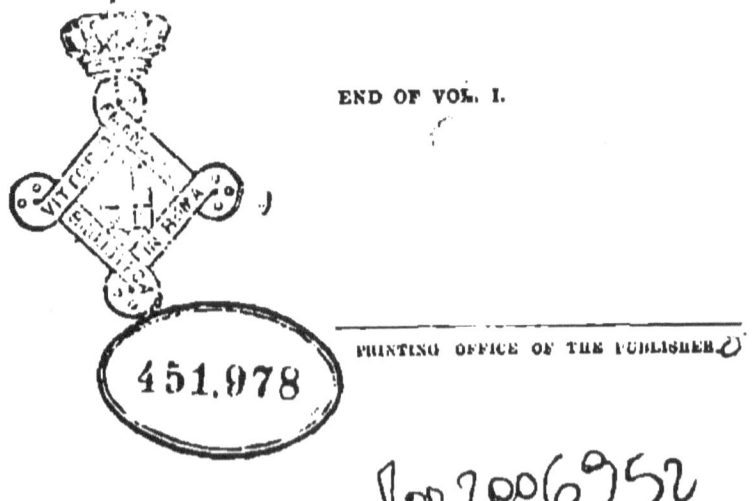

PRINTING OFFICE OF THE PUBLISHER.

www.ingramcontent.com/pod-product-compliance
Lightning Source LLC
Chambersburg PA
CBHW030403230426
43664CB00007BB/721